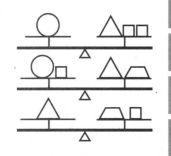

MATH
OLYMPIAD
Since 1979

## VOLUME 1

$$
\begin{array}{r}
H\ E \\
H\ E \\
H\ E \\
+\ H\ E \\
\hline
A\ H
\end{array}
$$

# MATH OLYMPIAD
# CONTEST
# PROBLEMS

## FOR ELEMENTARY AND MIDDLE SCHOOLS

## (VOLUME 1)

# DR. GEORGE LENCHNER

| 5 |    | 13 |
|---|----|----|
|   | ?  |    |
| 9 | 7  |    |

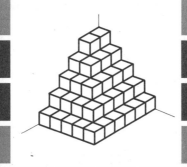

$$
\cfrac{1}{2 + \cfrac{1}{2 + \cfrac{1}{2 + \cfrac{1}{2}}}}
$$

## About the Author

Dr. George Lenchner (1917-2006) was formerly the Director of Mathematics for the Valley Stream High School District, and Consultant to the three associated Elementary School Districts in Long Island, NY. He was the founder of the Nassau County Interscholastic Mathematics League (Mathletes) in 1955. He also organized the Mathematical Olympiads for Elementary and Middle Schools (MOES) in 1979 and served as its Executive Director until his retirement in 1996.

Dr. Lenchner was the author of many mathematics textbooks and articles appearing in national publications. He brought to this book over forty years of experience as a mathematics teacher, supervisor, teacher-trainer, and creator of problems. Harvard University honored him for Outstanding and Distinguished Secondary School Teaching.

## Publisher

Math Olympiads for Elementary and Middle Schools, Inc., Bellmore, NY 11710

## Editors

Gilbert W. Kessler and Lawrence J. Zimmerman

## Layout and Graphics

David M. Lenchner, MicroComp, Santa Rosa, CA

## Cover Design

Gregory Andreyev, Agrecolor Inc., Mineola, NY

## Printer

Tobay Printing Company, Inc., Copiague, NY

First Edition, published in New York 1990. Printed in the U.S.A.: 1990, 1992, 1995.
Revised and Expanded Edition, published in New York 1997. Printed in the U.S.A., 1997, 1999, 2001, 2004, 2006, 2008, 2010.

All paper in this book is acid-free and meets the guidelines for permanence and durability of the Committee on Production Guidelines for Book Longevity of the Council on Library Resources.

Library of Congress Catalog Number: 96-77380

ISBN: 0-9626662-1-1; 9780962666216

This book is dedicated to the
children and teachers
who participate in
the Math Olympiads for
Elementary and Middle Schools.

# Contents

# Preface

Learning to solve problems is the underlying reason for studying mathematics. It is the principal mathematical skill that needs to be developed in children.

Exposure to challenging problems, interesting puzzles, and associated rich mathematical topics is essential for the development of skill in problem solving. This book is a collection of 400 problems authored by George Lenchner for the Mathematical Olympiads for Elementary and Middle Schools over the sixteen-year period from 1979 through 1995. More than 100,000 children participate annually in the Olympiads. These children represent 4000 teams in the U.S.A. and 25 other countries.

Each Olympiad is an interschool competition which is held five times during the school year at monthly intervals beginning in November. Each contains five problems with specified time limits. The value of the Olympiad problems is related to their special appeal to reasoning, creativity, resourcefulness, ingenuity, and important principles of mathematics.

The author believes that mathematics problems should:
- · stimulate children's interest and enthusiasm for problem solving,
- · broaden their mathematical intuition and develop their "brain power",
- · introduce them to interesting and important mathematical ideas, and
- · let them experience the satisfaction, pleasure, fun, and thrill of discovery associated with creative problem solving.

The problems in this book were reviewed by a select group of mathematicians and teachers for ambiguity, language, and level of difficulty over the sixteen-year period 1979-1995. Special thanks are in order for these reviewers. Their names are: Harry Sitomer (deceased), Harry Ruderman (deceased), Dr. Hamilton S. Blum, and Mary D. Morrison.

I am especially grateful to Gilbert W. Kessler and Larry J. Zimmerman for their significant contributions to the production of this book. Their excellent editorial advice helped to enrich this work. They are well known in the circle of mathematics competitions especially for their authorship of many of the NYSML (New York State Mathematics League) competitions and the ARML (American Regions Mathematics League) competitions.

I hope you find this book interesting, valuable, and enjoyable.

George Lenchner

# Introduction

# The Problem Solving Process

### Understanding the Problem

Before you try to solve a problem, make sure that you understand the wording of the problem, its question, and any special words it might contain such as factor, digit, diagonal, and so forth. Does the problem give you too little, just enough, or too much information? Can you restate the problem in your own words? Can you guess what the answer will look like?

### Planning to Solve the Problem

You need to have a plan of action to solve a problem. Such plans are called *strategies*. The following are some strategies that are used more frequently than others.

> Find a Pattern
> Draw a Picture or Diagram
> Make an Organized List
> Make a Table
> Work Backward
> Use Reasoning

### Carrying Out the Plan

You will observe that each problem in this book has a suggested time limit which begins after you have read the problem and are ready to begin. Select a strategy from the above list or use one of your own choice. You may also want to use a combination of strategies. Now try to solve the problem. If you are not able to do the problem within the recommended time limit, ignore the time limit and continue to work on the problem until you have a solution. Speed is not important! As you become more experienced with different strategies, mathematical ideas and principles, and develop your skills, the amount of time you need to do a problem will decrease naturally. If you have difficulty with a computation, get help from your teacher, a parent, or another student. If your strategy doesn't seem to be working, try a different strategy. If you are still "stumped", go on to another problem. Later, you may want to again try to do the problem that stumped you. Perhaps you will think of a way of doing the problem in the time that has elapsed. If that doesn't help, read *Using Different Parts of the Book* which begins on page 15.

# The Problem Solving Process

**Looking Back**

When you get an answer, compare it to what you thought your answer should look like. Is your answer reasonable? Reread the problem and the question that is being asked. Now write your answer in a complete sentence. Compare it with the answer given in the Answer section. If you are satisfied with your answer, try to find a different strategy that could be used to solve the problem. Try to relate this problem to other problems you may have solved in the past. If you used different strategies to solve the problem, compare them and try to decide which strategy is best for you. If you were able to solve the problem but exerienced some difficulty, try it again at a later date to see if you remember how you overcame your difficulties.

# Strategies and Problems

Knowledge of Algebra and its associated techniques are helpful but not necessary for solving any of the Olympiad problems. Try to solve the problems without using Algebra initially, even if you have experience in Algebra. You may make some interesting discoveries involving the variables of the problem.

### Find a Pattern
<u>Problem:</u> Express the following sum as a simple fraction in lowest terms.

$$\frac{1}{1\times2}+\frac{1}{2\times3}+\frac{1}{3\times4}+\frac{1}{4\times5}+\frac{1}{5\times6}+\frac{1}{6\times7}$$

Look at the partial sums beginning with the first fraction, then the sum of the first two fractions, and then the sum of the first three fractions. Examine each of the simplified sums carefully and look for a pattern which relates each of these sums to the individual fractions in the sum. The pattern will be discussed in the next section titled *Solutions to Problems,* page 13.

### Draw a Picture or Diagram
<u>Problem:</u> Four distinct straight lines are drawn across a rectangle, thus subdividing the interior of the rectangle into regions which do not overlap. What is the greatest number of regions that the four lines can produce?

Draw a diagram of the rectangle and experiment with the placement of the four lines across the interior of the rectangle. See *Solutions to Problems,* page 13.

### Make an Organized List
<u>Problem:</u> Five students hold a checkers tournament. In the first round, each of the students plays each of the other students just once. How many different games are played?

Designate the five students as A, B, C, D, and E. Let a pair of letters such as AB represent the game played by A and B. Notice that AB and BA represent the same game. Now list, in an organized way, the different games that can be played. See *Solutions to Problems*, page 14.

# Strategies and Problems

**Make a Table**

Problem: The toll for an automobile to cross a certain bridge is 40¢. A toll machine in an EXACT CHANGE lane will accept any combination of coins that has a total value of 40¢ but will not accept any pennies. In how many ways can the driver pay the 40¢ toll in the EXACT CHANGE lane?

Make a table of the different combinations of coins that can be used to pay the toll. Let the letters Q, D, and N denote the number of quarters, dimes, and nickels having a total value of 40¢. Check your list of combinations against the list in *Solutions to Problems,* page 14.

**Work Backward**

Problem: I have a Magic Money Box which will double any amount of money placed in it and then add $1 to the doubled amount. One day, I placed a certain amount of money in the Magic Money Box and got a new amount. I then placed the new amount in the Magic Money Box and got $75. How much money did I first place in the Box?

Let M represent the amount of money I placed in the Box the second time.

| Amount placed in the Box the second time | What the Magic Money Box did to the amount | | The new amount I received |
|---|---|---|---|
| M | 2×M + 1 | = | $75 |

If I subtract $1 from $75, I then have $74 which is 2×M. Then M must be $37. Therefore the amount placed in the Magic Money Box the second time was $37. Now repeat these operations to determine the amount placed in the Magic Money Box the first time. See *Solutions to Problems,* page 14.

**Use Reasoning**

Problem: A school has 731 students. Prove that there must be at least three students who have the same birthday.

Before you read ahead, think of how you can prove this. Suppose you questioned all 731 students and found three who had the same birthday. Would this be considered a proof that the same thing will always happen whenever a school has 731 students? See *Solutions to Problems,* page 14.

# Solutions to Problems

## Find a Pattern

The following are the three partial sums you were asked to investigate.

1) $$\frac{1}{1 \times 2} = \frac{1}{2}$$

2) $$\frac{1}{1 \times 2} + \frac{1}{2 \times 3} = \frac{2}{3}$$

3) $$\frac{1}{1 \times 2} + \frac{1}{2 \times 3} + \frac{1}{3 \times 4} = \frac{3}{4}$$

Observe how the sum on the right side of each equation is related to the last fraction on the left side. The two numbers in the denominator of the last fraction of the left side become the numerator and denominator of the fraction on the right side. According to this pattern, the partial sum of the first four fractions would be 4/5. The answer to the given problem is 6/7. However you should understand that there may be better ways to do this problem.

## Draw a Picture or Diagram

a. Draw four lines across the rectangle for the following cases:

Case 1) the four lines do not intersect in an interior point,

Case 2) the four lines intersect in one common point on a side of the rectangle, and

Case 3) the four lines intersect in one common point in the interior of the rectangle.

     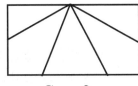     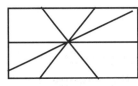

Case 1                  Case 2                  Case 3

There are 5 regions in Case 1, 5 regions in Case 2, and 8 regions in Case 3.

b. The greatest number of non-overlapping regions occurs when each of the four lines drawn across the rectangle intersects the other three lines in different points located in the interior of the rectangle.

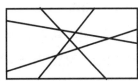

Answer: The greatest number of regions into which the interior of a rectangle can be subdivided by four straight lines is eleven.

---

# Solutions to Problems

## Make an Organized List

The different games that can be played are shown at the right. Notice how each pair in row 1 starts with A, how each pair in row 2 starts with B, and so forth. Doing this makes it easier to organize the list. The five students will play ten different games in the first round.

AB  AC  AD  AE

BC  BD  BE

CD  CE

DE

## Make a Table

The largest number of quarters (Q) we can use is 1. Rows 1 and 2 show the two combinations that can be made with 1 quarter. In row 3, the largest number of dimes (D) we can use is 4. We continue to use dimes in rows 4 through 6. This completes all combinations that can be made with dimes. In row 7, only nickels are used.

Answer: There are seven different combinations of coins that each have a value of 40¢ if no pennies are used.

|     | Q | D | N |
| --- | --- | --- | --- |
| 1)  | 1 | 1 | 1 |
| 2)  | 1 | 0 | 3 |
| 3)  | 0 | 4 | 0 |
| 4)  | 0 | 3 | 2 |
| 5)  | 0 | 2 | 4 |
| 6)  | 0 | 1 | 6 |
| 7)  | 0 | 0 | 8 |

## Work Backward

| Amount placed in the Box the first time | What the Magic Money Box did to the amount | | The new amount I received |
| --- | --- | --- | --- |
| N | $2 \times N + 1$ | $=$ | $37 |

If I subtract $1 from $37, I have the double of what was placed in the Box the first time. Then $36 is $2 \times N$ and N, the amount placed in the Box, was $18.

## Use Reasoning

There are 365 different birthdays in a year. Consider just 365 students of the 731. The possibility that all 365 students have different birthdays does exist although it is very, very small. Now consider 365 of the remaining 366 students. Again, the possibility of all 365 students of the second group having different birthdays does also exist although it is very, very, very small. This unlikely but not impossible situation results in there now being exactly 2 students for each of the 365 birthdays. The one student of the original 731 students who has not been considered at this point must have a birthday which will match just one of the 365 different pairs. Therefore: In a group of 731 students, there are at least 3 students who have the same birthday.

# Using Different Parts of the Book

There are four parts of this book which will help you solve problems. They are titled *Answers, Hints, Solutions,* and *Appendixes.* The following describe how to use these parts properly. Careful attention to these descriptions should improve your ability to solve problems, expand your mathematical background, and increase your enjoyment of mathematics. Other helpful parts are *Problem Types, Glossary,* and *Index.*

## When You Have a Solution

1) Compare your answer with the answer given in *Answers.* If the answers agree, compare the strategy you used with the strategies given in *Solutions.* Study the strategies that are different than yours. Try to decide which strategy is most efficient, which is most easily understood by you, and which is best for you at the present time. Try using a new strategy when you encounter a similar problem.

2) If the answers do not agree, go over your work carefully. You may have made an error in computation or in copying the given information onto your paper. If you decide that you have not made either of the errors described, read the reference for the problem in *Hints.* Redo the problem using the suggested hint. Remember to compare your answer with the given answer.

## When You Do Not Have a Strategy for Solution

1) If you are not familiar with certain terms or vocabulary in the problem, consult the *Glossary, Index,* or *Appendixes.* If any of these resources provides the information you need to know, then proceed with your solution.

2) If you understand the problem but do not know how to proceed, read the reference to the problem in *Hints.*

3) If *Hints* does not help you, go to *Solutions* and cover the solution of the problem with a sheet of paper. Reveal and read one line at a time until you think you can proceed on your own. If you are not able to proceed on you own, go over the solution or solutions and select the one you understand best. Study it. Try to write that solution in your own words without referring to *Solutions.* At a later date, try to solve the problem without referring to *Solutions.* This will indicate how much you have retained and learned by yourself.

# Using Different Parts of the Book

## Redoing and Sharing Problems

Many of the Olympiad problems will stimulate and challenge your mind. You may discover that rereading a problem and again solving it from time to time is an enjoyable experience and will strengthen your problem solving skill. Share the problems with your classmates, friends, teachers, and parents. They too may find the problems interesting and challenging. You may be able to help them with your own hints and strategies.

## Scoring the Olympiad

You can use the following scale to evaluate your problem solving ability for each Olympiad of five problems.

| Number correct | Rating |
|---|---|
| 5 | excellent |
| 4 | superior |
| 3 | very good |
| 2 | good |
| 1 | average |
| 0 | try again |

**Remember: Learning how to solve a problem is more important than getting the correct answer. But using an effective strategy to solve a problem and getting the correct answer is the best of all situations.**

# Olympiads

| Olympiad | Page | Olympiad | Page | Olympiad | Page |
|----------|------|----------|------|----------|------|
| 1 | 19 | 28 | 46 | 55 | 73 |
| 2 | 20 | 29 | 47 | 56 | 74 |
| 3 | 21 | 30 | 48 | 57 | 75 |
| 4 | 22 | 31 | 49 | 58 | 76 |
| 5 | 23 | 32 | 50 | 59 | 77 |
| 6 | 24 | 33 | 51 | 60 | 78 |
| 7 | 25 | 34 | 52 | 61 | 79 |
| 8 | 26 | 35 | 53 | 62 | 80 |
| 9 | 27 | 36 | 54 | 63 | 81 |
| 10 | 28 | 37 | 55 | 64 | 82 |
| 11 | 29 | 38 | 56 | 65 | 83 |
| 12 | 30 | 39 | 57 | 66 | 84 |
| 13 | 31 | 40 | 58 | 67 | 85 |
| 14 | 32 | 41 | 59 | 68 | 86 |
| 15 | 33 | 42 | 60 | 69 | 87 |
| 16 | 34 | 43 | 61 | 70 | 88 |
| 17 | 35 | 44 | 62 | 71 | 89 |
| 18 | 36 | 45 | 63 | 72 | 90 |
| 19 | 37 | 46 | 64 | 73 | 91 |
| 20 | 38 | 47 | 65 | 74 | 92 |
| 21 | 39 | 48 | 66 | 75 | 93 |
| 22 | 40 | 49 | 67 | 76 | 94 |
| 23 | 41 | 50 | 68 | 77 | 95 |
| 24 | 42 | 51 | 69 | 78 | 96 |
| 25 | 43 | 52 | 70 | 79 | 97 |
| 26 | 44 | 53 | 71 | 80 | 98 |
| 27 | 45 | 54 | 72 |  |  |

**1.**

**4 min.**

Suppose today is Tuesday. What day of the week will it be 100 days from now?

Thursday

$$7\overline{|100}$$
$$\frac{7}{30}$$
$$\frac{28}{2}$$
$$\frac{14}{}$$

✓

**2.**

**5 min.**

I have four 3¢-stamps and three 5¢-stamps. Using one or more of these stamps, how many different amounts of postage can I make?

$$7+6+5+4+3+2+1 = 28$$

28 amounts

✗

**3.**

**5 min.**

Find the sum of the counting numbers from 1 to 25 inclusive. In other words, if $S = 1 + 2 + 3 + \cdots + 24 + 25$, find the value of S.

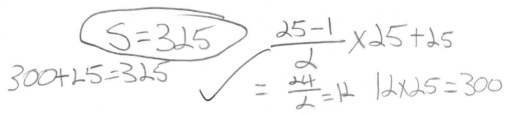

$$S = 325$$

$$300 + 25 = 325$$

$$\frac{25-1}{2} \times 25 + 25$$

$$= \frac{24}{2} = 12 \quad 12 \times 25 = 300$$

✓

**4.**

**6 min.**

In a stationery store, pencils have one price and pens have another price. Two pencils and three pens cost 78¢. But three pencils and two pens cost 72¢. How much does one pencil cost?

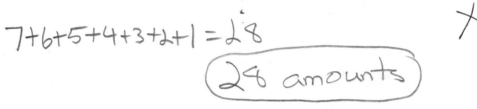

$$2p + 3d = 78$$
$$3p + 2d = 72$$
$$12 ¢$$

$$15 \times 2 + 16 \times 3 = 78$$
$$12 \times 2 + 17 \times 3$$
$$12 \times 2 + 18 \times 3 = 78$$

✓

**5.**

**5 min.**

A work crew of 3 people requires 3 weeks and 2 days to do a certain job. How long would it take a work crew of 4 people to do the same job if each person of both crews works at the same rate as each of the others? Note: each week contains six work days.

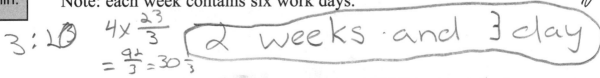

$$3:20$$
$$4 \times \frac{23}{3}$$
$$= \frac{92}{3} = 30\frac{2}{3}$$

2 weeks and 3 day

19

**1.**

**4 min.**

A girl bought a dog for $10, sold it for $15, bought it back for $20, and finally sold it for $25. Did the girl make or lose money, and how much did she make or lose?

made-$5 ✗

**2.**

**5 min.**

I have 30 coins consisting of nickels and quarters. The total value of the coins is $4.10. How many of each kind do I have?

**3.**

**5 min.**

Rectangular cards, 2 inches by 3 inches, are cut from a rectangular sheet 2 feet by 3 feet. What is the greatest number of cards that can be cut from the sheet?

6 in²    6 ft²

6 ft² = 24 in × 36 in = 780 in²

780 ÷ 6 = 130 (130 cards)

**4.**

**5 min.**

In three bowling games, Alice scores 139, 143, and 144. What score will Alice need in a fourth game in order to have an average score of 145 for all four games? ✓

145
×4
580

139
143
144
426

580
-426
154

(154)

**5.**

**6 min.**

A book has 500 pages numbered 1, 2, 3, and so on. How many times does the digit 1 appear in the page numbers?

4 + 100 + 10 + 10 + 10 + 10 + 10 ✗

= 104 + 50 + 40

= (194 times)

**1.**

4 min.

A set of marbles can be divided in equal shares among 2, 3, 4, 5, or 6 children with no marbles left over. What is the least number of marbles that the set could have?

720 marbles

$2 \cdot 3 \cdot 4 \cdot 5 \cdot 6$
$= 6 \times 20 \times 6$  X
$= 120 \times 6$
$= 720$

**2.**

5 min.

A motorist made a 60-mile trip averaging 20 miles per hour. On the return trip, he averaged 30 miles per hour. What was the motorist's average speed for the entire trip?

5 hours in 120 miles
$120 \div 5 = \boxed{24}$   24 mph ✓

**3.**

4 min.

The four-digit numeral 3AA1 is divisible by 9. What digit does A represent?

A = 4   $3+4+4+1 = 12$   X

**4.**

7 min.

Express the following sum as a simple fraction in lowest terms.

$$\frac{1}{1 \times 2} + \frac{1}{2 \times 3} + \frac{1}{3 \times 4} + \frac{1}{4 \times 5} + \frac{1}{5 \times 6}$$

$\frac{1}{2} + \frac{1}{6} + \frac{1}{12} + \frac{1}{20} + \frac{1}{36} = \frac{90}{180} + \frac{30}{180} + \frac{15}{180} + \frac{9}{180} + \frac{5}{180}$

$= \boxed{\frac{149}{180}}$

**5.**

5 min.

If we count by 3s starting with 1, the following sequence is obtained: 1, 4, 7, 10, ... . What is the 100th number in the sequence?

1 4 7 10 13 16 19 22 25 28 31 34   X

301   $(100 \times 3) + 1 = 301$

**1.**

**5 min.**

100 pounds of chocolate is packaged into boxes each containing 1¼ pounds of chocolate. Each box is then sold for $1.75. What is the total selling price for all of the boxes of chocolate?

$219.75

**2.**

**5 min.**

In the multiplication problem at the right, A and B stand for different digits. Find A and B.

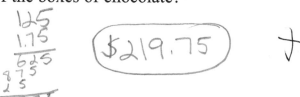

A = 3
B = 8

$$
\begin{array}{r}
A\,B \\
\times\ B\,A \\
\hline
1\ 1\ 4 \\
3\ 0\ 4 \\
\hline
3\ 1\ 5\ 4
\end{array}
$$

**3.**

**5 min.**

In the rectangle at the right, line segment MN separates the rectangle into 2 sections. What is the largest number of sections into which the rectangle can be separated when 4 line segments are drawn through the rectangle?

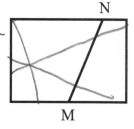

8

**4.**

**6 min.**

If $\dfrac{1}{3} = \dfrac{1}{A} + \dfrac{1}{B}$ where A and B are different whole numbers, find the value of A and the value of B.

A = 4
B = 12

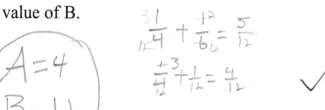

**5.**

**5 min.**

P and Q represent numbers, and P * Q means $\dfrac{P+Q}{2}$ . What is the value of 3 * (6 * 8)?

**1.**

**4 min.**

The numbers 2, 4, 6, and 8 are a set of four consecutive even numbers. Suppose the sum of five consecutive even numbers is 320. What is the smallest of the five numbers?

(60) ✓

**2.**

**5 min.**

Amy can mow 600 square yards of grass in 1½ hours. At this rate, how many minutes would it take her to mow 600 square feet?

30 minutes ✗

**3.**

**6 min.**

Express the extended fraction at the right as a simple fraction in lowest terms.

$$\cfrac{1}{2+\cfrac{1}{2+\cfrac{1}{2+\cfrac{1}{2}}}}$$

$\frac{14}{29}$ ✓

**4.**

**5 min.**

There are many numbers that divide 109 with a remainder of 4. List all two-digit numbers that have that property.

35, 21, 15 ✓

**5.**

**6 min.**

A dealer packages marbles in two different box sizes. One size holds 5 marbles and the other size holds 12 marbles. If the dealer packaged 99 marbles and used more than 10 boxes, how many boxes of each size did he use?

$\frac{12}{5} = \boxed{2}$  $\boxed{14}$  24 ✗

**1.**

**3 min.**

X and Y are two different numbers selected from the first fifty counting numbers from 1 to 50 inclusive.

What is the largest value that $\dfrac{X+Y}{X-Y}$ can have?

99 ✓

**2.**

**5 min.**

A chime clock strikes 1 chime at one o'clock, 2 chimes at two o'clock, 3 chimes at three o'clock, and so forth. What is the total number of chimes the clock will strike in a twelve-hour period?

69 ✗

**3.**

**4 min.**

The average of five weights is 13 grams. This set of five weights is then increased by another weight of 7 grams. What is the average of the six weights?

12 ✓

**4.**

**6 min.**

From a pile of 100 pennies(P), 100 nickels(N), and 100 dimes(D), select 21 coins which have a total value of exactly $1.00. In your selection you must also use at least one coin of each type. How many coins of each of the three types(P,N,D) should be selected?

P = 5    N = 13    D = 3 ✓

**5.**

**5 min.**

In a group of 30 high school students, 8 take French, 12 take Spanish and 3 take both languages. How many students of the group take neither French nor Spanish?

10 ✗

**1.**

**4 min.**

A palimage of a counting number is the number that has the same digits as the given number but in reverse order. For example, 659 and 956 are palimages; so are 1327 and 7231. Now add 354 and its palimage. Call this sum X. Add X and its palimage. Call this sum Y. Add Y and its palimage. Call this sum Z. What is the value of Z?

*15156 666*

**2.**

**5 min.**

A boy has the following seven coins in his pocket: 2 pennies, 2 nickels, 2 dimes, and 1 quarter. He takes out two coins, records the sum of their values, and then puts them back with the other coins. He continues to take out two coins, record the sum of their values, and put them back. How many different sums can he record at most?

**3.**

**4 min.**

Suppose all the counting numbers are arranged in columns as shown at the right. Under what column-letter will 1000 appear?

| A | B | C | D | E | F | G |
|---|---|---|---|---|---|---|
| 1 | 2 | 3 | 4 | 5 | 6 | 7 |
| 8 | 9 | 10 | 11 | 12 | 13 | 14 |
| 15 | 16 | 17 | 18 | 19 | _ | _ |

*142 R6*

*142.857¹*

*7⟌1000*

**4.**

**4 min.**

Twelve people purchased supplies for a ten-day camping trip with the understanding that each of the twelve will get equal daily shares. They are then joined by three more people, but make no further purchases. How long will the supplies then last if the original daily share for each person is not changed?

*12 - 1 each*
*15 - 1 each*

**5.**

**5 min.**

The U-shaped figure at the right contains 11 squares of the same size. The area of the U-shaped figure is 176 square inches. How many inches are in the perimeter of the U-shaped figure?

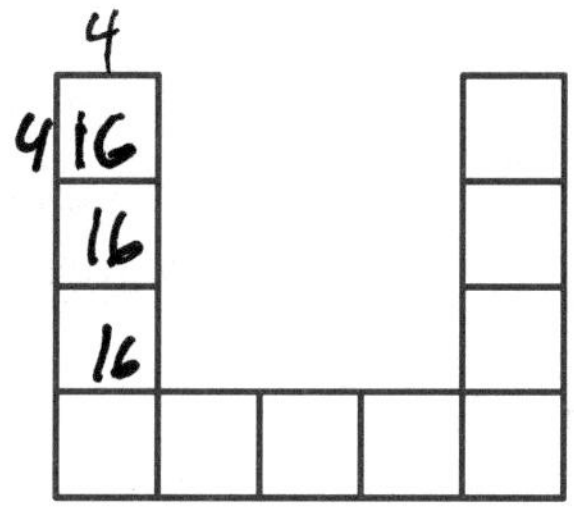

*24 inches*

**1.**

**4 min.**

A bag contains 500 beads, each of the same size, but in 5 different colors. Suppose there are 100 beads of each color and I am blindfolded. What is the fewest number of beads I must pick to be absolutely sure there are 5 beads of the same color among the beads I have picked blindfolded?

**2.**

**5 min.**

If 20 is added to one-third of a number, the result is the double of the number. What is the number?

*12* ✓

**3.**

**5 min.**

Each of the boxes in the figure at the right is a square. How many different squares can be traced using the lines in the figure?

*38*

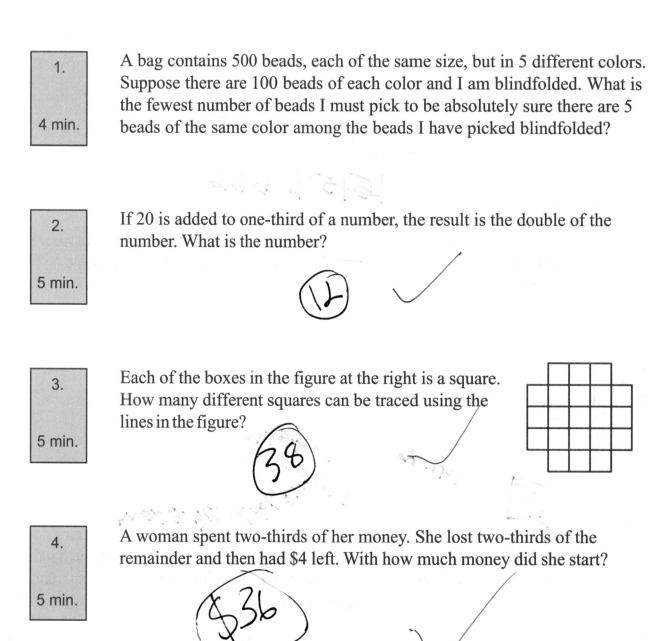

**4.**

**5 min.**

A woman spent two-thirds of her money. She lost two-thirds of the remainder and then had $4 left. With how much money did she start?

*$36* ✓

**5.**

**5 min.**

If a number ends in zeros, the zeros are called *terminal zeros*. For example, 520,000 has four terminal zeros, but 502,000 has just three terminal zeros. Let N equal the product of all counting numbers from 1 through 20:

$$N = 1 \times 2 \times 3 \times 4 \times \cdots \times 20.$$

How many terminal zeros will N have when it is written in standard form?

**1.**

5 min.

In the "magic-square" at the right, five more numbers can be placed in the boxes so that the sum of the three numbers in each row, in each column, and in each diagonal is always the same. What value should X have?

| 15 |    | 35 |
|----|----|----|
| 50 | 30 | 10 |
| 25 | X  | 45 |

X = 20

**2.**

4 min.

If I start with 2 and count by 3s until I reach 449, I will get: 2, 5, 8, 11, ... , 449 where 2 is the first number, 5 is the second number, 8 is the third number and so forth. If 449 is the Nth number, what is the value of N?

149

149
×3

149
×3
447

**3.**

5 min.

The perimeter of a rectangle is 22 inches and the inch-measure of each side is a counting number. How many different areas in square inches can the rectangle have?

1 10
2 9
3 8
4 7
5 6

5

**4.**

5 min.

A man drives from his home at 30 miles per hour to the shopping center which is 20 miles from his home. On the return trip he encounters heavy traffic and averages 12 miles per hour. How much time does the man take in driving to and from the shopping center?

40 + 84 = 124

**5.**

6 min.

In the division problem at the right, the blanks represent missing digits. If A and B represent the digits of the quotient, what are the values of A and B?

```
      AB
  5_)_0___
      6_
     432
     432
       0
```

**1.** 4 min.

In the addition problem at the right, each letter stands for a digit and different letters stand for different digits. What digits do the letters H, E, and A each represent?

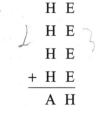

```
    H E
    H E
    H E
  + H E
  -----
    A H
```

A=9   H=2   E=3

**2.** 5 min.

The product of two numbers is 144 and their difference is 10. What is the sum of the two numbers?

26

**3.** 5 min.

A and B are whole numbers, and $\frac{A}{11}+\frac{B}{3}=\frac{31}{33}$. Find the value of A and the value of B.

A = 3   B = 1

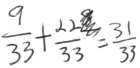

$\frac{9}{33}+\frac{22}{33}=\frac{31}{33}$

$\frac{3a}{33}+\frac{11b}{33}=\frac{31}{33}$

**4.** 5 min.

The XYZ club collected a total of $1.21 from its members with each member contributing the same amount. If each member paid for his or her share with 3 coins, how many nickels were contributed?

11

**5.** 6 min.

During a school year, a student was given an award of 25¢ for each math test he passed and was fined 50¢ for each math test he failed. At the end of the school year, the student had passed 7 times as many tests as he had failed, and received $3.75. How many tests did he fail?

**1.**

**5 min.**

Julius Caesar wrote the Roman Numerals I, II, III, IV, and V in a certain order from left to right. He wrote I before III but after IV. He wrote II after IV but before I. He wrote V after II but before III. If V was not the third numeral, in what order did Caesar write the five numerals from left to right?

*IV | II | I | V | III*     *I V | I | III*

**2.**

**5 min.**

In the multiplication problem at the right, each blank space represents a missing digit. Find the product.

$$\begin{array}{r} 4\_6 \\ \times \ 3\ 7 \\ \hline \_\ 9\ 8\ 2 \\ 1\ 2\ \_\ 8 \\ \end{array}$$

*416*
*37*

product: *15762*

**3.**

**4 min.**

Glen, Harry, and Kim each have a different favorite sport among tennis, baseball, and soccer. Glen does not like baseball or soccer. Harry does not like baseball. Name the favorite sport of each person.

*G = T*
*H = S*
*K = B*

**4.**

**4 min.**

An acute angle is an angle whose measure is between 0° and 90°. Using the rays in the diagram, how many different acute angles can be formed?

  *4+3+1=8*

**5.**

**6 min.**

Thirteen plums weigh as much as two apples and one pear. Four plums and one apple have the same weight as one pear. How many plums have the weight of one pear?

*4q + a = p*     *13q = 2a + p*

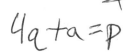

*4q = p − a*     *q = 4.5*

**1.**

**4 min.**

Arrange the digits 1, 1, 2, 2, 3, 3, as a six-digit number in which the 1s are separated by one digit, the 2s are separated by two digits, and the 3s are separated by <u>three digits</u>. There are two answers. Find one.

12132  312132 ← other one

231213

**2.**

**3 min.**

Suppose five days before the day after tomorrow was Wednesday. What day of the week was yesterday?

~~Thursday~~

Friday

**3.**

**5 min.**

At the right, ABCD is a square whose sides are each 2 units long. The length of the shortest path from A to C following the lines of the diagram is 4 units. How many different shortest paths are there from A to C?

6 paths

**4.**

**4 min.**

A dollar was changed into 16 coins consisting of just nickels and dimes. How many coins of each kind were in the change?

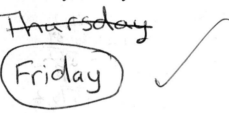

12 nickels
4 dimes

$$x + y = 16$$
$$5x + 10y = 100$$

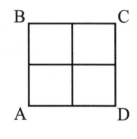

$$5x + 5y = 80$$
$$5x + 10y = 100$$
$$0 + 5y = 20$$
$$y = 4 \quad x = 12$$

**5.**

**6 min.**

A number has a remainder of 1 when divided by 4, a remainder of 2 when divided by 5, and a remainder of 3 when divided by 6. What is the smallest number that has the above properties?

57

**1.**

**4 min.**

Each of the boxes in the figure at the right is a square. Using the lines of the figure, how many different squares can be traced? $15+6+1=22$ ways

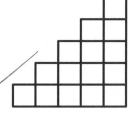

**2.**

**5 min.**

In the multiplication problem at the right, different letters stand for different digits, and ABC and DBC each represent a three-digit number. What number does DBC represent? (Two answers are possible; give one.)  875

$$A \ B \ C \ 5$$
$$\times \ C \ 5$$
$$8 \ D \ B \ C \ 5$$

$$\begin{array}{r} 175 \\ \times 5 \\ \hline 875 \end{array}$$

**3.**

**4 min.**

Consecutive numbers are whole numbers that follow in order such as 7, 8, 9, 10, 11, and 12. Find three consecutive numbers such that the sum of the first and third is 118.   58, 59, 60

**4.**

**6 min.**

When Anne, Betty, and Cynthia compared the amount of money each had, they discovered that Anne and Betty together had $12, Betty and Cynthia together had $18, and Anne and Cynthia together had $10. Who had the least amount of money, and how much was it?

$b+(10-a)=18$

$a+b=12 \quad a=-b+12$
$b+c=18 \quad b=-c+18$
$a+c=10 \quad c=-a+10$

**5.**

**5 min.**

A total of fifteen pennies are put into four piles so that each pile has a different number of pennies. What is the smallest possible number of pennies that could be in the largest pile?

3  4  5  6    six

2  3  4  5

**1.**

**4 min.**

The perimeter of a rectangle is 20 feet and the foot-measure of each side is a whole number. How many rectangles with different shapes satisfy these conditions?

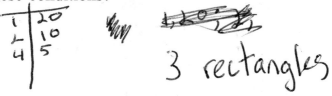

3 rectangles

**2.**

**5 min.**

In a math contest of 10 problems, 5 points was given for each correct answer and 2 points was deducted for each incorrect answer. If Nancy answered all 10 problems and scored 29 points, how many correct answers did she have?

$x + y = 10$   $5x + 5y = 50$

$5x - 2y = 29$   $5x - 2y = 19$

$7 \text{ correct answers}$   $0 \quad 7y = 79$

**3.**

**4 min.**

The counting numbers are arranged in four columns as shown at the right. Under which column letter will 101 appear?

D

| A | B | C | D |
|---|---|---|---|
| 1 | 2 | 3 | 4 |
| 8 | 7 | 6 | 5 |
| 9 | 10 | 11 | 12 |
| … | … | 14 | 13 |

**4.**

**6 min.**

Three water pipes are used to fill a swimming pool. The first pipe alone takes 8 hours to fill the pool, the second pipe alone takes 12 hours to fill the pool, and the third pipe alone takes 24 hours to fill the pool. If all three pipes are opened at the same time, how long will it take to fill the pool?

**5.**

**5 min.**

In the "magic square" at the right, the four numbers in each column, in each row, and in each of the two diagonals, have the same sum. What value should N have?

|   |    | 7  | 12 |
|---|----|----|----|
| N | 4  | 9  |    |
|   | 5  | 16 | 3  |
| 8 | 11 |    |    |

**1.**

4 min.

A train can hold 78 passengers. The train starts out empty and picks up 1 passenger at the first stop, 2 passengers at the second stop, 3 passengers at the third stop, and so forth. After how many stops will the train be full?

9   10   11
47   57   68

*12 stops* ✓

**2.**

5 min.

The complete outside including the bottom of a wooden 4 inch cube is painted red. The painted cube is then cut into 1 inch cubes. How many of the 1 inch cubes do not have red paint on any face?

*4 cubes* ✗

46
+8
54

**3.**

5 min.

The number of two-dollar bills I need to pay for a purchase is 9 more than the number of five-dollar bills I need to pay for the same purchase. What is the cost of the purchase?

*$30* ✓

**4.**

4 min.

If 24 gallons of water are poured into an empty tank, then 3/4 of the tank is filled. How many gallons does a full tank hold?

*32 gallons* ✓

**5.**

6 min.

3×3, 3×3×3, and 3×3×3×3 are "multiplication strings" of two 3s, three 3s, and four 3s respectively. When each string multiplication is done, 3×3 ends in 9, 3×3×3 ends in 7, and 3×3×3×3 ends in 1. In what digit will a multiplication string of thirty-five 3s end?

*7* ✓

**1.**

**3 min.**

The last Friday of a particular month is on the 25th day of the month. What day of the week is the first day of the month?

*Tuesday* ✓

**2.**

**4 min.**

The age of a man is the same as his wife's age with the digits reversed. The sum of their ages is 99 and the man is 9 years older than his wife. How old is the man?

*54* ✓

**3.**

**4 min.**

A group of 21 people went to the county fair with 9 people on a stagecoach and 3 people in each buggy. On the return trip, 4 people rode in each buggy. How many people returned on the stagecoach?

*5 people* ✓

**4.**

**5 min.**

At the right are three views of the same cube. What letter is on the face opposite (1) H, (2) X, and (3) Y? (Give your answer in the same order.)

*E, A, N* ✓

**5.**

**6 min.**

D is the sum of the odd numbers from 1 through 99 inclusive, and N is the sum of the even numbers from 2 through 98 inclusive:

$$D = 1 + 3 + 5 + \cdots + 99 \text{ and } N = 2 + 4 + 6 + \cdots + 98$$

Which is greater, D or N, and by how much?

*N, by 49* ✗

$3x + 6y = 3.6$
$x + 6y = 1.8$
$2x = 1.8$ $x = \frac{1.8}{2}$ = $\frac{180}{2} = 90$¢

Very bad

**1.**

**4 min.**

I have exactly ten coins whose total value is \$1. If three of the coins are quarters, what are the remaining coins?

7 coins → 25¢
2 d 5c
(2 Dimes + 5 pennies)

**2.**

**4 min.**

One loaf of bread and six rolls cost \$1.80. At the same prices, two loaves of bread and four rolls cost \$2.40. How much does one loaf of bread cost?

$x + 6y = 1.80$
$3x + 6y = 3.6$  $2x + 4y = 2.40$
$2x = 60$¢   $x = 30$¢

$2x + 12y = 3.60$
$2x + 4y = 2.40$
$8y = 1.20$
$y =$

16.48
3

**3.**

**5 min.**

The small boxes in Figures A and B at the right are congruent squares. The perimeter of Figure A is 48 inches. What is the perimeter of Figure B? (The perimeter of a figure is the distance around it.)

A

B

20

56 inches

**4.**

**5 min.**

If a kindergarten teacher places her children 4 on each bench, there will be 3 children who will not have a place. However, if 5 children are placed on each bench, there will be 2 empty places. What is the smallest number of children the class could have?

$6 \times 4 = 24$ × × ×
13
23
27 children

**5.**

**4 min.**

If the digits A, B, and C are added, the sum is the two-digit number AB as shown at the right. What is the value of C?

1
3
9
13

1
4
9

9

A
B
+ C
A B

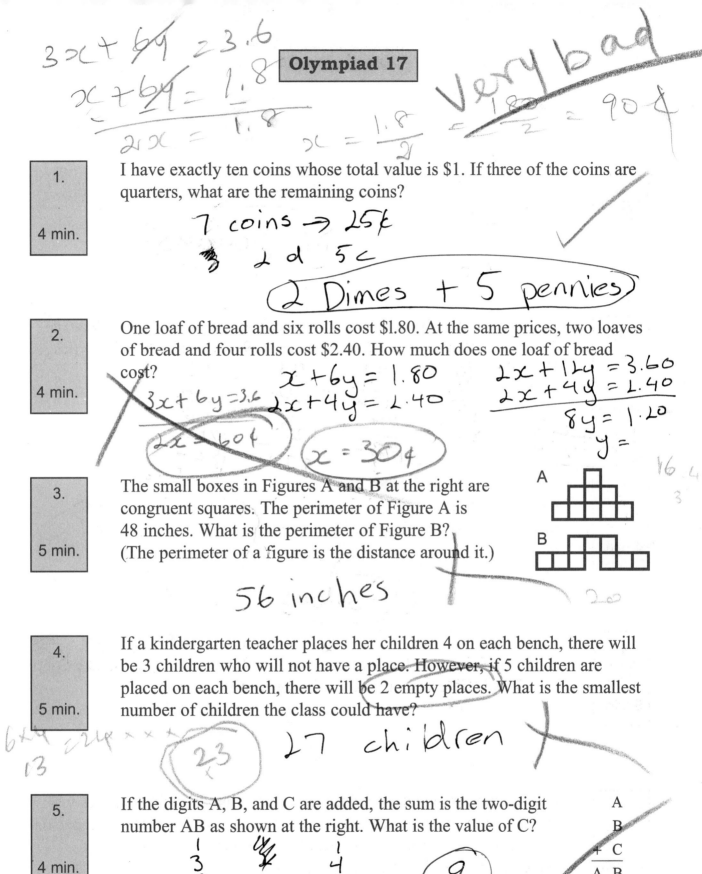

**1.**

**4 min.**

The sum of the weights of Tom and Bill is 138 pounds and one boy is 34 pounds heavier than the other. How much does the heavier boy weigh?

$$\begin{array}{r} 69 \\ 17 \\ \hline 86 \end{array}$$

86 pounds ✓

**2.**

**5 min.**

When I open my mathematics book, there are two pages which face me and the product of the two page numbers is 1806. What are the two page numbers?

42 + 43

$$\begin{array}{r} 15 \\ 15 \\ \hline 75 \\ 15 \\ \hline 225 \end{array}$$

$$\begin{array}{r} 44 \\ 44 \\ \hline 176 \\ 176 \\ \hline 1936 \end{array}$$

$$\begin{array}{r} 43 \\ 44 \\ \hline 172 \\ 12 \\ \hline 1892 \end{array}$$

$$\begin{array}{r} 43 \\ 42 \\ \hline 86 \\ 172 \\ \hline 1806 \end{array}$$ ✓

**3.**

**4 min.**

Eight one-inch cubes are put together to form the T-figure shown at the right. The complete outside of the T-figure is painted red and then separated into one-inch cubes. How many of the cubes have exactly four red faces?

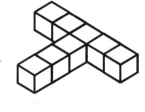

4 cubes ✓

**4.**

**5 min.**

The members of an Olympiad team contributed a total of $1.69 for refreshments for their weekly practice. Each member contributed the same amount and paid for his or her share in five coins. How many nickels were contributed by all of the members?

**5.**

**5 min.**

Consecutive numbers are counting numbers that follow in order as in 7, 8, 9, 10, and so forth. Suppose the average of 15 consecutive numbers is 15. What is the average of the first five numbers of the set?

8, 9, 10, 11, 12

 10 ✓

 ( 8  9  10  11  12 ) 13  14  15  16  17  —

**1.**

**4 min.**

A camera and case together cost $100. If the camera costs $90 more than the case, how much does the case cost?

$x + y = 100$          $x + y = 100$
$x = 90 + y$          $x - y = 90$
                    _____
($5)  ✓             $\phi \, 2y = 10$
                         $y = 5$   $x = 95$

**2.**

**3 min.**

In the addition problem at the right A, B, and C are digits. If C is placed in the tens column instead of the units column as shown at the far right, the sum is 97. What are the values of A, B, and C?

```
A B        A B
+ C        + C
___        ___
5 2        9 7
```

4  7  5
A  B  C

```
47        47
+5       +50
__        __
52        97
```

**3.**

**5 min.**

Suppose K, L, and M represent the number of points assigned to the three target regions shown at the right. The sum of K and L is 11, the sum of L and M is 19, and the sum of K and M is 16. How many points are assigned to M?

$K + L = 11$
$L + M =$

**4.**

**5 min.**

Mrs. Winthrop went to a store, spent half of her money and then $10 more. She went to a second store, spent half of her remaining money and then $10 more. But she then had no money left. How much money did she have to begin with when she went to the first store?

$0 + 10 + 10 + 10 + 30 = 60$

$60  ✓

**5.**

**5 min.**

A4273B is a six-digit number in which A and B are digits, and the number is divisible by 72 without remainder. Find the value of A and the value of B.

**1.**

**4 min.**

A train is moving at the rate of 1 mile in 1 minute and 20 seconds. If the train continues at this rate, how far will it travel in one hour?

45 miles

80⟌3600
 320
 400
 400
 000

**2.**

**5 min.**

If a number is divided by 3 or 5, the remainder is 1. If it is divided by 7, there is no remainder. What number between 1 and 100 satisfies the above conditions?

91

**3.**

**5 min.**

Toytrain cars made of blocks of wood either 6 inches long or 7 inches long can be hooked together to make longer trains. Which of the following train-lengths cannot be made by hooking together either 6-inch train cars, 7-inch train cars, or a combination of both:

29 inches, 30 inches, 31 inches, 32 inches, 33 inches?

14 + 18

**4.**

**5 min.**

A circular track is 1000 yards in circumference. Cyclists A, B, and C start at the same place and time, and race around the track at the following rates per minute: A at 700 yards, B at 800 yards, and C at 900 yards. What is the least number of minutes it must take for all three to be together again?

**5.**

**6 min.**

Alice and Betty each want to buy the same kind of ruler. But Alice is 22¢ short and Betty is 3¢ short. When they combine their money, they still do not have enough money. What is the most the ruler could cost?

24¢

**1.**

**4 min.**

Six dollars were exchanged for nickels and dimes. The number of nickels was the same as the number of dimes. How many nickels were there in the change?

$n = d$

$5n + 10d = 600$

$120t$

$5n - 5d = 0$

$5n + 10d = 600$

$0 \quad 5d = 600$

$d = 120$

**2.**

**4 min.**

In the multiplication example at the right, A, B, and H represent different digits. What is the sum of A, B, and H?

$$
\begin{array}{r}
B\ A \\
\times\ 7 \\
\hline
H\ A\ A
\end{array}
$$

**3.**

**5 min.**

A total of 350 pounds of cheese is packaged into boxes each containing 1¾ pounds of cheese. Each box is then sold for $1.75. What is the total selling price of all of the boxes of cheese?

$350

**4.**

**4 min.**

A wooden block is 4 inches long, 4 inches wide, and 1 inch high. The block is painted red on all six sides and then cut into sixteen 1 inch cubes. How many of the cubes each have a total number of red faces that is an even number?

8 cubes

**5.**

**6 min.**

$1200 is divided among four brothers so that each gets $100 more than the brother who is his next younger brother. How much does the youngest brother get?

$x, x+100, x+200, x+300$

$150, 250, 350, 450$

$400 \qquad 800$

$150

**1.**

**3 min.**

Suppose two days ago was Sunday. What day of the week will 365 days from today then be?

*Tu*  $7\overline{)365}$  52

Wednesday

**2.**

**5 min.**

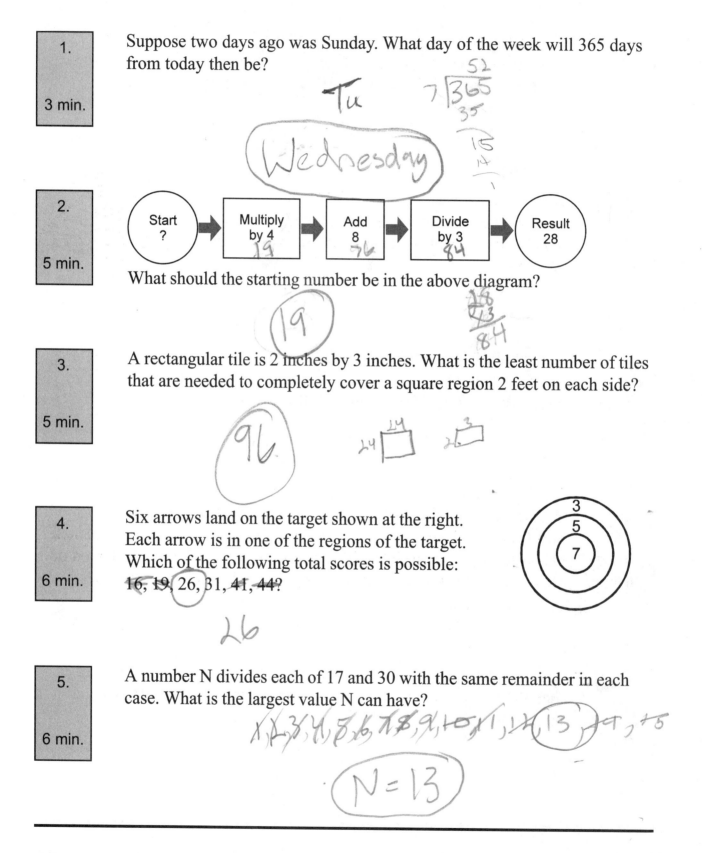

What should the starting number be in the above diagram?

19

**3.**

**5 min.**

A rectangular tile is 2 inches by 3 inches. What is the least number of tiles that are needed to completely cover a square region 2 feet on each side?

96

**4.**

**6 min.**

Six arrows land on the target shown at the right. Each arrow is in one of the regions of the target. Which of the following total scores is possible: 16, 19, 26, 31, 41, 44?

26

**5.**

**6 min.**

A number N divides each of 17 and 30 with the same remainder in each case. What is the largest value N can have?

N = 13

**1.**

**4 min.**

The average of five numbers is 18. Let the first number be increased by 1, the second number by 2, the third number by 3, the fourth number by 4, and the fifth number by 5. What is the average of the set of increased numbers?

16, 17, 18, 19, 20
17, 19, (21), 23, 25

**2.**

**5 min.**

The set of stairs shown at the right is constructed by placing layers of cubes on top of each other. What is the total number of cubes contained in the staircase?

48 cubes

**3.**

**6 min.**

When a counting number is multiplied by itself, the result is a square number. Some examples of square numbers are 1, 4, 9, 16, and 25. How many square numbers are there between 1,000 and 2,000?

**4.**

**5 min.**

The owner of a bicycle store had a sale on bicycles (two-wheelers) and tricycles (three-wheelers). Each cycle had two pedals. When he counted the total number of pedals of the cycles, he got 50. When he counted the total number of wheels of the cycles, he got 64. How many tricycles were offered in the sale?

14 tricycles

$x + y = 50$
$2x + 3y = 64$

$2x + 2y = 100$ (50)
$2x + 3y = 64$
$y = 14 \quad x = 11$

**5.**

**5 min.**

A jar filled with water weighs 10 pounds. When one-half of the water is poured out, the jar and remaining water weigh 5¾ pounds. How much does the jar weigh?

$x + y = 10$
$x + \frac{y}{2} = 5\frac{3}{4}$
$2x + y = 11\frac{1}{2}$

$y = 10 - x$
$y = 11\frac{1}{2} - 2x$
$y = -2x$

**1.**

**4 min.**

Person A was born on January 15, 1948.
Person B was born on January 15, 1962.
If both are alive now, in what year was person A
twice as old as person B?

16, 2    20, 6    24, 10    28, 14

1976

**2.**

**5 min.**

A square piece of paper is folded in half as shown
and then cut into two rectangles along the fold. The
perimeter of each of the two rectangles is 18 inches.
What is the perimeter of the original square?

24    inches

**3.**

**5 min.**

In the division example at the right A and B represent
different digits. What is the sum of A and B if the
remainder is zero?

$$AB \overline{)\underline{\phantom{--}}\,\underline{\phantom{-}}\,1}^{\displaystyle BA}$$

$$=\!=\!=$$
$$\underline{\phantom{--}}\,1$$
$$=\!=\!=$$

**4.**

**5 min.**

The product of two whole numbers is 10,000. If neither number contains
a zero digit, what are the two numbers?

**5.**

**7 min.**

A train traveling at 30 miles per hour reaches a tunnel which is 9 times as
long as the train. If the train takes 2 minutes to completely clear the
tunnel, how long is the train? (1 mile = 5,280 feet)

586
9 ) 5280
45
78
72
60
54

586
×9
4

**1.**

**4 min.**

My age this year is a multiple of 7. Next year it will be a multiple of 5. I am more than 20 years of age but less than 80. How old will I be 6 years from now?

$55$

$49$
$+6$
$\overline{55}$

**2.**

**5 min.**

Six people participated in a checker tournament. Each participant played exactly three games with each of the other participants. How many games were played in all?

$15$
$\times 6$
$\overline{90}$

$90$ games

**3.**

**6 min.**

Consecutive numbers are counting numbers that follow in order as in the case of 3, 4, 5, 6, and 7. Find three consecutive numbers whose product is 15,600.

$5200$
$3\overline{)15600}$
$15$
$006$

**4.**

**5 min.**

Of three numbers, two are 1/2 and 1/3. What should the third number be so that the average of all three is 1?

$$\frac{x + \frac{4}{6}}{3} = 1$$

$x + \frac{4}{6} = 3$

$x = 2\frac{1}{3}$

**5.**

**6 min.**

The four-digit number A 5 5 B is divisible by 36. What is the sum of A and B?

---

**1.** The month of January has 31 days. Suppose January 1 occurs on Monday. What day of the week is February 22 of the next month?

4 min.

$$7\overline{)53}$$ handwritten work: $49$, $4$

M T W T F

(Friday)

**2.** How many times does x occur in the diagram at the right?

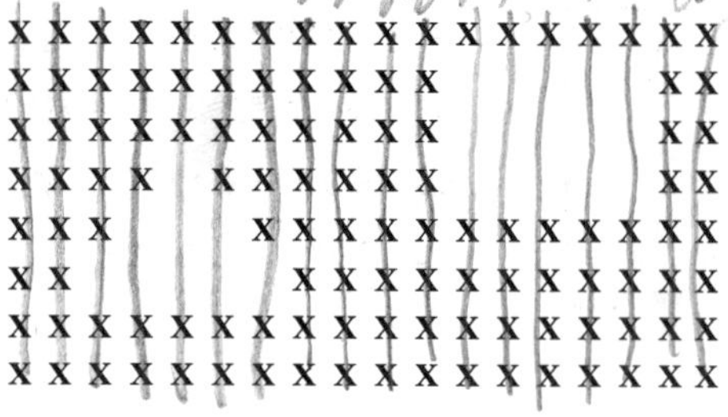

5 min.

(120)

handwritten work with x diagram

**3.** The product of three counting numbers is 24. How many different sets of 3 numbers have this property if the order of the 3 numbers in a set does not matter?

4 min.

(1, 2, 12)  (2, 2, 6)
(1, 3, 8)
(1, 4, 6)
(2, 3, 4)

(5 sets)

**4.** A group of 12 girl scouts had enough food to last for 8 days when they arrived in camp. However, 4 more scouts joined them without the amount of food being increased. How long will the food last if each scout is given the same daily ration as originally planned?

4 min.

(6 days)

96 ÷ 12 = 8 days
96 ÷ 16 = 6 days

**5.** Let N be a number that divides 171 with a remainder of 6. List all the two-digit numbers that N can be.

5 min.

**1.**

**3 min.**

Carol spent exactly $1 for some 5¢-stamps and some 13¢-stamps. How many 5¢-stamps did she buy?

$x + y = 100$    65

⑦    5  13s
      7  55

**2.**

**5 min.**

A square has an area of 144 square inches. Suppose the square is partitioned into six congruent rectangles as shown at the right. How many inches are there in the perimeter of one of the six rectangles?

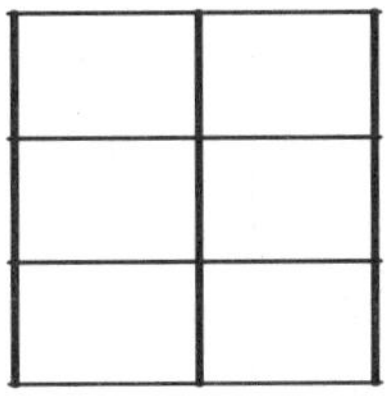

⟨20 inches⟩

**3.**

**5 min.**

In the addition problem at the right, there are three two-digit numbers in which different letters represent different digits. What digits do A, B, and C represent?

```
    A  A
    B  B
+   C  C
-------
  B  A  C
```

**4.**

**5 min.**

The result of multiplying a counting number by itself is a square number. For example 1, 4, 9, and 16 are each square numbers because 1×1 = 1, 2×2 = 4, 3×3 = 9, and 4×4 = 16. What year in the 20th century (the years 1901 through 2000) was a square number?

㊹ ⟨1936⟩

**5.**

**5 min.**

The digits of a two-digit number are interchanged to form a new two-digit number. The difference of the original number and the new number is 45. Find the largest two-digit number which satisfies these conditions.    3 8    8 3

```
  8 3
  3 8
-----
  4 5
```

**1.**

**3 min.**

A and B are two different numbers selected from the first forty counting numbers, 1 through 40 inclusive.

What is the largest value that $\dfrac{A \times B}{A - B}$ can have?

39

40
‾‾
00
156
‾‾‾
1560

1560

**2.**

**6 min.**

A twelve-hour clock loses 1 minute every hour. Suppose it shows the correct time now. What is the least number of hours from now when it will again show the correct time?

720 hours

**3.**

**5 min.**

A certain counting number is divisible by 3 and also by 5. When the number is divided by 7, the remainder is 4. What is the smallest number that satisfies these conditions?

60

**4.**

**5 min.**

The figure shown consists of 3 layers of cubes with no gaps. Suppose the complete exterior of the figure (including the bottom) is painted red and then separated into individual cubes. How many of these cubes have exactly 3 red faces?

**5.**

**6 min.**

Alice needs 1 hour to do a certain job. Betty, her older sister, can do the same job in 1/2 hour. How many minutes will it take them to do the job if they work together at the given rates?

**1.**

**4 min.**

3, 6, 9, 12, ... are some multiples of 3. How many multiples of 3 are there between 10 and 226?

**2.**

**5 min.**

ABCD is a rectangle with area equal to 36 square units. Points E, F, and G are midpoints of the sides on which they are located. How many square units are there in the area of triangle EFG?

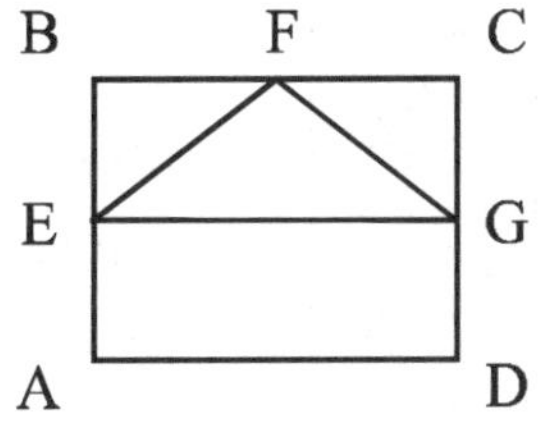

**3.**

**4 min.**

When the sum of two whole numbers is multiplied by the difference of the numbers, the result is 85. If the difference of the two numbers is not 1, what is their sum?

**4.**

**5 min.**

30! represents the product of all counting numbers from 1 through 30 inclusive: $1 \times 2 \times 3 \times 4 \times 5 \times \cdots \times 28 \times 29 \times 30$. If the product is factored into primes, how many 5s will the factorization contain?

**5.**

**6 min.**

A printer has to number the pages of a book from 1 to 150. Suppose the printer uses a separate piece of type for each digit in each number. How many pieces of type will the printer have to use?

**1.**

**3 min.**

Many whole numbers between 10 and 1,000 have 2 or 7 as the units digit. How many such numbers are there between 10 and 1,000?

198

**2.**

**4 min.**

Peter has one of each of the following coins in his pocket: a penny, a nickel, a dime, a quarter, and a half-dollar. Four of these coins are taken out of the pocket and the sum of their values is calculated. How many different sums are possible?

**3.**

**4 min.**

The front wheel of a vehicle has a circumference of 3 feet, the rear wheel has a circumference of 4 feet. How many more complete turns will the front wheel make than the rear wheel in travelling a distance of 1 mile on a straight road? (1 mile = 5280 feet)

**4.**

**6 min.**

In the multiplication example at the right, each of A, B, and C stands for a different digit and each of the blank spaces represents a non-zero digit. What digits do A, B, and C each represent?

```
    A B C
  × A B C
  * * * 9
  * * * 4
* * * 1
```

**5.**

**5 min.**

Ann gave Betty as many cents as Betty had. Betty then gave Ann as many cents as Ann then had. At this point, each had 12 cents. How much did Ann have at the beginning?

**1.** 5 min.

The weight of a whole brick is the same as 4 pounds plus the weight of 1/3 of the whole brick. How many pounds does the whole brick weigh?

*6 pounds*

**2.** 5 min.

Consecutive odd numbers are odd numbers that differ by 2 and follow in order such as 1, 3, 5, 7, 9, or, 17, 19, 21. Find the first of seven consecutive odd numbers if the average of the seven numbers is 41.

*35*

**3.** 5 min.

When the order of the digits of 2552 is reversed, the number remains the same. How many counting numbers between 100 and 1000 remain the same when the order of the number's digits is reversed?

*| | | | | | | | | | = 10*

*90 #s*

**4.** 5 min.

A tractor wheel is 88 inches in circumference. How many complete turns will the wheel make in rolling one mile on the ground? (1 mile = 5,280 feet)

*720 turns*

$$88\overline{)63360}$$

*5280 × 12 = 10560, 5280, 63360*

**5.** 5 min.

In the addition problem at the right, each letter represents a digit and different letters represent different digits. What four-digit number does D E E R represent?

```
    I N
+ R I D
-------
D E E R
```

**1.**

**4 min.**

Tom multiplied a number by 2½ and got 50 as an answer. However, he should have divided the number by 2½ to get the correct answer. What is the correct answer?

8

**2.**

**5 min.**

Consider the counting numbers from 1 to 1000: 1, 2, 3, 4, ... , 1000. Which one of these numbers multiplied by itself, is closest to 1985?

44

$$
\begin{array}{r} 45 \\ 45 \\ \hline 225 \\ 180 \\ \hline 2025 \end{array}
\qquad
\begin{array}{r} 44 \\ 44 \\ \hline 176 \\ 176 \\ \hline 1936 \end{array}
$$

**3.**

**6 min.**

The sum of the ages of Al and Bill is 25; the sum of the ages of Al and Carl is 20; the sum of the ages of Bill and Carl is 31. Who is the oldest of the three and how old is he?

$$a+b=25$$
$$a+c=20$$
$$b+c=31$$

**4.**

**6 min.**

A square is divided into three congruent rectangles as shown at the right. Each of the three rectangles has a perimeter of 16 meters. How many meters are in the perimeter of the square?

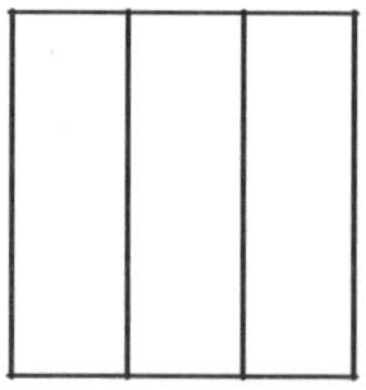

**5.**

**6 min.**

Abracadabra has four different coins with values as shown at the right. Suppose you had just one of each of the four different coins. How many different amounts can be made using one or more of the four different coins?

1    2

4    8

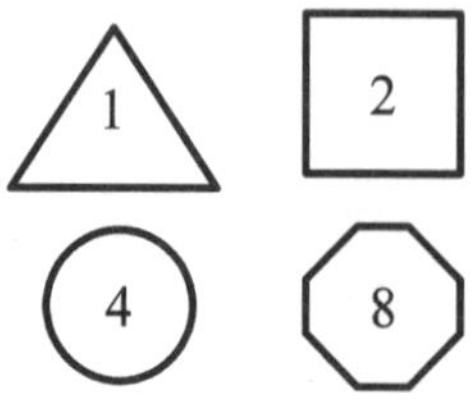

**1.**

**4 min.**

The weight of a glass bowl and the marbles it contains is 50 ounces. If the number of marbles in the bowl is doubled, the total weight of the bowl and marbles is 92 ounces. What is the weight of the bowl?
(Assume that each of the marbles has the same weight.)

$$x+y=50 \qquad -y=-42 \qquad y=42$$
$$x+2y=92 \qquad x=\boxed{8 \ ounces}$$

**2.**

**5 min.**

A number is greater than 10 and has the property that, when divided either by 5 or by 7, the remainder is 1. What is the smallest odd counting number that has this property?

$\boxed{71}$

**3.**

**6 min.**

The tower at the right is made up of five horizontal layers of cubes with no gaps. How many individual cubes are in the tower?

$$5+8+9+8+5$$
$$=\boxed{35}$$

**4.**

**6 min.**

A certain slow clock loses 15 minutes every hour. Suppose the clock is set to the correct time at 9 AM What will the correct time be when the slow clock first shows 10 AM?

$$10{:}15 \ AM$$

**5.**

**6 min.**

Said Anne to Betty: "If you give me one marble, we will each have the same number of marbles." Said Betty to Anne: "If you give me one marble, I will have twice as many marbles as you will then have."
How many marbles did Anne have before any exchange was made?

$$A+1=B-1 \qquad a+1=b-1 \quad b=a+2$$
$$B+1=2a \qquad b+1=2a \quad b=2a-1$$
$$\qquad\qquad\qquad\qquad 3b=5a$$

**1.**

**4 min.**

The sum of the first twenty-five counting numbers is 325:
$$1 + 2 + 3 + 4 + \cdots + 25 = 325.$$
What is the sum of the next twenty-five counting numbers:
$$26 + 27 + 28 + 29 + \cdots + 50 = ?$$

**2.**

**5 min.**

Eric has just three types of coins in his change-purse: nickels, dimes, and quarters. The purse contains more dimes than quarters, and more quarters than nickels and there are seven coins in all. What is the total value of the seven coins?

**3.**

**6 min.**

Square ABCD and rectangle AEFG each have an area of 36 square meters. E is the midpoint of AB. What is the perimeter of rectangle AEFG?

**4.**

**6 min.**

If <u>a</u> is divided by <u>b</u>, the result is 3/4. If <u>b</u> is divided by <u>c</u>, the result is 5/6. What is the result when <u>a</u> is divided by <u>c</u>?

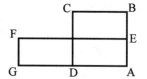

**5.**

**6 min.**

Find the greatest counting number that divides 364, 414, and 539 with the same remainder in each case.

**1.**

**3 min.**

In the XYZ contest, a school may enter 1, 2, 3, or, at most, 4 teams. Suppose 347 teams are entered in the XYZ contest. What is the smallest number of schools that could have entered the XYZ contest?

347 teams

**2.**

**4 min.**

What is the total of:
one plus two plus three plus four plus five plus six plus
one plus two plus three plus four plus five plus six plus
one plus two plus three plus four plus five plus six plus
one plus two plus three plus four plus five plus six plus
one plus two plus three plus four plus five?

5 + 10 + 15 + 20 + 25 + 24 = 99

**3.**

**5 min.**

Express the sum at the right as a simple fraction in lowest terms.

$$\frac{1}{2+\dfrac{1}{2}}+\frac{1}{3+\dfrac{1}{3}}$$

$= \dfrac{2}{5} + \dfrac{3}{10} = \dfrac{7}{10}$

$= \dfrac{1}{\frac{5}{2}} + \dfrac{1}{\frac{10}{3}}$

**4.**

**5 min.**

Alice started a Math Club during the first week of school. As the only member, she decided to recruit two new members during the following week of school. Each new member, during the week following the week when he or she became a member, recruits two new members. How many members will the club have at the end of five weeks?

**5.**

**6 min.**

One light flashes every 2 minutes and another light flashes every 3½ minutes. Suppose both lights flash together at noon. What is the first time after 1 PM that both lights will flash together?

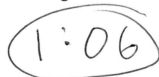

1:06

**1.**

4 min.

In the subtraction problem at the right, each letter represents a digit, and different letters represent different digits. What digit does C represent?

$$
\begin{array}{r}
A\ B\ A \\
-\ C\ A \\
\hline
A\ B
\end{array}
$$

**2.**

4 min.

Each of the small boxes in the figure at the right is a square. The perimeter of square ABCD is 36 cm. What is the perimeter of the figure shown with darkened outline?

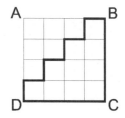

**3.**

5 min.

$2^3$ means $2 \times 2 \times 2$ or 8.
$3^3$ means $3 \times 3 \times 3$ or 27.
$N^3$ means $N \times N \times N$.
Suppose $N^3 = 4,913$.
What is the value of N?

**4.**

6 min.

Carl shot 3 arrows; 2 landed in the A ring and 1 landed in circle B for a total score of 17. David also shot 3 arrows; 1 landed in A and 2 in B for a total score of 22. How many points are assigned to circle B?

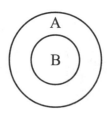

**5.**

5 min.

In the following sequence of numbers, each number has one more 1 than the preceding number: 1, 11, 111, 1111, 11111, ... . What is the tens digit of the sum of the first 30 numbers of the sequence?

**1.**

**4 min.**

There are 4 separate large boxes, and inside each large box there are 3 separate small boxes, and inside each of these small boxes there are 2 separate smaller boxes. How many boxes, counting all sizes, are there altogether?

**2.**

**6 min.**

When asked how many gold coins he had, the collector said:
    If I arrange them in stacks of five, none are left over.
    If I arrange them in stacks of six, none are left over.
    If I arrange them in stacks of seven, one is left over.
What is the least number of coins he could have?

**3.**

**6 min.**

The length of the shortest trip from A to B along the edges of the cube shown is the length of 3 edges. How many different 3-edge trips are there from A to B?

6 trips

**4.**

**5 min.**

How many two-digit numbers are there in which the tens digit is greater than the ones digit?

**5.**

**6 min.**

Alice and Betty run a 50-meter race and Alice wins by 10 meters. They then run a 60-meter race, and each girl runs at the same speed she ran in the first race. By how many meters will Alice win?

$$\frac{a}{1} \qquad \frac{a+10}{1}$$

# Olympiad 38

**1.**
**4 min.**

At the right, the sum of two 3-digit numbers is represented. A, B, and C represent the digits 2, 3 and 5 but not necessarily in the same order, and different letters represent different digits. What is the largest value the indicated sum could have?

$$\begin{array}{r} 5\ 2\ 3 \\ \text{B A C} \\ \text{+ C A B} \\ \hline 8 4 8 \end{array}$$

**2.**
**5 min.**

$(5273)^2$ means $5273 \times 5273$; $(5273)^3$ means $5273 \times 5273 \times 5273$; and so forth. Suppose $(5273)^6$ is completely multiplied out.
What will the units (or ones) digit be in the resulting product?

3, 9, 7, 1          ⑨

**3.**
**5 min.**

A baseball league has nine teams. During the season, each of the nine teams plays exactly three games with each of the other teams.
What is the total number of games played?

**4.**
**5 min.**

June has 30 days. One year, June had exactly four Sundays. On which two days of the week could June 30 not have occurred that year?

Friday and Saturday

**5.**
**5 min.**

The six faces of a three-inch wooden cube are each painted red. The cube is then cut into one-inch cubes along the lines shown in the diagram. How many of the one-inch cubes have red paint on at least two faces?

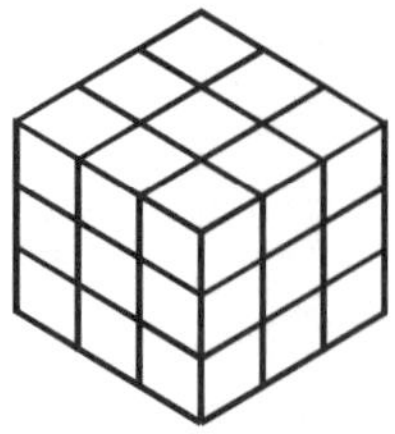

20 cubes

56

**1.**

**4 min.**

The serial number of my camera is a four-digit number less than 5,000 and contains the digits 2, 3, 5, and 8 but not necessarily in that order. The "3" is next to the "8", the "2" is not next to the "3", and the "5" is not next to the "2". What is the serial number?

5 3 8 2    2 8 3 5

**2.**

**5 min.**

One day, Carol bought apples at 3 for 25¢ and sold all of them at 2 for 25¢. If she made a profit of $1 that day, how many apples did she sell?

**3.**

**5 min.**

As shown, ABCD and AFED are squares with a common side AD of length 10 cm. Arc BD and arc DF are quarter-circles. How many square cm. are in the area of the shaded region?

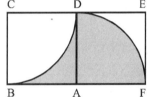

**4.**

**6 min.**

When the same whole number is added to both the numerator and denominator of 2/5, the value of the new fraction is 2/3. What number was added to both the numerator and denominator?

**5.**

**6 min.**

The sum of the ages of three children is 32. The age of the oldest is twice the age of the youngest. The ages of the two older children differ by three years. What is the age of the youngest child?

**1.**

**4 min.**

A slow clock loses 3 minutes every hour. Suppose the slow clock and a correct clock both show the correct time at 9 A.M. What time will the slow clock show when the correct clock shows 10 o'clock the evening of the same day?

**2.**

**5 min.**

The figure at the right is a "magic square" with missing entries. When complete, the sum of the four entries in each column, each row, and each diagonal is the same. Find the value of A and the value of B.

| A |  | 7 | 12 |
|---|---|---|---|
|  | 4 | 9 |  |
|  | 5 | 16 |  |
| 8 | 11 |  | B |

**3.**

**5 min.**

The digit 3 is written at the right of a certain two-digit number thus forming a three-digit number. The new number is 372 more than the original two-digit number. What was the original two-digit number?

**4.**

**6 min.**

ABCD is a square with area 16 sq. meters. E and F are midpoints of sides AB and BC, respectively.
What is the area of trapezoid AEFC, the shaded region?

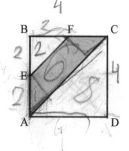

**5.**

**6 min.**

Peter agreed to work after school for 8 weeks at a fixed weekly rate. But instead of being given only money, he was to be given $85 and a bicycle. However, Peter worked only 5 weeks at the fixed weekly rate and was given $25 and the bicycle. How much was the bicycle worth?

**1.**

**3 min.**

Suppose the time is now 2 o'clock on a twelve-hour clock which runs continuously. What time will it show 1,000 hours from now?

**2.**

**4 min.**

The average of five numbers is 6. If one of the five numbers is removed, the average of the four remaining numbers is 7. What is the value of the number that was removed?

**3.**

**5 min.**

If you start with 3 and count by 7s, you get the terms of the sequence 3, 10, 17, ... , 528 where 3 is the 1st term, 10 is the 2nd term, 17 is the 3rd term, and so forth up to 528 which is the Nth term. What is the value of N?

**4.**

**5 min.**

When a counting number is multiplied by itself, the result is a perfect square. For example 1, 4, and 9 are perfect squares because $1\times1 = 1$, $2\times2 = 4$, and $3\times3 = 9$. How many perfect squares are less than 10,000?

**5.**

**6 min.**

A restaurant has a total of 30 tables which are of two types. The first type seats two people at each table; the second type seats five people at each table. A total of 81 people are seated when all seats are occupied. How many tables for two are there?

**1.**

**4 min.**

The cost of a book is $1 and a whole number of cents. The total cost of six copies of the book is less than $8. However, the total cost of seven copies of the same book at the same price per book is more than $8. What is the least a single copy of the book could cost?

**2.**

**5 min.**

The sum of all digits in the numbers 34, 35, and 36 is 24 because (3+4) + (3+5) + (3+6) = 24. Find the sum of all digits in the first twenty-five counting numbers: 1, 2, 3, 4, 5, ... , 23, 24, 25

**3.**

**5 min.**

Alice earned a total of $65 for working five days after school. Each day after the first day, she earned $2 more than she earned the day before. How much did she earn on the first day?

**4.**

**5 min.**

Each of the small boxes in the figure at the right is a square and the area of the figure is 52 square units. How many units are there in the outer perimeter of the figure?

**5.**

**5 min.**

A work team of four people completes half of a job in 15 days. How many days will it take a team of ten people to complete the remaining half of the job? (Assume that each person of both teams works at the same rate as each of the other people.)

**1.**

**2 min.**

Two cash registers of a store had a combined total of $300. When the manager transferred $15 from one register to the other register, each register then had the same amount. How much did the register with the larger amount have before the transfer was made?

$160

**2.**

**4 min.**

The product of two numbers is 128 and their quotient is 8. What are the numbers?

32 and 4

**3.**

**6 min.**

In the figure at the right, each number represents the length of the segment which is nearest it. How many square units are in the area of the figure if there is a right angle at each corner of the figure?

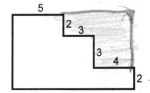

**4.**

**5 min.**

In the addition problem at the right, different letters stand for different digits. AH represents a two-digit number and HEE represents a three-digit number. What number does HEE represent?

```
  A H
+ A
-----
H E E
```

**5.**

**6 min.**

Barbara has 20 coins consisting of nickels and dimes. If the nickels were dimes and the dimes were nickels, she would have 30¢ more than she has now. How many dimes did she have to begin with?

**1.**

**4 min.**

I am less than 6 feet tall but more than 2 feet tall. My height in inches is a multiple of 7 and is also 2 inches more than a multiple of 6. What is my height in inches?

56 in.

**2.**

**5 min.**

In the multiplication example at the right, A and B represent different digits, AB is a two-digit number and BBB is a three-digit number. (* means multiply.) What two-digit number does AB represent?

$$\begin{array}{r} A\ B \\ *\ \ 6 \\ \hline B\ B\ B \end{array}$$

**3.**

**5 min.**

Tom went to a store and spent one-third of his money. He went to a second store where he spent one-third of what remained, and then had $12 when he left. How much money did he have to begin with at the first store?

**4.**

**6 min.**

The tower at the right has no gaps. Suppose it is painted red on all exterior sides including the bottom, and then cut into cubes along the indicated lines. How many cubes will each have red paint on just three faces?

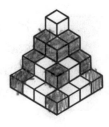

9

**5.**

**6 min.**

A9543B represents a six-digit number in which A and B are digits different from each other. The number is divisible by 11 and also by 8. What digit does A represent?

**1.**

**4 min.**

In Nogatco, a primitive country, "OC" means a bundle of 8 sticks, "OCTA" means a bundle of 8 OCs, "OCTIL" means a bundle of 8 OCTAs, and "OCTILLA" means a bundle of 8 OCTILs. How many sticks are in an OCTILLA?

36928

**2.**

**5 min.**

When certain numbers are placed in the empty boxes, the sum of the three numbers in each of the three rows, three columns, and two diagonals is the same. What number should be in the center box?

| 5 | 7 | 13 |
|---|---|----|
|   |   |    |
| 9 | 7 |    |

**3.**

**6 min.**

In hoopball, a field goal is worth 2 points and a foul shot is worth 1 point. Suppose a team scored 72 points and made 6 more field goals than foul shots. How many foul shots did the team make?

**4.**

**5 min.**

The square at the right is divided into four congruent rectangles. The perimeter of each of the four congruent rectangles is 25 units. How many units are there in the perimeter of the square?

**5.**

**6 min.**

$1^2$ means $1 \times 1$, $2^2$ means $2 \times 2$, $3^2$ means $3 \times 3$, and so forth.
$$1^2 + 2^2 + 3^2 + 4^2 + \cdots + 25^2 = 5525, \text{ and}$$
$$2^2 + 4^2 + 6^2 + 8^2 + \cdots + 50^2 = N.$$
Find the value of N.

**1.**

**4 min.**

A purse contains 4 pennies, 2 nickels, 1 dime, and 1 quarter. Different values can be obtained by using one or more coins in the purse. How many different values can be obtained?

*8 different values*

**2.**

**5 min.**

Tickets for a concert cost $2 each for children and $5 each for adults. A group of thirty people consisting of children and adults paid a total of $87 for the concert. How many adults were in the group?

*9 adults*

**3.**

**6 min.**

The tower shown at the right is made of horizontal layers of unit cubes, not all being visible in the diagram. How many unit cubes are contained in the tower? *30 + 18 + 12 + 12 + 8 + 0 =*

*30*

*70 cubes*

**4.**

**5 min.**

The average of five numbers is 16. Suppose 10 is added to the five numbers. What is the average of the six numbers?

*15*

**5.**

**6 min.**

For the division problem at right:
A, B, and C are different digits, each of AB and 7C is a 2-digit number, and each blank space represents a missing digit. What is the value of each of A, B, and C?

*A =*
*B =*
*C =*

```
         7C
   AB) ____
       ==
       ____
        2_
         0
```

**1.**

**4 min.**

A certain brand of sardines is usually sold at 3 cans for $2. Suppose the price is changed to 4 cans for $2.50. Will the new cost for 12 cans be more or less than the usual cost for 12 cans, and by how much?

**2.**

**5 min.**

N is the number of buttons in a sewing box.
a). N is more than 40 but less than 80.
b). When N is divided by 5, the remainder is 2.
c). When N is divided by 7, the remainder is 4.
Find the value of N.

**3.**

**4 min.**

Consecutive numbers are whole numbers that follow in order such as 3, 4, 5. Find the smallest of the five consecutive numbers whose sum is 100.

**4.**

**5 min.**

A dog takes 3 steps to walk the same distance for which a cat takes 4 steps. Suppose 1 step of the dog covers 1 foot. How many feet would the cat cover in taking 12 steps?

**5.**

**6 min.**

In the addition problem at the right, different letters represent different digits. It is also given that N is 6 and T is greater than 1. What four-digit number does T H I S represent?

```
  T H I S
+   I S
-------
  K E E N
```

**1.**

**5 min.**

(1,1,8) is a triple of counting numbers which has a sum of 10. Consider (1,8,1) and (8,1,1) to be the same triple as (1,1,8). How many different triples of counting numbers have a sum of 10? Include (1,1,8) as one of your triples.

**2.**

**5 min.**

Patricia has $12 more than Rhoda and $15 more than Sarah. Together all three have $87. How much does Patricia have?

**3.**

**6 min.**

The "staircase" at the right is 4 units tall and contains 10 unit squares. Suppose the staircase were extended until it was 12 units tall. How many unit squares would it then contain all together?

**4.**

**6 min.**

If I start with the number 7 and count by 4s, the following sequence is obtained: 7, 11, 15, 19, 23, and so forth. A new sequence is formed when I start with a different number and count by a different number. Suppose the 2nd number of the new sequence is 8 and the 5th number is 17. What is the 10th number of the new sequence?

**5.**

**7 min.**

The entire treasury of the Alpha club, consisting of $240, was to be divided into equal shares for each club member. When it was discovered that one member was not eligible for a share, the share of each of the remaining members increased by $1. How many eligible members got a share of the $240?

**1.**

**4 min.**

There are many three-digit numbers that are each divisible by 7 and also by 8 without remainder in each case. What is the largest of these three-digit numbers?

✓ 952

**2.**

**5 min.**

Twenty-four meters of fencing is used to fence a rectangular garden. Let M represents the number of square meters in the area of the garden. What is the largest value that M could have?

**3.**

**6 min.**

When a certain number N is divided by 3, the result is the same as when N is decreased by 8. What is the number N?

✓ 12

**4.**

**5 min.**

A package weighs P pounds, P being a whole number. To ship this package by express costs $1.65 for the first five pounds and 12¢ for each additional pound. The total shipping cost was $3.45. How many pounds did the package weigh?

15   6.80 pounds

**5.**

**5 min.**

The sum $\frac{1}{2} + \frac{.1}{2} + \frac{1}{.2}$ is equal to the decimal A.BC where A, B, and C may be the same or different digits. What number does A.BC represent?

✗ 5.55

**1.**

**4 min.**

In the U.S.A., the symbol 5/2 means the 5th month, 2nd day, or May 2. But in England, 5/2 means the fifth day, 2nd month, or February 5. How many days of the year each have the same symbol in both the U.S.A. and England?

Good thinking !

√ 12

**2.**

**4 min.**

The product of two numbers is 504 and each of the numbers is divisible by 6. However, neither of the two numbers is 6. What is the larger of the two numbers?

√ 42

**3.**

**6 min.**

A rectangular garden is 14 ft. by 21 ft. and is bordered by a concrete walk 3 ft. wide as shown. How many square feet are in the surface area of just the concrete walk?

WALK

GARDEN

WALK

**4.**

**6 min.**

Four numbers are arranged in order of size and the difference between any two adjacent numbers is the same. Suppose 1/3 is the first and 1/2 is the fourth of these numbers. What are the two numbers between 1/3 and 1/2?

**5.**

**7 min.**

Each of the three diagrams at the right shows a balance of weights using different objects. How many ⬜s will balance a ◯?

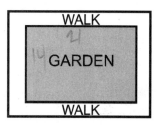

**1.**

5 min.

How many times does the letter x occur in the diagram at the right?

$\sqrt{71}$

```
x x x
x x x x x
x x x x x x x
x x x x x x x x x
x x x          x x x
 x x x x      x x x x x
x x x x x x  x x x x x x
x x x x x x x x x x x x x x x x x x
```

**2.**

5 min.

A jar contains a large number of pennies. The pennies can be divided into equal shares among 3, 4, 5, 6, 7, or 8 children with no pennies left over each time. What is the least number of pennies the jar could contain?

19760 840

**3.**

5 min.

If a counting number is multiplied by itself, the result is called a perfect square. Thus, 1, 4, 9, 16, 25, 36, 49, ... are perfect squares and also consecutive because they follow in order. The number 1000 is between two consecutive perfect squares. Which one of these two squares is closer to 1000?

**4.**

6 min.

I spent 2/3 of my money in store A. I then spent 1/3 of what remained in store B. When I left store B, I had $4. How much money did I have when I entered store A?

**5.**

6 min.

If 6 is placed at the right end of a two-digit number AB, the value of the three-digit number thus formed is 294 more than AB. What is the original two-digit number AB?

**1.**

5 min.

When 24 is added to a number, the result is the same as when the number is multiplied by 3. What is the number?

$x + 24 = 3x$

$24 = 2x$

$12 = x$

$\boxed{12}$

**2.**

4 min.

Suppose all counting numbers are arranged in columns as shown at the right. Under what letter will the number 300 appear?

$7\overline{)300}$ r6
$\quad 42$ r6
$\quad \underline{28}$
$\quad \phantom{0}20$
$\quad \phantom{0}\underline{14}$
$\quad \phantom{00}6$

$\boxed{D}$

| A | B | C | D | E | F | G |
|---|---|---|---|---|---|---|
| 1 | | 2 | | 3 | | 4 |
| | | 7 | | 6 | | 5 |
| 8 | | 9 | | 10 | | 11 |
| | | 14 | | 13 | | 12 |
| 15 | | 16 | | ... | | |

**3.**

5 min.

Mrs. Bailey has equal numbers of nickels and quarters but the value of the quarters is $1.80 more than the value of the nickels. What is the total value of all coins together in dollars and cents?

**4.**

6 min.

In the addition problem at the right, AB and BA each represent a two-digit number, and A and B stand for different digits. Find the value of A.

```
  B A
  A B
+ A B
-----
C A A
```

**5.**

6 min.

Let all the odd numbers from 1 through 301 inclusive be written. How many times will the digit 3 appear?

42 times

**1.**

**5 min.**

A container has 10 red disks, 10 white disks, and 10 blue disks, all of the same size. Suppose I am blindfolded when I pick disks from the container. What is the least number of disks I must pick in order to be absolutely certain that there are three disks of the same color among those I have picked?

7

**2.**

**5 min.**

In the target at the right, ring A, ring B, and circle C have different point values. The sum of the point values of A and B is 23, of B and C is 33, and of A and C is 30. What is the sum of the point values of A, B, and C?

$A + B = 23$
$B + C = 33$
$A + C = 30$

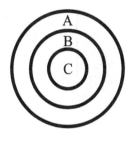

**3.**

**5 min.**

T and V in the four-digit number T37V represent different digits, and T37V is divisible by 88 without remainder. What digit is represented by T? (Hint: find the value of V first)

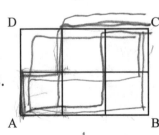

**4.**

**6 min.**

ABCD is a rectangle whose sides are 3 units and 2 units long. The length of the shortest path from A to C following the lines of the diagram is 5 units. How many different shortest paths are there from A to C?

10

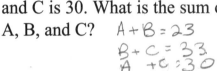

**5.**

**6 min.**

There are twice as many liters of water in one container as in another. If 8 liters of water are removed from each of the two containers, there will be three times as many liters of water in one container as in the other. How many liters of water did the smaller container have to begin with?

16

**1.**

5 min.

The quotient of two numbers is 4 and their difference is 39. What is the smaller number of the two?

**2.**

5 min.

Express the extended fraction at the right as a simple fraction in lowest terms.

$$\cfrac{1}{3+\cfrac{1}{3+\cfrac{1}{3}}}$$

**3.**

5 min.

The structure at the right is made of unit cubes piled on top of each other. Some cubes are not visible. What is the number of cubes in the structure?

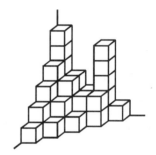

**4.**

5 min.

546 is one of six three-digit numbers each of which is different and has the digits 4, 5, and 6. What is the sum of these six numbers?

**5.**

6 min.

ABCD is a square with diagonal AC 8 units long. How many square units are in the area of the square?

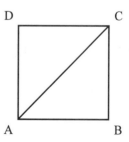

**1.**

5 min.

In the multiplication problem at the right, A, B, C, and D represent different digits. ABC is a three-digit number, and * means multiplication. What three-digit number does ABC represent?

$$\begin{array}{r} A\ B\ C \\ *\ \ D \\ \hline 1\ 6\ 7\ 3 \end{array}$$

**2.**

5 min.

Different rectangles can be traced using the lines in the figure given at the right. How many different rectangles can be traced?

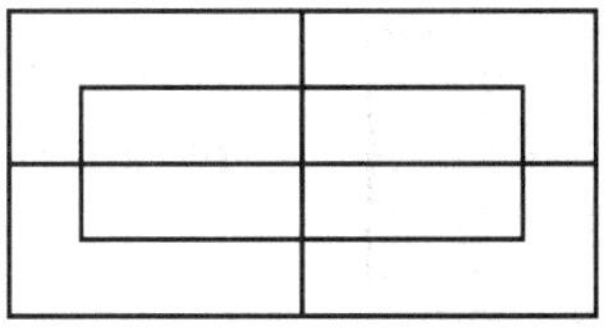

**3.**

5 min.

Two students are needed to work in the school store during the lunch hour every day, and four students volunteer for this work. What is the greatest number of days that can be arranged in which no pair of the four students works together more than once?

**4.**

5 min.

2, 3, 5, 7, 11, ... are examples of prime numbers; each number has only itself and 1 as factors. Suppose the number of units in each of the length and width of a rectangle are prime numbers and the perimeter is 36 units. What is the largest number of square units the area could have?

**5.**

6 min.

When Paul crossed the finish line of a 60 meter race, he was ahead of Robert by 10 meters and ahead of Sam by 20 meters. Suppose Robert and Sam continue to race to the finish line without changing their rates of speed. By how many meters will Robert beat Sam?

**1.**

5 min.

ABCD represents a four-digit number. The product of its digits is 70. What is the largest four-digit number that ABCD can represent?

**2.**

4 min.

What is its value of the expression at the right in simplest form?

$$(5\frac{1}{3} - 2\frac{1}{2}) + (5\frac{1}{2} - 3\frac{1}{3})$$

**3.**

5 min.

At the right is a 3 by 3 by 3 cube. Not all of the cubes are visible. Suppose the entire outside of the cube is painted red including the bottom. How many different 2 by 2 by 2 cubes with exactly three red faces can be found in the shown cube?

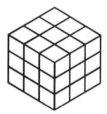

**4.**

6 min.

The cold water faucet of a bath tub can fill the tub in 15 minutes. The drain, when opened, can empty the full tub in 20 minutes. Suppose the tub is empty and the faucet and drain are both opened at the same time. How long will it take to fill the tub?

**5.**

5 min.

In the multiplication example at the right, different letters represent different digits and a blank space may represent any digit. The product WHAT is a four-digit number less than 5000. Find the number that WHAT represents.

```
        U  T
    ×   U  T
    ─────────
        _  6
    _   _
    _   8
    ─────────
    W  H  A  T
```

**1.**

**3 min.**

A stamp collector bought a rare stamp for $30, sold it for $42, bought it back for $50, and finally sold it for $48. Did the stamp collector make or lose money and how many dollars were made or lost?

**2.**

**4 min.**

The numbers M and N are different numbers selected from the first twenty-five counting numbers: 1, 2, 3, 4, ... , 24, 25. If M is larger than N, what is the smallest value that the expression at the right can have?

$$\frac{M \times N}{M - N}$$

**3.**

**5 min.**

ABCD is a square which contains nine small congruent squares as shown. The area of square ABCD is 36 square units. What is the area of triangle ACE in square units?

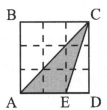

**4.**

**5 min.**

A prime number is a whole number, greater than 1, that is divisible only by itself and 1. Some examples of prime numbers are 2, 3, 5, 7, 11, and 13. What is the largest prime number, P, such that 9 times P is less than 400?

**5.**

**6 min.**

A person made a purchase for D dollars and C cents, and gave the cashier a $20 bill. The cashier incorrectly charged the person C dollars and D cents, and returned $4.88 in change. If the cashier had charged the correct price, what would the correct change have been?

**1.**

3 min.

Suppose the counting numbers from 1 through 100 are written on paper. What is the total number of 3s and 8s that will appear on the paper?

**2.**

4 min.

Given the expression: 1990×1991 – 1989×1990. What counting number is equivalent to the expression?

**3.**

5 min.

Suppose 3! means 3×2×1, 4! means 4×3×2×1, 5! means 5×4×3×2×1, and so forth. What is the value of the expression at the right in simplest form?

$$\frac{8! - 6!}{3! \times 5!}$$

**4.**

6 min.

ABCD is a square; E, F, G, and H are midpoints of AP, BP, CP, and DP respectively. What fractional part of the area of square ABCD is the area of square EFGH?

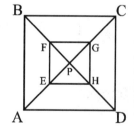

**5.**

7 min.

A bus was rented at a fixed cost by a group of 30 people. When 10 people were added to the group, the fixed cost of the bus did not change, but the charge for each person in the original group was $2 less than before. If each person paid the same charge as each of the others, find the fixed cost of renting the bus.

**1.**

**3 min.**

Suppose two days before yesterday was Wednesday. What day of the week will it be 100 days from today?

**2.**

**5 min.**

The first fifteen multiples of 6 are: 6, 12, 18, 24, ... , 84, 90. What is the sum of these multiples of 6?

**3.**

**7 min.**

A, B, and C represent different digits, C ≠ 0 and a blank space may represent any digit in the division problem at the right. What digits do A, B, and C each represent?

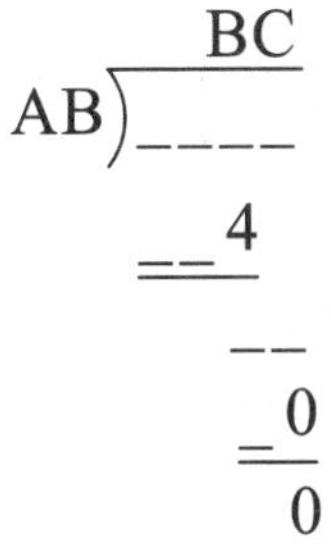

$$
\begin{array}{r}
BC \\
AB{\overline{\smash{\big)}\,----}} \\
\underline{==\,4} \\
-- \\
\underline{=\,0} \\
0
\end{array}
$$

**4.**

**6 min.**

Find the largest factor of 2520 that is not divisible by 6.

**5.**

**6 min.**

Five disks, numbered 1, 2, 4, 8, and 16, are placed in a bag. Three disks are withdrawn from the bag, the sum of their numbers is recorded, and the three disks are then returned to the bag. Suppose this process is repeated indefinitely. What is the largest number of different sums that can be recorded?

**1.**

**3 min.**

Consecutive odd numbers are odd numbers that follow in order such as 5, 7, 9, and 11. The sum of five consecutive odd numbers is 85. What is the largest number of the five?

**2.**

**5 min.**

The three-digit number 104 has a digit-sum of 1+0+4, or 5. How many different three-digit numbers, including 104, each have a digit-sum of 5?

**3.**

**5 min.**

A light flashes every 2 minutes, a second light flashes every 2.5 minutes, and a third light flashes every 3 minutes. Suppose all three lights flash together at 9 AM. What is the next time of the day they will all flash together?

**4.**

**5 min.**

ABCD is a square with each side divided into three segments of length 1 unit, 8 units, and 1 unit repectively, as shown in the diagram. What is the sum of the areas of the four shaded triangles?

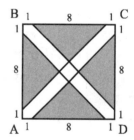

**5.**

**6 min.**

A fast clock gains one minute per hour and a slow clock loses two minutes per hour. At a certain time, both clocks are set to the correct time. Less than 24 hours later, the fast clock registers 9 o'clock at the same moment that the slow clock registers 8 o'clock. What is the correct time at that moment?

**1.**

**4 min.**

Suppose you enter an elevator at a certain floor. Then the elevator moves up 6 floors, down 4 floors, and up 3 floors. You are then at floor 7. At which floor did you initially enter the elevator?

**2.**

**4 min.**

The cube at the right is constructed of congruent boards, each being of the same size and shape. How many boards does the cube contain?

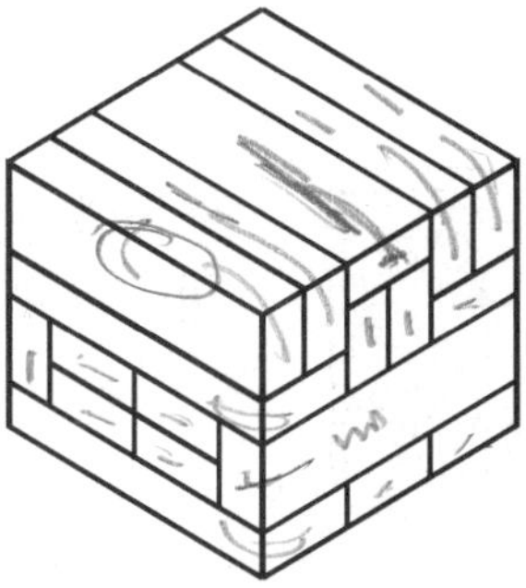

**3.**

**5 min.**

A certain examination of 12 questions was graded by giving 10 points for each correct answer and by then deducting 5 points for each incorrect answer. David attempted all 12 questions, leaving no question unanswered and scored a total of 75 points. How many wrong answers did he have?

**4.**

**5 min.**

A set of 10 coins may contain any combination of pennies, nickels, dimes, quarters, or half-dollars. In how many different ways can the set of 10 coins have a total value of 59¢ ?

**5.**

**7 min.**

The set of the consecutive odd numbers 1, 3, 5, 7, ... , N has a sum of 400. How many numbers are in the set?

# Olympiad 62

**1.** (3 min.)

6, 14, and 15 are factors of the counting number N. What is the smallest value that N can have?

```
15    15         35
30    14      6)210
45    60        18
60    15        30
75   210
90
```

210 ✓

**2.** (4 min.)

Suppose five days after the day before yesterday is Friday. What day of the week will tomorrow then be?

Tuesday

**3.** (5 min.)

A fisherman sold some big fish at $4 each and twice as many small fish at $1 each. He received a total of $72 for the big and small fish. How many big fish did he sell?

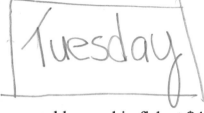

```
x   2x
4x + 2x = 72
   6x = 72
    x = 12
```

12 big fish

**4.** (6 min.)

A "Magic Square" has the property that the sum of the three numbers in each and every row, column, and diagonal is the same. What number should be in the center box of the Magic Square shown at the right?

| 9 | 7 | 17 |
|---|---|---|
| 19 | ? | 3 |
| 5 | 15 | 13 |

11 ✓

**5.** (6 min.)

Two dogs run around a circular track 300 feet long. One dog runs at a steady rate of 15 feet per second, the other at a steady rate of 12 feet per second. Suppose they start at the same point and time. What is the least number of seconds that will elapse before they are again together at the starting point?

80

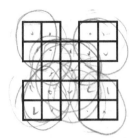

**1.**

5 min.

Each of the small boxes in the diagram at the right is a square and congruent to each of the others. How many different squares can be traced using the lines of the diagram as sides?

21

30

$\boxed{30}$ ✓

**2.**

5 min.

A box contains over 100 marbles. The marbles can be divided into equal shares among 6, 7, or 8 children with 1 marble left over each time. What is the least number of marbles that the box can contain?

$\boxed{169}$ ✓

**3.**

6 min.

Mr. Chin went to a store where he spent one-half of his money and then $14 more. He then went to another store where he spent one-third of his remaining money and then $14 more. He then had no money left. How much did he have when he entered the first store?

$\boxed{\$98}$

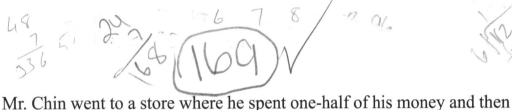

**4.**

5 min.

If 48 is added to one-third of a number, the triple of the number is the result. What is the number?

$\frac{1}{3}x + 48 = 3x$

$48 = \frac{8}{3}x$

$18 = x$

✓ $\boxed{18}$

**5.**

7 min.

In the multiplication example at the right, different letters represent different digits. What two-digit number does AB represent?

$\boxed{75}$

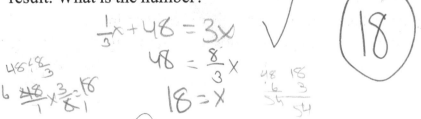

```
    A B
  × A B
  -----
  C A B
B D B
-------
B E D B
```

**1.**

**3 min.**

The average of six numbers is 7. If two of the six numbers are removed, the average of the remaining numbers is 8. What is the sum of the two numbers which were removed?

**2.**

**5 min.**

If you start with 4 and count by 3s, you get the sequence 4, 7, 10, ... , N where 4 is the first number, 7 is the second number, 10 is the third number, and so forth. If N is the fiftieth number, what number does N represent?

**3.**

**6 min.**

$7^1 = 7$, $7^2 = 7 \times 7 = 49$, $7^3 = 7 \times 7 \times 7 = 343$, and so forth.
When multiplied out, $7^2$ has a units digit of 9, $7^3$ has a units digit of 3, and so forth. What is the units digit of $7^{20}$ ?

**4.**

**5 min.**

In the five-digit number A6A41, each of the As represents the same digit and A6A41 is divisible by 9. What digit does A represent?

**5.**

**6 min.**

Eight people want to play a 48-minute game as a team but only a team of exactly five is allowed to play. However, during the game, a player may be replaced by someone else. Suppose each of the eight people plays in the game for the same amount of time. How many minutes will each of the eight people play?

**1.**

4 min.

What number multiplied by itself is equal to the product of 32 and 162?

**2.**

5 min.

Square ABCD has all four of its vertices on a circle with diameter 10 units in length. Segments AC and BD are diameters. How many square units of area does square ABCD have?

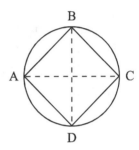

**3.**

5 min.

In the addition example at the right, different letters represent different digits. What digit does A represent?

$$\begin{array}{ccc} & A & A \\ + & A & A \\ \hline C & A & B \end{array}$$

**4.**

6 min.

The fraction F at the right is an extended fraction. What simple fraction in lowest terms is equal to F?

$$F = \cfrac{1}{1 + \cfrac{1}{2 + \cfrac{1}{3}}}$$

**5.**

6 min.

The sum of the first 25 multiples of 4 is: $4 + 8 + 12 + \cdots + 100$.
The sum of the first 25 multiples of 3 is: $3 + 6 + 9 + \cdots + 75$.
What number is equal to the difference of the two sums?

**1.**

**3 min.**

When I open my Math book, two pages face me and the sum of the two page numbers is 317. What is the number of the very next page?

**2.**

**5 min.**

The sum of the ages of Alice, Betty, and Clara is 29 years. Betty is 4 years older than Alice and Clara is 6 years older than Betty. What is Alice's age?

**3.**

**5 min.**

A car can travel 1 mile in 1 minute 12 seconds. How many miles will the car travel in 1 hour at the given rate?

**4.**

**5 min.**

Henry was able to buy some 23¢ stamps and some 15¢ stamps for a total of exactly $2.50. How many 15¢ stamps did he buy?

**5.**

**6 min.**

In the figure at the right, all corner angles are right angles and each number represents the unit-length of the segment which is nearest to it. How many square units of area does the figure have?

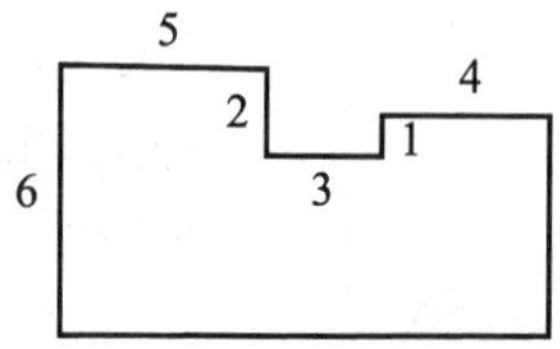

**1.**

**3 min.**

A counting number is a multiple of 13 and is also divisible by 4 and by 6. What is the smallest number that satisfies these conditions?

**2.**

**5 min.**

If a class of children is separated into groups of 5 children, 2 children will be left over. If the class is separated into groups of 6 children, 3 children will be left over. What is the smallest number of children the class could have?

**3.**

**5 min.**

When a counting number is multiped by itself, the result is a square-number. Since 1×1 = 1, 2×2 = 4, 3×3 = 9, 4×4 = 16, 1, 4, 9, 16, ... are square-numbers. How many counting numbers less than 500 are square-numbers?

**4.**

**5 min.**

The three-digit number AB8 is 296 more than the two-digit number AB. What is the value of the two-digit number AB?

**5.**

**5 min.**

The tower shown at the right is made by placing congruent cubes on top of each other. Not all cubes of the tower are visible. How many cubes does the tower contain?

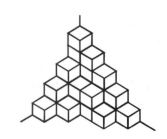

**1.** 3 min.

The sum of the heights of Paul and Rachel is 94 inches. Rachel is 8 inches taller than Paul. How many inches tall is Paul?

$x + x + 8 = 94$
$2x + 8 = 94$
$2x = 86$
$x = 43$

**43 inches**

**2.** 5 min.

A bicyclist wants to make a 600-mile trip on his two-wheel bicycle. He has a spare wheel which is used to replace either of the other two wheels. Suppose each of the three wheels is to have the same mileage for the trip. How many miles should each wheel travel?

**200 miles**

**3.** 5 min.

To write the counting numbers from 10 to 12 inclusive, we would write 10, 11, 12, and observe that a total of 6 digits is written. We then actually write the counting numbers from 1 to 150 inclusive. What is the total number of digits that must be written?

| 1-9 | 10-20 | 20-800 | 100-150 |
|-----|-------|--------|---------|
| 9 | 22 | 162 | 102 |

**295**

**4.** 5 min.

Three squares each have sides of length 6 units and overlap each other as shown at the right. The points where the sides cross are midpoints. Find the area of the shaded figure in square units.

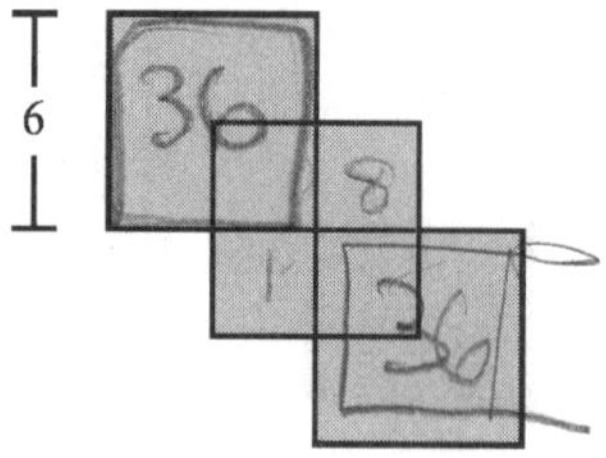

**90 units²**

**5.** 6 min.

There are exactly six different three-digit numbers that can be formed using each of the digits 4, 5, and 6 exactly once in each number. Find the average of these six three-digit numbers.

456
465
564
546
645
654

6)3330

**555**

3330

*Awues*

*Awesomeness*

**1.**

**4 min.**

The product 7×7 may be written as $7^2$, 6×6×6 as $6^3$, and 5×5×5×5 as $5^4$. Let A = $2^5$, B = $3^4$, C = $4^3$, and D = $5^2$. Write A, B, C, and D in order of their values beginning with the smallest value at the left.

*D, A, C, B*

*2, 2, 2, 2²*   *27*   *3×3×3×3*   *1⅔*   *25, 48, 81, 32*
*D     C        B    A*

**2.**

**4 min.**

The cost of mailing a letter first-class is 29¢ for the first ounce and 23¢ for each additional ounce. A letter weighs exactly N ounces where N is a counting number, and the total mailing cost is $1.90. What is the value of N?

**3.**

**6 min.**

A fast clock gains 12 minutes every normal hour, and the fast clock shows the correct time at 1 PM. What is the correct time when the fast clock first registers 2 PM?

*1:48*

**4.**

**5 min.**

A crew of 8 people can build a concrete wall in 6 days. Suppose 4 more people had joined the crew at the start. Assume that each person works at the same rate as each of the other people. How many days would it have taken the new crew to build the same wall?

*8:6*
*4:3*

**5.**

**6 min.**

In the multiplication example at the right ABCD and DCBA represent 4-digit numerals, and different letters represent different digits. What 4-digit number does ABCD represent?

$$\begin{array}{r} A\ B\ C\ D \\ \times\ 9 \\ \hline D\ C\ B\ A \end{array}$$

**1.**

**3 min.**

How many even numbers between 1 and 101 are multiples of 3?

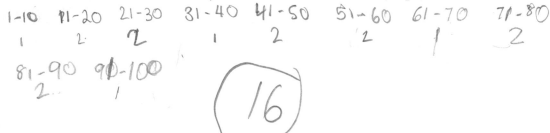

1-10   11-20   21-30   31-40   41-50   51-60   61-70   71-80
  1      2       2       1       2       2       1       2

81-90   90-100
  2       1

(16)

**2.**

**5 min.**

A person exchanged 390 pennies for quarters, dimes and nickels. The number of dimes in the exchange was twice the number of quarters and the number of nickels was twice the number of dimes. How many quarters were in the exchange?

**3.**

**5 min.**

A light flashes every 1 minute 15 seconds. Another flashes every 1 minute 40 seconds. Suppose they flash together at a certain time. What is the shortest amount of time that will elapse before both lights will again flash together?

**4.**

**5 min.**

A rectangular picture frame is 12 inches wide and 18 inches high. This includes a 2-inch border (shaded region) around the picture itself. How many square inches are in the border?

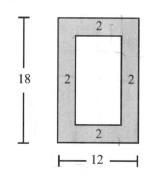

**5.**

**5 min.**

N is the 5-digit number 8A65B in which A and B are digits, and N is divisible by 24. What is the smallest number N can be?

**1.**

**5 min.**

In the subtraction problem at the right, all five of the digits 3, 5, 6, 7, and 9 are to be placed, one in-each box. What is the smallest difference that can be the result?

**2.**

**5 min.**

Five brothers, each born in a different year, share a gift of $100 according to the following arrangement: each boy, except the youngest, gets $5 more than his next younger brother. How much does the youngest boy get?

**3.**

**5 min.**

| START ? | SUBTRACT 3 | MULTIPLY BY 4 | ADD 8 | RESULT 40 |

What number in the "start" box will yield the result 40?

**4.**

**6 min.**

(1,1,9) is a triple of counting numbers whose sum is 11. We consider (1,1,9), (1,9,1) and (9,1,1) to be the same triple because each triple has the same three numbers. How many other triples of counting numbers have a sum of 11?

**5.**

**6 min.**

At the right is a 4×4×4 cubic block of wood. Suppose all six faces of the cube are painted red and the cube is then cut into 1×1×1 cubes along the lines shown. How many 1×1×1 cubes will have red paint on just two faces?

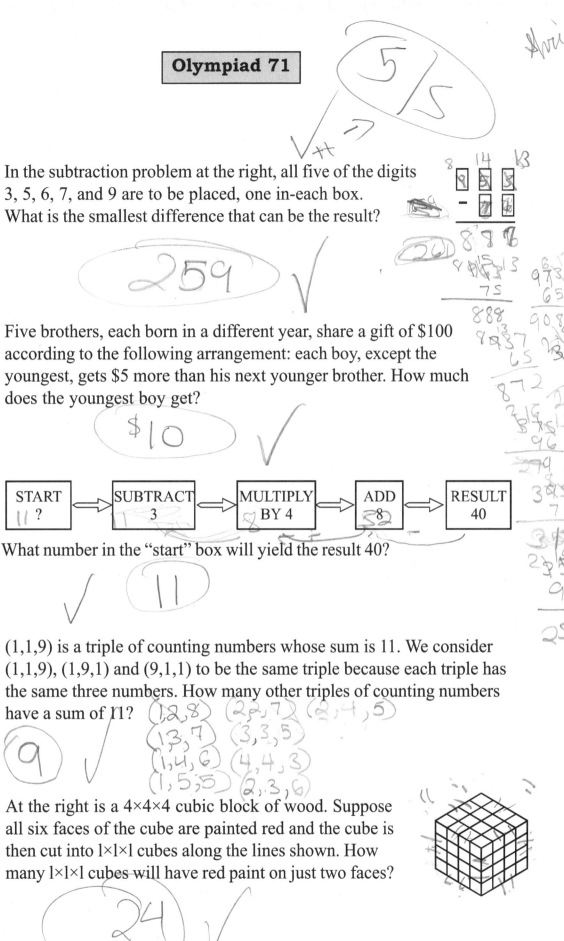

**1.**

**4 min.**

A counting number N has a remainder of 3 when divided by 7 and also has a remainder of 4 when divided by 5. What is the smallest value N can have? *#has 2 end with 4 or 9*

*24÷5= 4 r4*
*24÷7=3 r3*

√ **24**

**2.**

**5 min.**

ABCD is a square, and E and F are midpoints of sides AD and AB respectively as shown. What fractional part of the total area of the square is the area of triangle AEF?

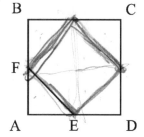

**1/8** √

**3.**

**5 min.**

Mary's average grade on 5 Math tests was 88. If her lowest grade was dropped, her average on the other 4 tests would be 90. What was Mary's lowest grade in the original set of 5 grades?

**4.**

**5 min.**

A $5 bill is exchanged for 72 coins having a total value of $5. Some of the coins are nickels and the rest are dimes. How many dimes are in the exchange? *500 ¢* *25 dimes*

**5.**

**5 min.**

In the following sequence, there are 10 numbers. Each number has one more 2 than the preceding number:

2, 22, 222, 2222, ... , 2222222222

What is the hundreds digit of the sum of these 10 numbers?

**8** √

**1.**

**3 min.**

There is an even number between 200 and 300 that is divisible by 5 and also by 9. What is that number?

**2.**

**5 min.**

A kangaroo chases a rabbit which starts 150 feet ahead of the kangaroo. For every 12-foot leap of the kangaroo, the rabbit makes a 7-foot leap. How many leaps will the kangaroo have to make to catch up to the rabbit?

**3.**

**6 min.**

A prime number is a counting number greater than 1 that has no divisors other than 1 and the number itself. The first five prime numbers are: 2, 3, 5, 7, and 11. How many different pairs of prime numbers have a sum of 36 if the order of the numbers in a pair does not matter?

**4.**

**5 min.**

The figure at the right is divided into 8 congruent squares as shown. The area of the figure is 72 square feet. What is the length of the darkened border in feet?

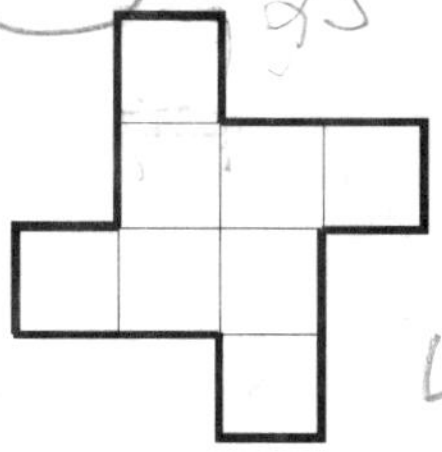

**5.**

**6 min.**

Peter had a 12:00 noon appointment that was 60 miles from his home. He drove from his home at an average rate of 40 miles per hour and arrived 15 minutes late. At what time did Peter leave home for the appointment?

## Olympiad 74

**1.**

**3 min.**

A group of 30 bikers went on a trip. Some rode bicycles and the others rode "tandems". (A tandem is a bicycle that is ridden by 2 people at the same time.) If the total number of bicycles and tandems was 23, how many tandems were used?

$8+14=22$
$7+16=13$

7 tandems

**2.**

**5 min.**

The following number sequence is formed by starting with 7 and then adding 3 to each term to get the next term: 7, 10, 13, 16, 19, ... . The 1st term of the sequence is 7, the 2nd term is 10, and so forth. What is the 100th term?

$7 \cdot 100$

**3.**

**5 min.**

The cost of sunglasses and a case for them is $10. If the sunglasses cost $9 more than the case, what is the cost of the case?

case = x    glasses x+9

$2x + 9 = 10$
$2x = 1 \frac{1}{2}$
$x = \frac{1}{2}$

$0.50

**4.**

**6 min.**

The tower shown at the right is made of unit cubes stacked on top of each other. Some of the unit cubes are not visible. How many unit cubes are not visible?

20 unit cubes    16 + 20

$1+2+3 = 6$    $10$

**5.**

**6 min.**

What is the greatest number of points of intersection that can occur when 2 different circles and 2 different straight lines are drawn on the same piece of paper?

    10    10 points

**1.**

**3 min.**

Suppose 6 days after the day before yesterday is Thursday. What day of the week is the day after tomorrow?

**2.**

**5 min.**

The number 2 is the first even number, 4 is the second even number, 6 is the third even number, and so forth. What is the sum of the first twenty-five even numbers?

**3.**

**5 min.**

In the addition problem at the right, different letters stand for different digits. What five-digit number does S E R V E represent?

$$
\begin{array}{c}
V \ C \ R \\
+ \ V \ C \ C \ T \\
\hline
S \ E \ R \ V \ E
\end{array}
$$

**4.**

**6 min.**

A school has 90 children. During the day, each child attends 4 classes. Each class has 15 children and 1 teacher. During the day, each teacher teaches 3 classes. What is the smallest number of teachers the school can have?

**5.**

**6 min.**

David and Eric each shot 6 arrows at the target shown. David shot 4 arrows into A and 2 into B; his score was 18 points. Eric shot 3 into A and 3 into B; his score was 21 points. How many points were given for an arrow in B?

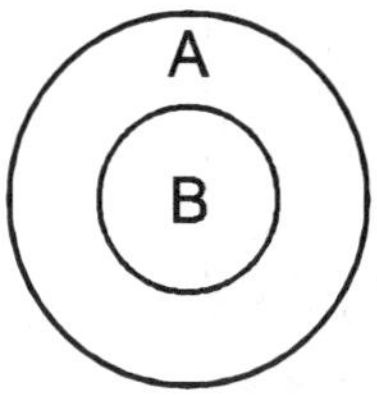

**1.**

**3 min.**

How many times does the letter x appear in the diagram at the right?

*36 times*

```
X X X X X X X
X X X   X X X
X X       X X
X           X
X X       X X
X X X   X X X
X X X X X X X
```

**2.**

**4 min.**

In the addition problem at the right, different letters represent different digits and E is twice H.
What two-digit number does AH, the sum, represent?

*93*

```
  3H E
  3H E
 +3H E
  9A3H
```

**3.**

**5 min.**

List all of the different counting numbers that each leave a remainder of 2 when divided into 83.

*9, 27, 3*

**4.**

**5 min.**

A study of 50 high school students showed that exactly 25 of them took Biology, exactly 20 of them took Chemistry, and exactly 12 of them took both subjects. How many of the 50 students took neither Biology nor Chemistry?

*17 students*

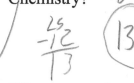

**5.**

**5 min.**

When a counting number is multiplied by itself, the result is called a perfect-square. Since 1×1 = 1, 2×2 = 4, 3×3 = 9 and so forth, 1, 4, 9 and so forth are perfect-squares. What year in the 18th century (the years 1701 through 1800) was a perfect square?

*1764*

**1.**

**4 min.**

In a group of 5 children, the average weight of each child was 72 pounds. When a sixth child joined the group, the average weight of each child became 73 pounds. What was the weight of the sixth child?

**2.**

**5 min.**

From a pile of coins containing nickels (N), dimes (D), and quarters (Q), Tom picked 10 coins with total value of $1.00. The 10 coins had a different number of each of the three types and at least 1 coin of each type. How many coins of each type did he pick?

**3.**

**5 min.**

In the multiplication example at the right, different letters represent different digits and blanks represent non-zero digits. What 4-digit number should the product be?

$$
\begin{array}{r}
A\ B \\
\times\ B\ A \\
\hline
\_\ \_\ 3 \\
\_\ \_\ \_ \\
\hline
\end{array}
$$

product: $\_\ \_\ \_\ \_$

**4.**

**4 min.**

Betty wants to purchase a bicycle but is $23 short. Claire wants to purchase the same bicycle but is $25 short. If they combine their money, they will have just enough to buy the bicycle. What is the cost of the bicycle?

**5.**

**5 min.**

At the right, there are two large congruent squares with sides 7 units long and four small congruent squares with sides 3 units long. If the shaded figure is also a square, what is its area in square units?

**1.**

**4 min.**

At the post office, a person spent a total of $2.00 to get some 29¢-stamps and some 5¢-stamps, and received no change. How many 5¢-stamps did the person buy?

*five ¢ Stamps*

**2.**

**5 min.**

Rectangle ABCD contains 3 small congruent rectangles. If the smaller dimension of one of the small rectangles is 5 units, what is the area of rectangle ABCD in square units?

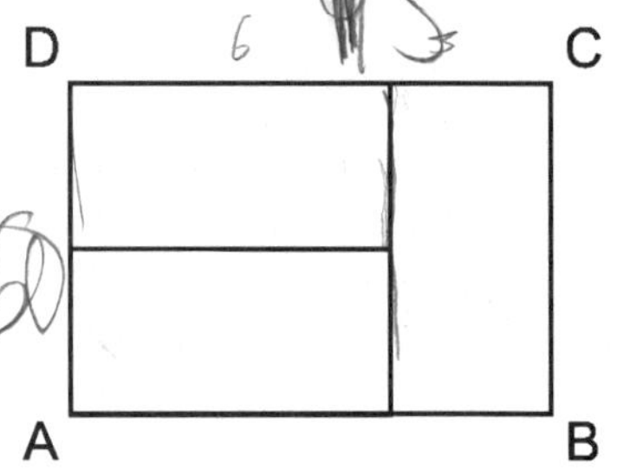

*150 units*

**3.**

**5 min.**

An Olympiad team is made up of students from the 4th, 5th, and 6th grades only. Seven students are 5th graders, eleven students are 6th graders, and one-third of the entire team are 4th graders. How many students are on the team?

*24 students*

**4.**

**5 min.**

A light flashes every 4 seconds, a second light flashes every 5 seconds, and a third light flashes every 6 seconds. If all three lights flash together at 8 o'clock, what is the very next time on the clock that they will again flash together?

*8:01 and 20 seconds*

**5.**

**6 min.**

Suppose all the counting numbers are written in columns in the pattern shown at the right. Name the letter of the column in which the number 1000 will appear.

*A*

| A | B | C | D | E | F | G |
|---|---|---|---|---|---|---|
| 1 |   | 2 |   | 3 |   | 4 |
|   |   | 7 |   | 6 |   | 5 |
| 8 |   | 9 |   | 10 |   | 11 |
|   |   | 14 |   | 13 |   | 12 |
| ... | ... |

**1.**

**4 min.**

A freight train travels 1 mile in 1 minute 30 seconds. At this rate, how many miles will the train travel in 1 hour?

$1 : 90$
$? : 3600$

40

40 ✓

**2.**

**5 min.**

A person has four special coins whose values in cents are shown at the right. How many different amounts can the person make using one or more of the coins?

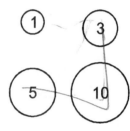

1, 3, 5, 10, 4, 6, 11, 8, 13, 15, 16, 14, 9, 19

14

**3.**

**5 min.**

If I add 5 to 1/3 of a number, the result is 1/2 of the number. What is the number?

$\frac{1}{3}x + 5 = \frac{1}{2}x$

$5 = \frac{1}{6}x$

30 ✓

$\frac{3}{6} - \frac{2}{6}$

$\frac{5}{1}x$  30 = X

**4.**

**6 min.**

The length of AE is 20 cm. B is the midpoint of AC, C is the midpoint of BD, and D is the midpoint of BE. What is the length of DE in cm?

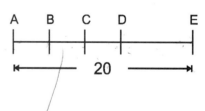

$20 = AB + BC + CD + DE$
$20 = 3AB + DE$

8 cm

**5.**

**6 min.**

What simple fraction is equal to the complex fraction shown at the right?

$\dfrac{1}{4+\dfrac{1}{2+\dfrac{1}{3}}}$

$\dfrac{7}{31}$ ✓

**1.**

**3 min.**

I have a drawer which contains 40 socks in the following numbers and colors: 12 tan, 9 brown, 11 gray, and 8 blue. Suppose I am blindfolded. What is the fewest number of socks I must pick from the drawer to be absolutely certain that I have two socks of the same color among those I have picked?

**2.**

**5 min.**

In the equation at the right, A and B represent counting numbers. What values of A and B will make the equation true? (List the value of A first, and then the value of B.)

$$\frac{A}{3} + \frac{B}{4} = \frac{11}{12}$$

**3.**

**6 min.**

Using the letters A and B, the following two-letter code words can be formed: AA, AB, BB, BA. Using the letters A, B, and C, how many different three-letter code words can be formed?

**4.**

**5 min.**

At the right, different letters represent different digits, ABC and DEF are three-digit numbers, and neither of the lead digits A and D is zero. If DEF is subtracted from ABC, what is the largest remainder that can occur?

```
   A  B  C
-  D  E  F
_____
```

**5.**

**6 min.**

Triangle ABC has its vertices A, B, and C on the sides of a rectangle 4 units by 5 units as shown. What is the area of triangle ABC in square units?

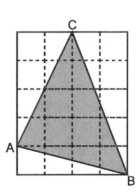

# Answers

**Olympiad 1:**  1) Thursday   2) 19   3) 325   4) 12¢   5) 15 days

**Olympiad 2:**  1) made $10   2) 17 nickels, 13 quarters   3) 144   4) 154   5) 200

**Olympiad 3:**  1) 60   2) 24 or 24mph   3) A = 7   4) 5/6   5) 298

**Olympiad 4:**  1) $140   2) A = 3, B = 8   3) 11   4) A = 4, B = 12   5) 5

**Olympiad 5:**  1) 60   2) 10 min   3) 12/29   4) 15,21,35   5) 15 small, 2 large

**Olympiad 6:**  1) 99   2) 78   3) 12 or 12 g   4) 5p,13n,3d, or 10p,4n,7d   5) 13

**Olympiad 7:**  1) 6666   2) 9   3) F   4) 8 days   5) 96

**Olympiad 8:**  1) 21   2) 12   3) 38   4) $36   5) 4

**Olympiad 9:**  1) 20   2) 150   3) 5   4) 140 min or 2 hr 20 min   5) A = 3, B = 8

**Olympiad 10:**  1) H = 2, E = 3, A = 9   2) 26   3) A = 3, B = 2   4) 22   5) 3

**Olympiad 11:**  1) IV, II, I, V, III   2) 15,762   3) Glenn-T, Harry-S, Kim-B   4) 10   5) 7

**Olympiad 12:**  1) 312132 or 231213   2) Friday   3) 6   4) 4d, 12n   5) 57

**Olympiad 13:**  1) 22   2) 625 or 875   3) 58, 59, 60   4) Anne; $2   5) 6

**Olympiad 14:**  1) 5   2) 7   3) D   4) 4 or 4 hr   5) 15

**Olympiad 15:**  1) 12   2) 8   3) $30   4) 32   5) 7

**Olympiad 16:**  1) Tuesday   2) 54   3) 5   4) E,A,N   5) D is greater by 50

**Olympiad 17:**  1) 5p, 2d   2) 90¢ or $.90   3) 60 or 60 in   4) 23   5) 9

**Olympiad 18:**  1) 86 or 86 lb   2) 42,43   3) 4   4) 26   5) 10

**Olympiad 19:**  1) 5 or $5   2) A = 4, B = 7, C = 5   3) M = 12   4) $60   5) A = 5, B = 6

**Olympiad 20:**  1) 45 or 45 mi   2) 91   3) 29 in   4) 10 or 10 min   5) 24 or 24¢

## Answers

**Olympiad 21:**    **1)** 40    **2)** 15    **3)** $350 or 350    **4)** 8    **5)** 150 or $150

**Olympiad 22:**    **1)** Wednesday    **2)** 19    **3)** 96    **4)** 26    **5)** 13

**Olympiad 23:**    **1)** 21    **2)** 48    **3)** 13    **4)** 14    **5)** 1.5 or 1½

**Olympiad 24:**    **1)** 1976    **2)** 24    **3)** 10    **4)** 16, 625; or $2^4, 5^4$    **5)** 1/10 mi or 528 ft

**Olympiad 25:**    **1)** 55    **2)** 45    **3)** 24,25,26    **4)** $2\frac{1}{6}$ or 13/6    **5)** 8

**Olympiad 26:**    **1)** Thursday    **2)** 120    **3)** 6    **4)** 6 or 6 days    **5)** 11, 15, 33, 55

**Olympiad 27:**    **1)** 7    **2)** 20    **3)** A = 9, B = 1, C = 8    **4)** 1936    **5)** 94

**Olympiad 28:**    **1)** 1,560    **2)** 720    **3)** 60    **4)** 16    **5)** 20

**Olympiad 29:**    **1)** 72    **2)** 9    **3)** 17    **4)** 7    **5)** 342

**Olympiad 30:**    **1)** 198    **2)** 5    **3)** 440    **4)** A = 7, B = 8, C = 3; or 7,8,3    **5)** 15 or 15¢

**Olympiad 31:**    **1)** 6    **2)** 35    **3)** 90    **4)** 720    **5)** 1009

**Olympiad 32:**    **1)** 8    **2)** 45    **3)** Bill, 18    **4)** 24    **5)** 15

**Olympiad 33:**    **1)** 8 or 8 oz.    **2)** 71    **3)** 35    **4)** 10:20 or 10:20 A.M.    **5)** 5

**Olympiad 34:**    **1)** 950    **2)** 95¢ or equivalent    **3)** 30 or 30 m    **4)** 5/8    **5)** 25

**Olympiad 35:**    **1)** 87    **2)** 99    **3)** 7/10    **4)** 31    **5)** 1:10

**Olympiad 36:**    **1)** 9    **2)** 36 or 36 cm    **3)** 17    **4)** 9    **5)** 2

**Olympiad 37:**    **1)** 40    **2)** 120    **3)** 6    **4)** 45    **5)** 12 or 12 m

**Olympiad 38:**    **1)** 848    **2)** 9    **3)** 108    **4)** Sun, Mon    **5)** 20

**Olympiad 39:**    **1)** 2835    **2)** 24    **3)** 100 or 100 sq cm    **4)** 4    **5)** 7

**Olympiad 40:**    **1)** 9:21 or 21:21    **2)** A = 1, B = 13    **3)** 41    **4)** 6    **5)** $75 or 75

**Olympiad 41:**    **1)** 6 o'clock    **2)** 2    **3)** 76    **4)** 99    **5)** 23

**Olympiad 42:**    **1)** $1.15 or 115¢    **2)** 127    **3)** 9 or $9    **4)** 40    **5)** 6

**Olympiad 43:**    **1)** $165    **2)** 4 and 32    **3)** 58    **4)** 100    **5)** 7

**Olympiad 44:**    **1)** 56    **2)** 74    **3)** 27 or $27    **4)** 11    **5)** A = 7

**Olympiad 45:**    **1)** 4096    **2)** 11    **3)** 20    **4)** 40    **5)** 22,100

**Olympiad 46:**    **1)** 49    **2)** 9    **3)** 70    **4)** 15    **5)** A = 1, B = 4, C = 9

**Olympiad 47:**    **1)** $.50 less or 50¢ less    **2)** 67    **3)** 18    **4)** 9    **5)** 7953

**Olympiad 48:**    **1)** 8    **2)** 38 or $38    **3)** 78    **4)** 32    **5)** 15

**Olympiad 49:**    **1)** 952    **2)** 36    **3)** 12    **4)** 20 or 20 lb    **5)** 5.55

**Olympiad 50:**    **1)** 12    **2)** 42    **3)** 246 or 246 sq ft    **4)** 7/18, 8/18, or equivalent    **5)** 6

**Olympiad 51:**    **1)** 71    **2)** 840    **3)** 32×32 or 1024 or $32^2$    **4)** 18 or $18    **5)** 32

**Olympiad 52:**    **1)** 12    **2)** D    **3)** $2.70 or 270¢    **4)** 4    **5)** 46

**Olympiad 53:**    **1)** 7    **2)** 43    **3)** 2    **4)** 10    **5)** 16

**Olympiad 54:**    **1)** 13    **2)** 10/33    **3)** 38    **4)** 3330    **5)** 32

**Olympiad 55:**    **1)** 239    **2)** 18    **3)** 6    **4)** 77    **5)** 12

**Olympiad 56:**    **1)** 7521    **2)** 5    **3)** 8    **4)** 60 min or 1 hr    **5)** 1296

**Olympiad 57:**    **1)** made 10 or $10    **2)** 25/24 or $1\frac{1}{24}$    **3)** 12    **4)** 43    **5)** $7.85 or 785¢

**Olympiad 58:**    **1)** 40    **2)** 3980    **3)** 55    **4)** 1/4    **5)** $240

**Olympiad 59:**    **1)** Monday    **2)** 720    **3)** A = 1, B = 8, C = 5    **4)** 315    **5)** 10

**Olympiad 60:**    **1)** 21    **2)** 15    **3)** 9:30 or 9:30 A.M.    **4)** 64    **5)** 8:40 or equivalent

**Olympiad 61:**   **1)** 2   **2)** 18   **3)** 3   **4)** 3   **5)** 20

**Olympiad 62:**   **1)** 210   **2)** Wednesday   **3)** 12   **4)** 11   **5)** 100

**Olympiad 63:**   **1)** 30   **2)** 169   **3)** $70   **4)** 18   **5)** 75

**Olympiad 64:**   **1)** 10   **2)** 151   **3)** 1   **4)** 8   **5)** 30

**Olympiad 65:**   **1)** 72   **2)** 50   **3)** 9   **4)** 7/10   **5)** 325

**Olympiad 66:**   **1)** 160   **2)** 5 or 5 yrs   **3)** 50   **4)** 9   **5)** 62

**Olympiad 67:**   **1)** 156   **2)** 27   **3)** 22   **4)** 32   **5)** 27

**Olympiad 68:**   **1)** 43 or 43 in   **2)** 400 or 400 mi   **3)** 342   **4)** 90   **5)** 555

**Olympiad 69:**   **1)** D,A,C,B or equivalent   **2)** 8   **3)** 1:50, 1:50 PM   **4)** 4, 4 da   **5)** 1089

**Olympiad 70:**   **1)** 16   **2)** 6   **3)** 300 sec or 5 min   **4)** 174   **5)** 82656

**Olympiad 71:**   **1)** 259   **2)** 10 or $10   **3)** 11   **4)** 9   **5)** 24

**Olympiad 72:**   **1)** 24   **2)** 1/8   **3)** 80   **4)** 28   **5)** 8

**Olympiad 73:**   **1)** 270   **2)** 30   **3)** 4   **4)** 48 or 48 units   **5)** 10:45 or 10:45 A.M.

**Olympiad 74:**   **1)** 7   **2)** 304   **3)** $.50 or 50¢ or half-dollar   **4)** 20   **5)** 11

**Olympiad 75:**   **1)** Tuesday   **2)** 650   **3)** 10390 or S = 1, E = 0, R = 3, V = 9   **4)** 8   **5)** B = 5

**Olympiad 76:**   **1)** 36   **2)** 72   **3)** 3,9,27,81   **4)** 17   **5)** 1764

**Olympiad 77:**   **1)** 78   **2)** 3,6,1   **3)** 7663   **4)** $48   **5)** 25

**Olympiad 78:**   **1)** 11   **2)** 150   **3)** 27   **4)** 8:01 or equivalent   **5)** D

**Olympiad 79:**   **1)** 40 or 40 mi   **2)** 15   **3)** 30   **4)** 8   **5)** 7/31

**Olympiad 80:**   **1)** 5   **2)** 2,1 or A = 2, B = 1   **3)** 27   **4)** 885   **5)** 9

# Hints

| Olympiads | Page |
|:---:|:---:|
| 1 - 5 | 107 |
| 6 - 10 | 108 |
| 11 - 15 | 109 |
| 16 - 20 | 110 |
| 21 - 25 | 111 |
| 26 - 30 | 112 |
| 31 - 35 | 113 |
| 36 - 40 | 114 |
| 41 - 45 | 115 |
| 46 - 50 | 116 |
| 51 - 55 | 117 |
| 56 - 60 | 118 |
| 61 - 65 | 119 |
| 66 - 70 | 120 |
| 71 - 75 | 121 |
| 76 - 80 | 122 |

## Olympiad 1

1) What day will it be 7 days from now? 14 days from now? 77 days from now?
2) Make an organized list of the different amounts starting with the 3¢-stamps.
3) Rewrite the series in reverse order placing each term directly under the term of the given series. Examine each vertical pair of terms.
4) How much will 5 pens and 5 pencils cost?
5) How long would it take one person to do the entire job alone?

## Olympiad 2

1) Act it out.
2) Try using half of the coins as nickels and the other half as quarters.
3) How many square inches are there in the rectangular sheet 2 feet by 3 feet?
4) If the average score for 4 games is 145, what is the total score for the 4 games?
5) If you counted from 1 on, how frequently would "1" appear in the units place? tens place? hundreds place?

## Olympiad 3

1) Try a simpler problem with 2, 3, or 4 children.
2) Average speed is the total distance divided by the total time.
3) If the sum of the digits of a number is divisible by 9, the number is also divisible by 9.
4) $\dfrac{1}{9 \times 10} = \dfrac{1}{9} - \dfrac{1}{10}$.
5) Compare the terms of the sequence with multiples of 3, starting with 3.

## Olympiad 4

1) Make 1.75 and 1¼ either both decimals or both mixed numbers.
2) $A \times AB = 114$. Try different values for A starting with 2.
3) Experiment with 2 lines and count the sections. Then try 3 lines, and then 4 lines.
4) Could A be less than 3?
5) Do (6*8) first.

## Olympiad 5

1) What is the average of the five numbers?
2) How many times larger than 600 square feet is 600 square yards?
3) Work from the bottom up.
4) What is the largest number that the two-digit numbers can divide exactly?
5) Try packaging some marbles in the larger boxes and examine what is left over.

## Olympiad 6

1) Make X + Y as large as possible and X – Y as small as possible.
2) Arrange the numbers to be summed as follows:  1  2  3  4  5  6
   Examine each of the vertical pairs.  12 11 10 9  8  7
3) What is the total weight of the original group of five weights?
4) Could you have as many as 15 pennies? What is the least number you could have?
5) Make a Venn diagram showing the relationship between French and Spanish students.

## Olympiad 7

1) Reread and follow the directions carefully.
2) Make a list of different pairs of coins arranged in order starting with (1,1), (1,5), and so on.
3) Divide each of the numbers in column A by 7. What do you observe?
4) If all of the supplies were used for just one person, how long would the supplies last?
5) What is the area of each small square? What is the length of a side of a small square?

## Olympiad 8

1) If I pick 5 beads blindfolded, can I be sure that I have 2 of the same color among those I have picked? If I then pick a 6th bead, can I then be sure that I have 2 of the same color?
2) How many thirds are there in 2?
3) Count the squares in an orderly fashion starting with 1×1 squares, 2×2 squares, and so on.
4) Work backward.
5) What prime factors must a number have so that it will end in one zero?

## Olympiad 9

1) What should be the sum of the numbers in each row, column, and diagonal?
2) Make a table which shows the order of terms, terms of the sequence, and multiples of 3.
3) List the possible dimensions in some orderly fashion.
4) Suppose you travel 60 miles at a rate of 30 miles per hour. How long will the trip take?
5) The product of the 2-digit number 5* and B is 432. What digit should B be?

## Olympiad 10

1) Can H be 3? What is the largest value that H can have? the smallest value?
2) List all pairs of counting numbers whose product is 144.
3) Change each of $^A/_{11}$ and $^B/_3$ to an equivalent fraction with denominator 33.
4) Test odd numbers as possible factors of 121 beginning with 3.
5) Suppose the student passed 7 tests and failed 1. How much would he then receive?

### Olympiad 11

1) Reread and follow the directions carefully.
2) What units digit in the top line times 7 will yield the 2 of the first partial product? What tens digit in the top line times 7 will yield the 8 in the first partial product?
3) Make a 3×3 table showing sports (t,b,s) and names (G,H,K). Enter Y for yes, and N for no.
4) Mark the rays a,b,c,d,e. List the angles in some order; for example, all angles that have ray a, then all angles that have ray b but not ray a, and so on.
5) In the first condition, replace 1 pear by 4 plums and 1 apple.

### Olympiad 12

1) Draw 6 blanks and place the digits in the blanks according to directions. Begin with 3s.
2) Mark 3 points on a line as Y, T, and W to represent yesterday, today, and tomorrow. Now locate points on the line referred to in the given information.
3) Draw a diagram for each path. Start by going to the right as far as possible and then up.
4) Suppose all of the coins were nickels. Exchange nickels for dimes until the total value is $1.
5) What would you add to the number being divided so that each remainder would be zero?

### Olympiad 13

1) What size squares can be found in the figure? How many of each are there?
2) C cannot be 0 or 1. Since C×C ends in C, what digits can C be?
3) You know the sum of the first and third numbers. What does their average represent?
4) If you add the different amounts of money that are given, what does the sum represent?
5) Try making the smaller piles as large as possible. (remember: 4th pile must be the largest.)

### Olympiad 14

1) Half of the perimeter is 10. How many different pairs of counting numbers have a sum of 10?
2) How many points less than a perfect score was Nancy's actual score?
3) Continue the entries in the table until 16 is reached. Divide the numbers in each column by 8 and examine just the remainders.
4) What part of the pool can each pipe fill in 1 hour? all together in 1 hour?
5) Find the sum that each column, row, and diagonal should have.

### Olympiad 15

1) What is the sum of the numbers of passengers that got on the train in the first 5 stops? the next 5 stops? How many more passengers are needed to have a total of 78?
2) Imagine removing all of the outer cubes. How many cubes are left?
3) What is the smallest purchase that can be paid for by either $2-bills or $5-bills?
4) How many gallons does $1/_4$ of the tank hold?
5) Look for a pattern in the units-digit of the different multiplication strings.

### Olympiad 16

1) What day of the month was the Friday before the 25th? 2 Fridays before the 25th?
2) If AB represents the man's age, what represents the wife's age? Which is greater, A or B? What is the sum of A and B?
3) How many buggies were used in going to the fair?
4) Which letters cannot be on the face opposite H?
5) How many numbers in the D-sum? Remove "1" from the D-sum. Now compare sums.

### Olympiad 17

1) Could the remaining coins be nickels?
2) Suppose the second purchase was cut in half. Compare this result with the first purchase.
3) How many sides of the unit-squares are contained in the perimeter of A?
4) Make a list of multiples of 4 each increased by 3, and a list of multiples of 5 each decreased by 2. Compare the two lists.
5) What is the sum of A and C?

### Olympiad 18

1) Let H represent the weight of the heavier boy and L the weight of the lighter boy. Then $H + L = 138$ and $H - L = 34$.
2) Could the page numbers be in the 40s? the 50s? What could the units digits be?
3) Place a dot on each cube that has 4 red faces.
4) 169 can be factored. Try odd numbers beginning with 11.
5) What is the middle number of the 15 consecutive numbers?

### Olympiad 19

1) Let C be the cost of the camera and S the cost of the case. Then $C + S = 100$ and $C - S = 90$.
2) Find B in the second addition.
3) $K + L = 11$ and $L + M = 19$. How much more than K is M?
4) Work backward.
5) The six-digit number is also divisible by 8 and 9.

### Olympiad 20

1) How many seconds in 1 min 20 sec? in 1 hour?
2) List the numbers less than 100 which have a remainder of 1 when divided by 15.
3) Can 29 be represented as a sum of 6s and 7s?
4) Where will each cyclist be 10 minutes after the starting time?
5) Make a table of costs of the ruler beginning with 22¢. Compute the amount Betty and Alice each have, and the total of the two amounts.

## Olympiad 21

1) What is the total value in cents of one nickel and one dime?
2) Can A be 0? Observe that the product 7×A ends in A. What digit must A be?
3) Express 1¾ as a decimal.
4) Place a dot on each cube that has 2 or 4 red faces.
5) If the dollar-share of the youngest is S, represent the other shares in terms of S.

## Olympiad 22

1) What day of the week is today? 7 days from today? 350 days from today?
2) Work backward.
3) How many square inches are there in the square region?
4) Each arrow lands on the target. What is the smallest score possible? largest score?
5) Try same problem with 5 and 8. Try it again with 7 and 11. What do you observe?

## Olympiad 23

1) What is the sum of the five numbers before each is increased?
2) Count the cubes in one slice.
3) What is the smallest square greater than 1000? largest square less than 2000? Express both squares in the exponential form $N^2$.
4) Suppose all the vehicles are bicycles. What is the total number of wheels they have?
5) What was the weight of the water poured out? the original weight of the water in the jar?

## Olympiad 24

1) How old is person A when person B is born?
2) Let the square's side have length s. What is the rectangle's perimeter in terms of s?
3) AB×A yields the second partial product which ends in 1. What digits must A and B be?
4) $10 = 2×5$; $10×10 = 100 = (2×5)×(2×5) = (2×2)×(5×5) = 4×25$.
5) How many train-lengths did the train travel from the time it entered to the time it cleared the tunnel?

## Olympiad 25

1) In what digit must the multiple of 7 end to satisfy the condition of divisibility of 5?
2) Let the 6 people be A, B, C, D, E, and F. Make a list of the different matches played in the first round.
3) $10×10×10 = 1000$; $20×20×20 = 8000$; $30×30×30 = 27,000$. Between which two products is 15,600 located?
4) If the average of all three numbers is 1, what must their sum be?
5) If a number is divisible by 36, it is also divisible by 4 and 9. What digits can B be?

## Olympiad 26

**1)** How many days are there from Jan. 1 to Feb. 22? On what days will Mondays occur?

**2)** How many Xs can fill the entire rectangle? How many Xs are actually missing?

**3)** Count (1,1,24) as one of the triples whose product is 24. How many different triples of counting numbers including (1,1,24) have a product of 24?

**4)** How many days would the food last if it was used by just one scout?

**5)** What is the largest number that each of the two-digit numbers will divide exactly?

## Olympiad 27

**1)** What was the cents-value of the 13¢-stamps that were purchased?

**2)** What is the length of a side of the square?

**3)** Examine the units column. What is the sum of A and B? What is B's value?

**4)** $30 \times 30 = ?$ $40 \times 40 = ?$ $50 \times 50 = ?$ What four-digit square number begins with 19**?

**5)** Let TU represent the largest two-digit number that satisfies the condition shown at the right. Suppose T = 9, what value does U have?

$$\begin{array}{r} T\,U \\ -\,U\,T \\ \hline 4\,5 \end{array}$$

## Olympiad 28

**1)** Make A×B as large as possible and A − B as small as possible.

**2)** How many minutes must the slow clock lose before it again shows the correct time?

**3)** If a number is divisible by 3 and 5, the number is a multiple of 15. List multiples of 15 in order with the smallest first. Divide each by 7.

**4)** Place a dot on each cube that has exactly 3 red faces. Start with the bottom layer.

**5)** What part of the job is done by Alice in 1 min.? Betty in 1 min.? together in 1 min.?

## Olympiad 29

**1)** Find the smallest and largest multiples of 3 between 10 and 226. Express each in the form 3×N.

**2)** Divide the rectangle into triangles which are each congruent to triangle BEF.

**3)** Express 85 as the product of two factors neither of which is 1. Which factor represents the sum of two numbers?

**4)** Remember that 25 is equal to 5×5.

**5)** How many pages require 1 piece of type for each page? 2 pieces of type for each page? 3 pieces of type for each page?

## Olympiad 30

**1)** How frequently do 3 or 7 appear as the units digit in the sequence of counting numbers?

**2)** When 4 coins are taken out of the pocket, how many are left in the pocket?

**3)** How many complete turns will the front wheel make in traveling 1 mile? the rear wheel?

**4)** What values can C have? Try one value and find the values of A and B that are then determined. If the 3 values of A, B, and C do not satisfy the problem, try another value for C.

**5)** Work backward.

## Olympiad 31
1) What fractional part of the weight of the brick was 4 pounds?
2) What is the middle number of the seven consecutive numbers?
3) List the numbers between 100 and 200 that have the required property. How many other numbers are there which have the required property?
4) How far will the wheel roll on the ground in making one complete turn?
5) Find the values of D, E, and R in that order.

## Olympiad 32
1) What number did Tom multiply by 2½ to get 50?
2) Between which two of the following products is 1985 located: 30×30, 40×40, 50×50?
3) What does the sum 25+20+31 represent?
4) What is the total perimeter of the 3 rectangles in terms of a side s of the square?
5) What is the largest amount that can be made using all four coins?

## Olympiad 33
1) What is the weight of the marbles that was added to the bowl and original set of marbles?
2) Find the smallest number which when divided by 5 or 7 has a remainder of 1.
3) Find the number of cubes in the tallest column.
4) When the correct clock advances 60 minutes, how many minutes will the slow clock advance?
5) Work backward.

## Olympiad 34
1) What is the average of the first 25 counting numbers? the next 25?
2) Suppose Eric has just one nickel. How does that affect the other coins?
3) What is the length of a side of square ABCD?
4) What does $\dfrac{a}{b} \times \dfrac{b}{c}$ equal?
5) Try the same problem with 5 and 8. How is your answer related to the given numbers?

## Olympiad 35
1) What is the largest number of schools that can enter exactly 4 teams in the XYZ contest?
2) Find the sum of the numbers in the first line.
3) Express each denominator as an improper fraction.
4) Make a table which shows the number of new members in each of the five weeks.
5) How frequently do both lights flash together?

## Olympiad 36
1) Find the value of A, B, and C in that order.
2) How many "vertical risers" does the staircase have? "horizontal treads"?
3) Between which two of the following products is N located: $10^3, 20^3, 30^3$?
4) What does the sum of Carl's and David's scores represent in terms of the target?
5) What is the sum of the 1s in the units column?

## Olympiad 37
1) Count the large, small and smaller boxes in that order.
2) If the coins were arranged in stacks of 30, would any be left over?
3) Make a diagram of each path. How many choices are there at the starting point?
4) How many numbers are in the set 00, 01, 02, ... , 99? Of these, how many have the same digit?
5) When Alice runs 50m, how far does Betty run? When Alice runs 5m, how far does Betty run?

## Olympiad 38
1) Experiment.
2) Which digit in the given four-digit number determines the units digit of the power?
3) Solve a simpler problem. Suppose each team played just one game with each of the other teams.
4) Could Sunday occur on the first day of the month? the second day of the month?
5) How many cubes have paint on three faces? on two faces?

## Olympiad 39
1) Take each condition and make a diagram. If there is more than one way to show the condition, make another diagram. Add the next condition to extends the diagram(s).
2) What is the smallest number of apples that Carol can buy and sell with none left over?
3) Compare the shaded regions with the unshaded regions.
4) Try adding the same number to the numerator and denominator starting with 1.
5) Make a table of the ages of the three children starting with youngest being 5 years of age.

## Olympiad 40
1) How many hours elapsed from 9AM to 10PM?
2) What is the sum of any set of the 3 numbers in any row, column, or diagonal?
3) Suppose the original two-digit number is TU. Express the problem's conditions using TU.
4) Find the area of triangles ABC and EBF. How is the area of the trapezoid related?
5) How much did Peter lose in dollars by working just five weeks?

## Olympiad 41

1) What time will the clock register 12 hours from now? 24 hours from now?
2) What is the sum of the five numbers?
3) Compare the terms of the sequence with multiples of 7 starting with 7.
4) What number multiplied by itself is 10,000?
5) Suppose each table had just 2 people seated at it. How many seats would then be empty?

## Olympiad 42

1) What would be the exact price of 1 book if 7 books were sold for exactly $8?
2) What is the sum of the digits of the first nine counting numbers? the next ten counting numbers?
3) What is the average amount that Alice earned for the days after school?
4) If the side of a small box is s, what is the length of the figure's outer boundary in terms of s?
5) How long would it take for one person, working alone, to complete half of the job?

## Olympiad 43

1) Work backward.
2) Pair the factors of 128 so that the product of each pair is 128.
3) Partition the figure into rectangles. (There are many ways to do this.)
4) Find the values of H, A, and E in that order.
5) How many more nickels than dimes did Barbara have to begin with?

## Olympiad 44

1) List the multiples of 6, each increased by 2, between 24 and 72. Compare with multiples of 7.
2) Can B be an odd number? Replace B by one of its possible values and multiply BBB by 6.
3) Work backward.
4) Concentrate on each layer starting on the bottom layer. Mark each cube having 3 red faces.
5) The six-digit number is divisible by 8 and by 11. Find B first.

## Olympiad 45

1) Calculate the number of sticks in OCTA, OCTIL, and OCTILLA in that order.
2) What number should be placed in the lower right-hand corner of the square?
3) The number of field goals was 6 more than the number of foul shots. What was the point-value of these 6 field goals?
4) Suppose the square's side has length s. What is the sum of the four perimeters in terms of s?
5) Express the first equation as $1 + 4 + 9 + 16 + \cdots + 625 = 5525$. Do the same with the second equation and compare the two, term for term.

## Olympiad 46

1) What is the largest amount that can be made? the 5 smallest amounts?
2) If the entire group of 30 people consisted solely of children, how much would the tickets cost?
3) Count the number of cubes in each horizontal layer starting at the top.
4) What is the sum of the original five numbers?
5) The first partial product is a two-digit number. What is the largest value that AB can have?

## Olympiad 47

1) Calculate the cost of the 12 cans at the old rate and also at the new rate.
2) According to b., what units-digits can N have? According to c., what values can N have?
3) What is the average of the five numbers?
4) How many steps should the dog take to cover the distance the cat covered in 12 steps?
5) What values may S have if N is 6? For each value of S, find the value of H, E, and I in that order.

## Olympiad 48

1) List the triples from smallest to largest starting with (1,1,8).
2) Add to Rhoda's and Sara's amounts so that each will have the same amount as Roberta. What will be the new sum that all three will then have together?
3) What is the average height of all twelve columns?
4) Let * 8 * * 17 be the first 5 numbers of the sequence. What are the 3rd and 4th numbers?
5) Find two factors of 240 that differ by 1. Reread the problem carefully.

## Olympiad 49

1) The largest multiple of 7 and 8 is also a multiple of 56.
2) The sum of the length (L) and width (W) of each of the different rectangles is 12. Calculate L×W for each rectangle.
3) Finding $\frac{1}{3}$ of a number is the same as decreasing the number by what part of itself?
4) How many pounds in excess of 5 pounds did the package weigh?
5) Change all three fractions to decimals or change all three to simple fractions.

## Olympiad 50

1) What is the first day of the year which has the same symbol in the U.S.A. and England?
2) Let the two numbers be 6A and 6B. What is their product? What value does A×B have?
3) How is the area of the walk related to the areas of the large and small rectangles?
4) Let the four numbers be $\frac{1}{3}$, *, *, $\frac{1}{2}$. How many increases are needed to go from $\frac{1}{3}$ to $\frac{1}{2}$?
5) Number the diagrams 1, 2, and 3 from the top down. Replace the circle in diagram 2 by its equal in diagram 1.

## Olympiad 51
1) Find the number of Xs in each row.
2) Find the LCM of the numbers.
3) First locate 1000 between a consecutive pair of the following: $30^2, 40^2, 50^2$.
4) Work backward.
5) When 6 is placed at the right of the two-digit number AB, you get AB6. Read the problem again.

## Olympiad 52
1) If N is the number, 24 is how many times N?
2) B≠0. Divide each number in the seven columns by 7, and replace each number by its remainder.
3) Pair each nickel with a quarter. What is the difference in the cents-value of the pair? of two pairs?
4) Study the units column. What value must B have? What value must A+B have in the tens column?
5) Count the number of 3s you find in the 1s-place, then the 10s-place, and then the 100s-place.

## Olympiad 53
1) If you pick 6 disks blindfolded, is it possible that you do not have 3 disks of the same color?
2) If A+B = 23 and B+C = 33, how much more than A is C?
3) Since 8 divides the number exactly, what value must V have?
4) Make a diagram of each of the different paths in some organized way.
5) Work backward. Start with one container being 3 times as large as the other.

## Olympiad 54
1) The larger number must be 4 times as large as the smaller number.
2) Work from the bottom up.
3) How many cubes does the tallest column have? the next tallest? and so on?
4) List the 6 three-digit number and add them.
5) Draw the other diagonal.

## Olympiad 55
1) D must be odd: 3, 5, 7, or 9. Which numbers can be eliminated?
2) Assign a different letter to each of the rectangle's 8 regions. Name each different rectangle by the letters it contains.
3) How many different pairs of students can be formed from the 4 students?
4) The semiperimeter of the rectangle is 18. Which 2 primes have a sum of 18?
5) In the time that Robert runs 5 meters, how many meters will Sam run?

## Olympiad 56

1) What are the four different digits whose product is 70?
2) Look only at the fractional parts of the numbers. Which are to be added, and which subtracted?
3) Find a cube with exactly three red faces. Where is it located?
4) In one minute, what part of the tub will the faucet fill, and what part will the drain empty?
5) What digit can T be if the product T×T ends in 6? Test it.

## Olympiad 57

1) How much did the stamp collector receive? pay out?
2) Make the denominator as large as possible.
3) Area of ACE can be obtained by subtracting the area of ECD from the area of ACD.
4) What number multiplied by 9 produces 400?
5) What was the incorrect change in dollars and cents?

## Olympiad 58

1) If you count by ones, how frequently will the digit 3 appear in the units place? tens place?
2) Use the Distributive Principle: A×B − A×C = A×(B−C).
3) Divide each of 8! and 6! by 5!. Take the difference and divide by 3!.
4) Draw lines connecting the midpoints of the sides AB, BC, CD, and DA in that order.
5) What was the total saved by the original group of 30 people when 10 people joined them?

## Olympiad 59

1) What day of the week is "today"?
2) What multiple of 6 is the average number of the 15 multiples of 6?
3) What digits can B be? What nonzero digit must C be? Test the digits in the problem.
4) The largest factor has either no 2s or no 3s. Which should it be?
5) Make an organized list of the numbers that the three disks can have.

## Olympiad 60

1) Find the average number of the five consecutive numbers.
2) The lead digit of the different three-digit numbers may be 1, 2, 3, 4, or 5. Make an organized list of the different three-digit numbers starting with 104.
3) How frequently do the three lights flash together after 9 AM? What time will that be?
4) Imagine that you can push the four triangles together. What will you see?
5) How many minutes apart are the 2 clocks after just 1 hour? 2 hours? 3 hours?

## Olympiad 61

**1)** Start at floor 7 and work backward.

**2)** Look at the bottom layer of the cube. What do you see?

**3)** If all answers are correct, what is the total score? If 1 answer is wrong, how many points are lost?

**4)** How many pennies can there be in the set of 10 coins?

**5)** Sum the first 2 terms, the first 3 terms, and the first 4 terms. What pattern do the sums form?

## Olympiad 62

**1)** Find the LCM of the three given numbers.

**2)** Make a line diagram with points marked YY for yesterday, TY for today, and TW for tomorrow.

**3)** Suppose just one big fish and two small fish were sold. How much would the fisherman receive?

**4)** Compare the sums of the entries in the top row and in the second column.

**5)** How many seconds does it take the first dog to get to the starting point? the second dog?

## Olympiad 63

**1)** What sizes can the squares be? Count the number of squares of each size.

**2)** Suppose no marbles are left over when they are distributed in equal shares among 6, 7, or 8 children. What is the least number of marbles the box can then contain?

**3)** Work backward.

**4)** Draw a rectangle divided into 3 congruent parts to represent the number. Then the triple of the number is represented by 3 congruent rectangles having 9 congruent parts.

**5)** Notice that B cannot be 0 or 1. What digits can B be?

## Olympiad 64

**1)** What is the sum of the original six numbers?

**2)** Make a table and look for a pattern.

**3)** To get the units digit of a power of 7, multiply just the units digit of the preceding power by 7.

**4)** If a number is divisible by 9, its digit-sum is a multiple of 9.

**5)** What is the total of the game-times played by each of the five active players?

## Olympiad 65

**1)** Rearrange the product as an equivalent product of a number multiplied by itself.

**2)** Any two of the four triangles can be rearranged to form a square.

**3)** Clearly A must be greater than or equal to 5. Which digit must it be?

**4)** Simplify the fraction from the bottom up.

**5)** Subtract the corresponding terms of the two sets: $(4-3) + (8-6) + (12-9) + \cdots + (100-75)$.

## Olympiad 66

1) If we add 1 to the sum, we get twice the page-number of the right page.
2) How much older than Alice is Clara?
3) How long will it take for the car to travel 5 miles?
4) When Henry purchases 23-cents stamps, what should the units digit of the cost be?
5) Partition the given figure by drawing two vertical lines.

## Olympiad 67

1) Find the smallest number that is divisible by 13, 4, and 6.
2) Multiples of 5 increased by 2 end in 2 or 7. Multiples of 6 increased by 3 are odd numbers.
3) What is the largest square number less than 500?
4) Subtract AB from AB8. The result must be 296.
5) Count the number of cubes in each vertical column.

## Olympiad 68

1) Find the average height of both people. How much less than the average is the shorter person?
2) What is the sum of the miles traveled by the front and rear wheels during the entire trip?
3) How many 1-digit numbers are written? 2-digit numbers? 3-digit numbers?
4) Extend the lines so that the shaded figure is completely covered by the small squares.
5) Write the 6 different 3-digit numbers, add them, and divide the sum by 6. Can you think of a shorter way?

## Olympiad 69

1) Calculate the values of A, B, C, and D.
2) What is the total cost of mailing the additional ounces?
3) If the fast clock moves 6 minutes, how many minutes will a normal clock move in that time?
4) If 2 men work 5 days, together they work a total of $2 \times 5 = 10$ individual work days. What is the total of individual work days that a crew of 8 will work in 6 days?
5) What is the value of A in the multiplicand?

## Olympiad 70

1) What is largest even multiple of 3 that is less than 101?
2) For every quarter, there are 2 dimes and 4 nickels.
3) One light flashes every 75 seconds and the other every 100 seconds.
4) How is the area of the border related to the areas of the outer and inner rectangles?
5) N is divisible by 8 and 3. Find the value of B first.

## Olympiad 71

1) Make the 3-digit number as small as possible and the 2-digit number as large as possible.
2) Find the average of the amounts that each boy gets.
3) Work backward.
4) Use an organized listing starting with (1,2,8).
5) How many edges does the given cube have?

## Olympiad 72

1) If a number has a remainder of 4 when divided by 5, what can the units digit of the number be?
2) Suppose a side of the square is 4 units. What is the area of the square and of the triangle?
3) What was Mary's total score on the five tests?
4) Suppose all 72 coins are nickels. How many cents short of 500 will the coins then be?
5) Suppose you listed the numbers in a column for addition. How many 2s are in the units column?

## Olympiad 73

1) What is the smallest two-digit number that 2, 5, and 9 will divide exactly?
2) If the kangaroo and the rabbit both make one leap from the same spot in the same direction, how many feet will the kangaroo gain?
3) Make a list of the prime numbers less than 36. What must be added to each to make the sum 36?
4) Find the length of a side of a small square.
5) How long will it take Peter to drive 60 miles?

## Olympiad 74

1) Suppose all the vehicles were bicycles. How many people would then have gone on the trip?
2) Make a table showing the order of numbers, given numbers, and consecutive multiples of 3. Look for a pattern.
3) What connection is there between the average of two numbers and their difference?
4) Make a list of the number of cubes not visible in each layer from the top down.
5) Make a diagram.

## Olympiad 75

1) Make a line diagram showing points T for today, Y for yesterday, and W for tomorrow. Then locate H, the point for Thursday.
2) Which term of the series is the average of the series?
3) Find the values of S, V, and E in that order.
4) Find the total number of classes that are given during the school day.
5) An arrow in B was worth more points than an arrow in A. How many more points?

## Olympiad 76

1) Count the number of Xs in the top three rows. How many are in the bottom three rows?
2) What values can E and H have?
3) The numbers will each divide 81 exactly.
4) How many students took Biology and not Chemistry? Chemistry and not Biology?
5) Is 40×40 too small, too large, or just right?

## Olympiad 77

1) What is the total weight of the original group of 5 children?
2) Could the ten coins contain three quarters?
3) The units digit of the product A×B is 3. What values must A and B have?
4) How much money does Betty have? Claire?
5) What is the length of the rectangle formed by the small four squares?

## Olympiad 78

1) How many 29¢-stamps must be purchased?
2) If the smaller dimension of one of the small rectangles is 5, what is the larger dimension?
3) What fractional part of the team do the 5th and 6th graders form?
4) How soon after the three lights flash together will they again flash together?
5) Divide each number in the table by 7 and replace the number by its remainder.

## Olympiad 79

1) How long will it take the train to travel 2 miles?
2) How many amounts can be made using just 1 coin? 2 coins? 3 coins? 4 coins?
3) How many sixths are in $1/_3$? $1/_2$? What fractional part of the number is 5?
4) Let d be the distance from A to B. What is the distance from B to C in terms of d? from C to D? from D to E? from A to E?
5) Work from the bottom up starting with $2 + \dfrac{1}{3}$.

## Olympiad 80

1) If I pick 4 socks blindfolded, is it possible that I do not have a pair of the same color among the 4?
2) Express each of A/3 and B/4 as an equivalent fraction with denominator 12.
3) Make a complete list of the three-letter codewords that begin with A. How many codewords are in this list? in a list with codewords beginning with B? with C?
4) Make the three-digit number ABC as large as possible and DEF as small as possible.
5) Find the area of the rectangle and each of the unshaded triangles.

# Solutions

| Olympiad | Page | Olympiad | Page | Olympiad | Page |
|----------|------|----------|------|----------|------|
| 1 | 125 | 28 | 160 | 55 | 196 |
| 2 | 127 | 29 | 161 | 56 | 197 |
| 3 | 129 | 30 | 162 | 57 | 198 |
| 4 | 130 | 31 | 163 | 58 | 199 |
| 5 | 131 | 32 | 164 | 59 | 200 |
| 6 | 133 | 33 | 165 | 60 | 201 |
| 7 | 134 | 34 | 167 | 61 | 203 |
| 8 | 135 | 35 | 169 | 62 | 204 |
| 9 | 136 | 36 | 170 | 63 | 205 |
| 10 | 137 | 37 | 171 | 64 | 207 |
| 11 | 138 | 38 | 173 | 65 | 208 |
| 12 | 141 | 39 | 174 | 66 | 209 |
| 13 | 143 | 40 | 176 | 67 | 211 |
| 14 | 144 | 41 | 176 | 68 | 212 |
| 15 | 146 | 42 | 178 | 69 | 214 |
| 16 | 148 | 43 | 178 | 70 | 215 |
| 17 | 149 | 44 | 179 | 71 | 217 |
| 18 | 150 | 45 | 181 | 72 | 217 |
| 19 | 151 | 46 | 182 | 73 | 219 |
| 20 | 153 | 47 | 183 | 74 | 220 |
| 21 | 154 | 48 | 184 | 75 | 221 |
| 22 | 155 | 49 | 186 | 76 | 223 |
| 23 | 156 | 50 | 187 | 77 | 224 |
| 24 | 157 | 51 | 190 | 78 | 225 |
| 25 | 158 | 52 | 191 | 79 | 226 |
| 26 | 159 | 53 | 192 | 80 | 227 |
| 27 | 160 | 54 | 194 | | |

## Solutions

### Olympiad 1

**1)** Every 7 days from "today" will be Tuesday. Since 98 is a multiple of 7, the 98th day from today will be Tuesday. Then the 100th day from today will be Thursday.

**2)** Method 1
List the amounts in an organized manner.

|  | Amounts | | | | Number |
|---|---|---|---|---|---|
| Amounts from 3¢-stamps: | 3, | 6, | 9, | 12 | 4 |
| Amounts from 5¢-stamps: | 5, | 10, | 15 | | 3 |
| Amounts from combining | | | | | |
| 3¢-stamps and 5¢-stamps: | 3+5, | 3+10, | 3+15 | | 3 |
| | 6+5, | 6+10, | 6+15 | | 3 |
| | 9+5, | 9+10, | 9+15 | | 3 |
| | 12+5, | 12+10, | 12+15 | | 3 |
| | | | | | Total 19 |

Method 2
The number of choices we have in using the 3¢-stamps is 5; we can use either 0, 1, 2, 3, or 4 of the 3¢-stamps. Similarly, we have 4 choices with respect to the 5¢-stamps; we can use either 0, 1, 2, or 3 of the 5¢-stamps. Each of the 5 choices for the 3¢-stamps can be combined with one of the four choices we have for the 5¢-stamps. This gives a total of 20 combinations. However, this total includes the combination of 0 3¢-stamps and 0 5¢-stamps. Since 1 or more of the stamps must be used, we exclude the combination of none of each. Therefore 19 different amounts of postage can be made.

**3)** Method 1

| Given | (1) | $S = 1 + 2 + 3 + \cdots + 23 + 24 + 25$ |
|---|---|---|
| Reverse order of right side of (1) | (2) | $S = 25 + 24 + 23 + \cdots + 3 + 2 + 1$ |
| Add (1) and (2) | (3) | $2S = 26 + 26 + 26 + \cdots + 26 + 26 + 26$ |
| Simplify the right side of (3) | (4) | $2S = 26 \times 25$ |
| Divide both sides of (4) by 2 | (5) | $S = 13 \times 25$ or $325$ |

The required sum is 325.

Method 2
Arrange the numbers in a square array as shown. Add the numbers in the left column (or bottom row). The sum of each of the other columns (or rows) can be easily determined by inspection. For example, each number in the second column is one more than its corresponding number in the first column. This is also true for other pairs of successive columns. The sum of the 5 columns (or rows) is 325.

| 21 | 22 | 23 | 24 | 25 | 115 |
|---|---|---|---|---|---|
| 16 | 17 | 18 | 19 | 20 | 90 |
| 11 | 12 | 13 | 14 | 15 | 65 |
| 6 | 7 | 8 | 9 | 10 | 40 |
| 1 | 2 | 3 | 4 | 5 | 15 |
| 55 | 60 | 65 | 70 | 75 | 325 |

**(Olympiad 1)**

**3)** <u>Method 3</u>
The sum of the numbers in the third column (or in the third row) is 65. This is the average of the sums of the five columns (or rows). Multiply 65 by 5 to get the complete sum: $65 \times 5 = 325$.

<u>Method 4</u>
Examine the array of numbers shown in Method 2. Observe that the average of all numbers is 13, the number in the middle of the array. Then the sum must be $13 \times 25 = 325$.

**4)** <u>Method 1</u>
By combining both purchases we find that 5 pencils and 5 pens cost 150¢. Then 1 pencil and 1 pen cost 30¢, or 2 pencils and 2 pens cost 60¢. Since 3 pencils and 2 pens cost 72¢, 1 pencil costs 12¢.

<u>Method 2</u>
The difference in the prices of the two purchases is equivalent to the difference in the costs of a pen and a pencil. Therefore, a pen costs 6¢ more than a pencil, or, 3 pens cost 18¢ more than 3 pencils. Thus, the first purchase of 2 pencils and 3 pens is equivalent to the purchase of 2 pencils and 3 pencils plus 18¢, or 5 pencils plus 18¢. Since the cost of this purchase was 78¢, 5 pencils alone cost 60¢. Therefore 1 pencil had a cost of 12¢.

<u>Method 3</u>
Algebra: Let C represent the cost of one pencil and N the cost of one pen.

| | | | | | |
|---|---|---|---|---|---|
| Given | (1) | $2C$ | $+ \quad 3N$ | $=$ | 78 |
| Given | (2) | $3C$ | $+ \quad 2N$ | $=$ | 72 |
| Multiply both sides of (2) by 3 | (3) | $9C$ | $+ \quad 6N$ | $=$ | 216 |
| Multiply both sides of (1) by 2 | (4) | $4C$ | $+ \quad 6N$ | $=$ | 156 |
| Subtract (4) from (3) | (5) | $5C$ | | $=$ | 60 |
| Divide both sides of (5) by 5 | (6) | | $C$ | $=$ | 12 |

Answer: A pencil costs 12¢

**5)** Each person of the work crew of three people worked 20 days. Thus the number of individual work days needed to do the job was 60. Then each member of the work crew of four people must work 15 days in order to provide a total of 60 individual work days.

### Olympiad 2

**1)** She paid out $10 + $20 = $30. She received $15 + $25 = $40. She made $10.

**2)** <u>Method 1</u>

Make a table. Let N represent the number of nickels and Q the number of quarters. Start with 30 nickels and 0 quarters. Then in each successive line, decrease the number of nickels by 1 and increase the number of quarters by 1 thus keeping the total number of coins as 30. Notice that every time we decrease the number of nickels by 1 and increase the number of quarters by 1, we increase the preceding total value by 20¢. Observe that the number of increases of 20 in the total value column is the same as the number of quarters on the same line. To increase 150 in the total value column to 410, we need to increase 150 by 260 or 13 × 20. Thus there were 13 quarters and 17 nickels in the 30 coins.

| N | Q | Total value in ¢ |
|----|----|------------------|
| 30 | 0 | 150 |
| 29 | 1 | 170 = 150 + **1** × 20 |
| 28 | 2 | 190 = 150 + **2** × 20 |
| 27 | 3 | 210 = 150 + **3** × 20 |
| ... | ... | ... ... ... |
| 17 | 13 | 410 = 150 + **13** × 20 |

<u>Method 2</u>

Let us look at the same problem in a different setting. Suppose 30 spiders had a total of 410 legs. Suppose further that some of the 30 spiders (nickelpeds) each have 5 legs and the others (quarterpeds) each have 5 rear legs and 20 forelegs. Suppose the nickelpeds always have their legs on the ground and the quarterpeds have just their 5 rear legs on the ground. Then the 30 spiders have just 150 legs on the ground and 260 legs in the air. But each quarterped has 20 legs in the air. Then there must be 260/20 = 13 quarterpeds. (Now compare method 1 and method 2; notice the similarities.)

<u>Method 3</u>

Algebra: Let N represent the number of nickels and Q the number of quarters.

| Given | (1) | N | + | Q | = | 30 |
|-------|-----|---|---|---|---|----|
| Given | (2) | 5N | + | 25Q | = | 410 |
| Divide both sides of (2) by 5 | (3) | N | + | 5Q | = | 82 |
| Subtract (1) from (3) | (4) | | | 4Q | = | 52 |
| Divide both sides of (4) by 4 | (5) | | | Q | = | 13 |
| Substitute from (5) into (1) | (6) | N | + | 13 | = | 30 |
| Subtract 13 from both sides of (6) | (7) | | | N | = | 17 |

Therefore there are 17 nickels and 13 quarters in the 30 coins.

**(Olympiad 2)**

**3)** <u>Method 1</u>

Make a diagram of the sheet showing one 2" strip. Notice that there are twelve 2" by 3" pieces in the 2" strip. Since there are 12 strips of 2" in 24", there are $12 \times 12 = 144$ 2" by 3" pieces in the 2' by 3' rectangle.

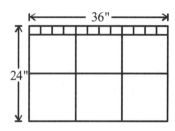

<u>Method 2</u>

The area of one card is 6 square inches. The area of the sheet is $24 \times 36$ square inches. Divide $24 \times 36$ by 6 to produce 144.

**4)** <u>Method 1</u>

If the average of four scores is 145, then their sum is $4 \times 145 = 580$. The sum of the three given scores is $139 + 143 + 144 = 426$. The fourth score is equal to $580 - 426$ or 154.

<u>Method 2</u>

The first score is 6 less than the average; the second score is 2 less than the average; and the third score is 1 less than the average. Thus the sum of the three scores is 9 less than the sum of three average scores. Thus the fourth score needs to be 9 above the average score which is $145 + 9 = 154$.

<u>Method 3</u>

Algebra:   Let S represent the fourth score.

| | | |
|---|---|---|
| Definition of average | (1) | $(139 + 143 + 144 + S) \div 4 = 145$ |
| Multiply both sides of (1) by 4 | (2) | $139 + 143 + 144 + S = 145 \times 4$ |
| Simplify (2) | (3) | $426 + S = 580$ |
| Subtract 426 from both sides of (3) | (4) | $S = 154$ |

Therefore the fourth score is 154.

**5)** Consider the frequency of appearance of the digit "1" in each of the places.

<u>units place:</u>   the digit "1" appears once in every ten. Since 500 has 50 tens, the digit "1" will appear 50 times in the units place.

<u>tens place:</u>   the digit "1" appears ten times in every hundred. Since 500 has 5 hundreds, the digit "1" will appear 50 times in the tens place.

<u>hundreds place:</u>   the digit "1" will appear 100 times in the hundreds place (100, 101, 102, ... , 199)

The digit "1" will appear a total of 200 times in the page numbers.

## Olympiad 3

**1)** The least number of marbles that the set could have is the least common multiple of 2, 3, 4, 5, and 6. LCM(2,3,4,5,6) = 60. (See Appendix 6, section 3.)

**2)** The average speed for any trip is the total distance divided by the total time spent in traveling. The total distance was 120 miles and the total time was 5 hours. The average speed equals (120 miles)/(5 hours) or 24 miles/hour or 24 mph.

Comment: It is interesting to observe that the average speed in this problem does not depend on the distance. In other words, the average speed in this problem would be the same no matter what distance was traveled at the given rates.

**3)** If a number is divisible by 9, then the sum of its digits is divisible by 9. The digit sum is $3+A+A+1 = 4+2A$. The digit sum cannot be 9, otherwise $A = 2\frac{1}{2}$. So $4+2A = 18$ which produces $A = 7$. (See Appendix 4, section 4.)

**4)** Any unit fraction whose denominator is the product of two consecutive numbers can be expressed as a difference of unit fractions as shown at the right. The second equation is the general rule.

$$\frac{1}{99\times100} = \frac{1}{99} - \frac{1}{100}$$

$$\frac{1}{n(n+1)} = \frac{1}{n} - \frac{1}{n+1}$$

Each of the fractions in the given sum can be expressed as the difference of two unit fractions like so:

$$\left(\frac{1}{1} - \frac{1}{2}\right) + \left(\frac{1}{2} - \frac{1}{3}\right) + \left(\frac{1}{3} - \frac{1}{4}\right) + \left(\frac{1}{4} - \frac{1}{5}\right) + \left(\frac{1}{5} - \frac{1}{6}\right)$$

Observe that when the addition is performed, all terms but the first and last drop out. Therefore the sum is $1 - \frac{1}{6}$ or $\frac{5}{6}$.

**5)** Since the successive terms of the sequence increase by 3, relate the sequence to the multiples of 3 and display the table at the right. Compare each of the terms of the sequence with the multiple of 3 directly below it. Notice that each term of the sequence is 2 less than the corresponding multiple of 3 directly below it. Since the 100th multiple of 3 is 300, the corresponding term of the sequence is $300-2 = 298$.

| order of terms | 1 | 2 | 3 | 4 | . . . | 100 |
|---|---|---|---|---|---|---|
| terms of sequence | 1 | 4 | 7 | 10 | . . . | ? |
| multiples of 3 | 3 | 6 | 9 | 12 | . . . | (300) |

## Olympiad 4

**1)** We need to know the number of boxes that were packaged in order to find the total selling price. The number of boxes is obtained by dividing 100 by 1¼: $100 \div 5/4 = 100 \times 4/5 = 80$. The selling price is $80 \times \$1.75 = \$140$.

**2)** The first partial product 114 is equal to the product of AB and A. The second partial product 304 is equal to the product of AB and B. Then A must be less than B.

Method 1
Since the product of AB and A is 114, A is a divisor of 114. Therefore A may be 2, 3, or 6. Since AB×A = 114, A cannot be 2 because AB×A would then be less than 60. Similarly, A cannot be 6 since AB×A would then be greater than 360. Therefore A must be 3 and AB must be $^{114}/_3$ or 38. Thus A = 3 and B = 8.

Method 2
From the first partial product, observe that B×A must end in 4. Since A is less than B, A = 2 and B = 7, or A = 3 and B = 8, or A = 4 and B = 6. But 27×2 = 54, 46×4 = 184, and 38×3 = 114. Only the third equation satisfies the given conditions. So A = 3 and B = 8.

Method 3
From the second partial product 304, we see that B×B ends in 4. Then B = 2 or 8. If B = 2, then A must be 1 because A is less than B. But 12×21 = 252. If B = 8 and AB×B = 304, then AB = 304/8 or 38 and 38×83 = 3154. Therefore A = 3 and B = 8.

**3)** Method 1
Make a diagram and draw 4 lines so that they intersect each other as shown. The number of different sections is 11.

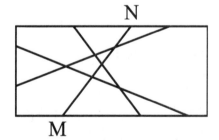

Method 2
Make a table. The original rectangle without lines added is considered to be one section.

| Total number of lines added | 0 | 1 | 2 | 3 | 4 |
| --- | --- | --- | --- | --- | --- |
| Total number of sections | 1 | 2 | 4 | 7 | ? |

### (Olympiad 4)

**3)** <u>Method 2</u>
Look for a pattern. Observe that the 1st added line results in increasing the preceding total of sections by 1, the 2nd added line increases the preceding total of sections by 2, the 3rd added line increases the preceding total of sections by 3. It seems that the 4th added line will increase the preceding total of sections by 4 and that there will be 7+4 or 11 sections. Examine the 4th line in the diagram at the right. When the 4th line intersects the first of the 3 interior

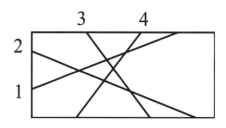

lines, it creates a new section. This happens each time the 4th line crosses an interior line. When the 4th line finally ends at a point on the rectangle, it creates a 4th new section. Thus the 4th line creates a total of 4 new sections. The answer to the given problem is 11.
(If a 5th line were added, it would increase the preceding total of sections by 5.)

**4)** A has to be larger than 3. Try A = 4: $\quad\dfrac{1}{3}=\dfrac{1}{4}+\dfrac{1}{B}$ or $\dfrac{1}{B}=\dfrac{1}{3}-\dfrac{1}{4}=\dfrac{1}{12}$
Therefore A = 4 and B = 12.

The following rule applies to all unit fractions: $\quad\dfrac{1}{N}=\dfrac{1}{N+1}+\dfrac{1}{N(N+1)}$ .

**5)** According to the order of operations, first perform the operation indicated in the parentheses.

$$6 * 8 = \frac{6+8}{2} \text{ or } 7. \quad \text{Then} \quad 3 * (6 * 8) = 3 * 7 = \frac{3+7}{2} \text{ or } 5.$$

### Olympiad 5

**1)** <u>Method 1</u>
The middle number of an odd number of consecutive numbers is always the average of the set. Then the average of the numbers is $^{320}/_5$ or 64 which also is the third or middle number. Count back by twos. The required number is 60.

<u>Method 2</u>
Represent the middle number by n. Then the five consecutive even numbers are n–4, n–2, n, n+2, and n+4. The sum of the five numbers is 5n. Since 5n = 320, n = 64. Thus n–4, the first number, is 60.

**2)** <u>Method 1</u>
1 sq yd = 9 sq ft. Then 600 sq yd = 600×9 sq ft. Since 600 sq ft is $^1/_9$ of 600×9 sq ft, the time needed to mow 600 sq ft is $^1/_9$ of the time required to mow 600 sq yd. Therefore $^1/_9$ of 1½ hrs is $^1/_9 \times ^3/_2 = ^1/_6$ hr or 10 min.

**(Olympiad 5)**

Method 2
Since 9 sq ft = 1 sq yd, 1 sq ft = $\frac{1}{9}$ sq yd. Then the time needed to mow 1 sq ft is $\frac{1}{9}$ of the time needed to mow 1 sq yd. Therefore, 600 sq ft will require $\frac{1}{9}$ of 1½ hr or $\frac{1}{6}$ hr or 10 min.

3) Work from the bottom up.

$$\cfrac{1}{2+\cfrac{1}{2+\cfrac{1}{2+\cfrac{1}{2}}}} = \cfrac{1}{2+\cfrac{1}{2+\cfrac{1}{5/2}}} = \cfrac{1}{2+\cfrac{1}{2+\cfrac{2}{5}}} = \cfrac{1}{2+\cfrac{1}{12/5}} = \cfrac{1}{2+\cfrac{5}{12}} = \cfrac{1}{29/12} = \cfrac{12}{29}$$

4) If 4 is subtracted from 109, the result is 105. Then each of the two-digit numbers that will divide 109 with a remainder of 4 will divide 105 exactly. Thus, the problem is equivalent to finding all two-digit divisors of 105. Since the prime factors of 105 are 3, 5, and 7, the divisors are 3×5, 3×7, and 5×7, or 15, 21, and 35.

5) Method 1
After some marbles are packaged in boxes for 12, the remaining marbles must be completely packaged in boxes for 5. The following table shows what happens when some marbles are packaged in boxes for 12. Only in two cases (marked with an asterisk) can all 99 marbles be completely packaged in 12-marble and 5-marble boxes. However, only the first of these two *cases will satisfy the condition that more than 10 boxes must be used. Therefore 2 of the large boxes and 15 of the small boxes were used.

| Number of boxes for 12 | Number of extra marbles | Number of boxes for 5 | Total number |
|---|---|---|---|
| 1 | 99 − 12 = 87 | 17; 2 m left over | -- |
| *2 | 99 − 24 = 75 | 15 | 17 |
| 3 | 99 − 36 = 63 | 12; 3 m left over | -- |
| . | . | . | . |
| . | . | . | . |
| *7 | 99 − 84 = 15 | 3 | 10 |

Method 2
Let S represent the number of 5-marble boxes and L the number of 12-marble boxes.

Then 5S + 12L = 99 or $S = \dfrac{99-12L}{5}$. In the second equation, 99 − 12L must be divisible by 5 if S is to be a whole number. This will happen only if L = 2 or 7. If L = 2, S = 15. If L = 7, S = 3. The number of boxes will be greater than 10 only when L = 2 and S = 15.

## Olympiad 6

1) The largest value will occur when the denominator is as small as possible and the numerator is as large as possible. This occurs when X is 50 and Y is 49. The largest value is $\frac{50+49}{50-49} = 99$.

2) <u>Method 1</u>
T, the total number of chimes, equals $1 + 2 + 3 + 4 + \cdots + 10 + 11 + 12$. The sum of this series is 78.

<u>Method 2</u>

$$\begin{array}{rl} T = & 1 + \ 2 + \ 3 + \ 4 + \ \cdots + 10 + 11 + 12 \\ T = & 12 + 11 + 10 + \ 9 + \ \cdots + \ 3 + \ 2 + \ 1 \\ 2T = & 13 + 13 + 13 + 13 + \ \cdots + 13 + 13 + 13 \end{array}$$

Notice that the series on the second line is the reverse of the series on the first line. Each time we add a term and the corresponding term above, the sum is 13. Then 2T is equal to 12×13 or 156. But 2T is twice the sum of the first series. Therefore, T = 78.

3) The average of the five weights is 13 gm. Then the total weight of the five weights is 5×13 or 65 gm. The sixth weight increases the total to 72 gm. The average of the six weights is $^{72}/_6$ or 12 gm.

4) *Case 1.* Since pennies must be used in the selection, the number of pennies used must be a multiple of 5. Suppose 5 pennies are selected. Then the remaining 16 coins must have a value of 95¢. If the 16 coins are nickels, their total value is 80¢. But this is 15¢ short of the desired 95¢. Exchange 3 of the 16 nickels for 3 dimes. Then we will have 13 nickels and 3 dimes which have a total value of 95¢. Therefore 5 pennies, 13 nickels, and 3 dimes is one possible answer.

*Case 2.* Suppose 10 pennies are selected. Then the remaining 11 coins must have a value of 90¢. Suppose that the 11 coins are nickels. Then their total value is 55¢ which is 35¢ short of the required 90¢. We need to exchange 7 of the 11 nickels for 7 dimes. Then we will have 4 nickels and 7 dimes which have a total value of 90¢. This produces another possible answer of 10 pennies, 4 nickels and 7 dimes.

*Case 3.* Suppose 15 pennies are selected. Then the remaining 6 coins must have a value of 85¢. But this is impossible since the largest value the remaining 6 coins could have is 60¢.

## (Olympiad 6)

5) A Venn diagram is helpful in explaining the solution. Let an oval patch represent the set of students taking French and another oval represent those taking Spanish. In the diagram, observe that the intersection (overlap) of the two oval patches represents the set of students taking both French and Spanish (see region B). We begin by placing 3 xs in region B, representing the students taking both French and Spanish. Region A represents the set taking French alone. Since the totals in regions A and B must be 8, we place 5 xs in region A. Similarly we place 9 xs in region C. D represents the set taking neither French nor Spanish. In the second Venn diagram, each x represents a student. Observe that the total number of xs in regions A, B, and C is 17. Therefore D has 30 − 17 = 13 students.

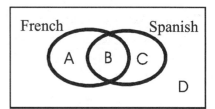

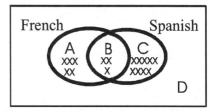

## Olympiad 7

1)

| 354 | 807 | 1515 |
|---|---|---|
| + 453 | +708 | +5151 |
| X = 807 | Y = 1515 | Z = 6666 |

2) The following pairs of numbers represent the values of the two coins the boy could take from his pocket:

$$(1,1) \qquad (1,5) \qquad (1,10) \qquad (1,25)$$
$$(5,5) \qquad (5,10) \qquad (5,25)$$
$$(10,10) \qquad (10,25)$$

Each of the above pairs has a sum that is different from the sum of each of the other pairs. Therefore there are 9 different sums.

3) Observe that each of the entries in the first column has the same remainder when it is divided by 7. The same can be said for each of the other columns. When 1,000 is divided by 7, the remainder is 6. Therefore 1,000 will appear in column F.

| A | B | C | D | E | F | G |
|---|---|---|---|---|---|---|
| 1 | 2 | 3 | 4 | 5 | 6 | 7 |
| 8 | 9 | 10 | 11 | 12 | 13 | 14 |
| 15 | 16 | 17 | 18 | 19 | -- | -- |

4) Since each person of the original group had 10 daily shares, the total supplies are equivalent to 120 daily shares. When 3 people join the group, the total number of people becomes 15. Then each person in the new group will have $^{120}/_{15}$ or 8 daily shares. The supplies will last 8 days.

5) The area of each square is $^{176}/_{11}$ or 16 square inches. Then the length of each side of a square is 4 inches. The perimeter of the U-shaped figure is equivalent to the total length of 24 sides or 96 inches.

## Olympiad 8

**1)** Suppose I select 5 beads blindfolded. The 5 beads could contain 1 bead of each color. Suppose I select 5 beads three more times with the same result. I will then have a total 20 beads consisting of 4 beads of each color. The selection of the 21st bead guarantees that there are now at least 5 beads of the same color among the 21 beads.

**2)** Method 1
Think of the double of the number as six-thirds (6/3) of the number. Since the double of the number results when 20 is added to 1/3 of the number, 20 must be 5/3 the number. Then 1/5 of 20 must be equal to 1/5 of 5/3 of the number; or 4 is 1/3 of the number. Then $3 \times 4 = 12$ is the required number.

Method 2
Let the double of the number be represented by the rectangle at the right. Divide the rectangle into 6 congruent sections, each one representing 1/3 of the number. Then 20 which is 5/3 of the number is represented by 5 boxes. Each of the boxes must have a value of 4. Since 3 boxes represent the number, the number must be 12.

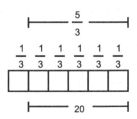

Method 3
Algebra: Let N represent the number.
Given                                   (1)      $\dfrac{N}{3} + 20 = 2N$

Multiply both sides of (1) by 3      (2)      $N + 60 = 6N$

Subtract N from both sides of (2)    (3)      $60 = 5N$

Divide both sides of (3) by 5        (4)      $12 = N$

The number is 12.

**3)** There are three different sizes for the squares that can be traced in the figure: $1\times1$, $2\times2$, and $3\times3$. The table at the right shows how many squares can be traced for each size.

| Sizes | Number of Squares |
|---|---|
| 1×1 | 21 |
| 2×2 | 12 |
| 3×3 | 5 |
| Total | 38 |

**4)** Method 1
Since $4 is $^1/_3$ of what she had left after losing money, then $12 is $^3/_3$ of what she had left after spending money. More simply, $12 is what she had left after spending money. But $12 is $^1/_3$ of what she had to begin with. Then $36 is the whole amount she had to begin with.

## (Olympiad 8)

4) Method 2
Make a diagram showing the transactions. The rectangle represents all the money that was available at the outset.

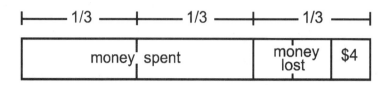

$4, the amount of money that was left, was $\frac{1}{3}$ of $\frac{1}{3} = \frac{1}{9}$ of the original amount of money. Then she started with $36.

Method 3
Let 9M represent the amount of money the woman had at the start. (If the original amount is denoted by M, each of the remaining representations will be in fractional form.) Record the transactions as follows:
Since M = 4, 9M = 36.

| Amount | Spent | Money Left | Money Lost | Money Left |
|--------|-------|------------|------------|------------|
| 9M | 6M | 3M | 2M | M |

5) Multiplication by 10 produces an additional terminal zero when a product is written in standard form. If $1 \times 2 \times 3 \times \cdots \times 20$ is written as a product of prime factors, it will contain four 5s and more than four 2s among many factors. Then part of the product can be written as: $(5 \times 2)(5 \times 2)(5 \times 2)(5 \times 2)$ which can also be represented as $10 \times 10 \times 10 \times 10$. Therefore there are four terminal zeros in the product.

## Olympiad 9

1) Method 1
From the first column, we see that the sum for each row, column, and diagonal should be 90. Then the missing number in the 3rd row is 40, and the missing number in the lead diagonal is 30. The sum for the second column is $40 + 30 + X$ or $70 + X$. Then X must be 20.

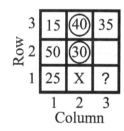

Method 2
Since the numbers in the two diagonals have equal sums and the same middle number, then the two numbers in the corners of each diagonal have equal sums; $25 + 35 = 15 + ?$ It follows that ?, the number in the lower right corner, is 45. Since the sums of the numbers in any row, column, or diagonal is 90, the bottom row sum $25 + X + 45 = 90$. Thus X is 20.

## (Olympiad 9)

**2)** Arrange the terms of the given sequence in order. Since the consecutive terms of the sequence increase by 3s, also display the corresponding multiples of 3 in the table. Notice that each multiple of 3 is 1 more than the corresponding term of the sequence. Then the multiple of 3 that corresponds to 449 is 1 more than 449 or 450.
Since 450 is the 150th multiple of 3, N must be 150.

| Order | 1 | 2 | 3 | 4 | ... | N |
|---|---|---|---|---|---|---|
| Terms of Sequence | 2 | 5 | 8 | 11 | ... | 449 |
| Multiples of 3 | 3 | 6 | 9 | 12 | ... | (450) |

**3)** If the perimeter is 22 inches, then the sum of the length and width, the half perimeter, is 11 inches. The table at the right shows what dimensions are possible and the resulting areas. Just 5 different areas are possible.

| One Side | Other Side | Area |
|---|---|---|
| 10 | 1 | 10 |
| 9 | 2 | 18 |
| 8 | 3 | 24 |
| 7 | 4 | 28 |
| 6 | 5 | 30 |

**4)** At 30 mi per 60 min, it will take 2 min to cover 1 mi or 40 min to cover 20 mi. On the return trip which averages 12 mi per 60 min or 2 mi per 10 min, 20 mi will be covered in 100 min. The round trip takes $40 + 100 = 140$ min or 2 hr 20 min.

**5)** In the following discussion, * represents a missing digit.
The product of 5* and B yields the second partial product 432. B is a divisor of 432 and greater than 6. If B = 6, the divisor becomes $432 \div 6 = 72$ which is impossible because the divisor is 5*. Other candidates for B are 8 and 9. We test 8 and 9 by dividing each into 432: $432 \div 8 = 54$, and $432 \div 9 = 48$. Only 54 satisfies the given condition that the divisor be 5*. Then B = 8. Observe that $54 \times A$ is equal to the first partial product * 6 *. The only value of A that satisfies this condition is 3. Then A = 3 and B = 8.

## Olympiad 10

**1)** In the tens column, H is less than 3. Otherwise the sum would be a three-digit number. H = 1 or 2. In the units column, the sum of 4 Es is an even number. Then H in the sum must be 2. It follows that E must be either 3 or 8. If E = 8, the sum will be a three-digit number. Thus E = 3, H = 2, and A = 9.

**2)** Examine the pairs of whole numbers whose product is 144. The only pair that has a difference of 10 is 18 and 8. Their sum is 26.

| 144 | 72 | 48 | 36 | 24 | 18 | 16 | 12 |
|---|---|---|---|---|---|---|---|
| 1 | 2 | 3 | 4 | 6 | 8 | 9 | 12 |

**3)** <u>Method 1</u>
Rewrite each fraction as an equivalent fraction with denominator 33.
If B = 1, 3A = 20 and A is then 20/3. But A must be a whole number. Therefore B ≠ 1. If B = 2, 3A = 9 and A = 3. Then A = 3 and B = 2.

$$\frac{3A}{33} + \frac{11B}{33} = \frac{31}{33}$$

## (Olympiad 10)

**3)** <u>Method 2</u>

Rewrite the equation in Method 1 as: $\dfrac{3A+11B}{33} = \dfrac{31}{33}$.

Then $3A + 11B = 31$. If $B = 1$, A will not be a whole number. If $B = 2$, $11B = 22$ and $3A = 9$. It follows that $A = 3$ and $B = 2$.

**4)** Since $121 = 11 \times 11$, the club has 11 members and each contributed 11¢. Each 11¢ share was paid in 3 coins which had to be 2 nickels and 1 penny. Then the 11 members contributed a total of 22 nickels.

**5)** <u>Method 1</u>

For every 8 tests the student took, his average performance was pass 7 and fail 1. On this basis he received $7 \times 25$¢ and paid $1 \times 50$¢ or $\$1.75 - \$.50 = \$1.25$ for each 8 tests. Since $1.25 is one-third of $3.75, he must have taken $3 \times 8$ or 24 tests, passed 21 and failed 3.

<u>Method 2</u>

Algebra: Let P represent the number of tests passed and F the number of tests failed.

| | | | | | | |
|---|---|---|---|---|---|---|
| Given | (1) | | | P | = | 7F |
| Given | (2) | 25P | − | 50 F | = | 375 |
| Divide both sides of (2) by 25 | (3) | P | − | 2F | = | 15 |
| Substitute from (1) into (3) | (4) | 7F | − | 2F | = | 15 |
| Simplify left side of (4) | (5) | | | 5F | = | 15 |
| Divide both sides of (5) by 5 | (6) | | | F | = | 3 |

Therefore the student failed 3 tests.

## Olympiad 11

**1)** 

| Statement in Problem | Order of Numerals |
|---|---|
| I before III but after IV | IV, I, III |
| II after IV but before I | IV, II, I, III |
| V after II but before III | IV, II, V, I, III, or IV, II, I, V, III |
| V is not the third numeral | IV, II, I, V, III |

**2)** <u>Multiplicand</u>

Since the units digit of the first partial product (fpp) is 2, the units digit of the multiplicand must be 6. The tens digit of the fpp is 8. This comes from multiplying the tens digit of the multiplicand by 7 and then adding the "carry" of 4 (from 7×6) to the product. The tens digit of the multiplicand must be 2.

```
      4 2 6   multiplicand
    ×   3 7   multiplier
    ─────────
      * * 8 2   fpp
  1 2 * *       spp
  ─────────
  * * * * *   product
```

<u>Multiplier</u>

The tens digit of the multiplier must be 3 to give the second partial product (spp). Complete the multiplication. The product is 15,762.

## (Olympiad 11)

**3)**  Method 1
Since Glenn likes neither baseball nor soccer, then tennis must be his favorite sport. Since Harry does not like baseball and can't like tennis (Glenn's favorite sport), then soccer is Harry's favorite. Glenn likes tennis, Harry likes soccer, and Kim must like baseball.

Method 2
In the table at the right, G, H, and K represent Glenn, Harry, and Kim respectively; t, b and s represent tennis, baseball, and soccer. Enter N (for No) in the table if the sport is not the associated person's favorite, and Y (for Yes) if it is. According to the given conditions, only one Y can appear in any row or column. Other letters in the row or column must be N. It follows that Glenn likes tennis, Harry likes soccer, and Kim likes baseball.

|   | t | b | s |
|---|---|---|---|
| G | Y | N | N |
| H | N | N | Y |
| K | N | Y | N |

**4)**  Method 1
Let a, b, c, d, and e represent the rays, and let (a,b) represent the angle formed by the rays a and b. Notice that (a,b) and (b,a) represent the same angle. The different angles that can be formed are: (a,b), (a,c), (a,d), (a,e), (b,c), (b,d), (b,e), (c,d), (c,e), (d,e). Ten angles can be formed.

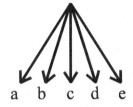

Method 2
The angles could be listed as follows:

(a,b), (b,c), (c,d), (d,e)
(a,c), (b,d), (c,e)
(a,d), (b,e)
(a,e)

Method 3
Make a diagram to show all possible pairings.

Each pairing is associated with the line segment joining two letters. Notice that there are 5×4 = 20 pairings. However, each pairing is repeated. For example, the pairing in the first of the five diagrams that represents (a,d) also appears in the fourth diagram as (d,a). Therefore we need to divide the total number of pairings in the above diagrams by 2. Thus, there are 10 different angles.

**(Olympiad 11)**

**5)**  Method 1
Let P, A, and R represent the respective weights of a plum, apple and pear. The initial given condition,
(1) $13P = 2A + 1R$, is shown as a balance of weights on a pan-balance. Condition (2) is $1R = 4P + 1A$.
The solution will be obtained by removing the same weight from both sides of the pan-balance and by
replacing a weight with its equivalent weight.

This is the initial condition:
(1)  $13P = 2A + 1R$

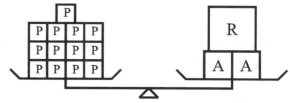

Since (2) $1R = 4P + 1A$, replace R by $4P + 1A$ on the
right side of the pan-balance. The diagram at the right
shows what occurs:  (3)  $13P = 3A + 4P$.

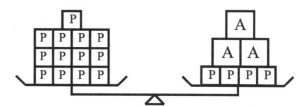

Remove 4P from both sides of the balance.
The diagram at the right shows the result:
$9P = 3A$ which is equivalent to (4) $3P = A$.

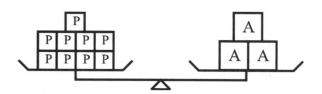

Substitute 3P for A in (2). Then $1R = 4P + 3P$ or $7P$.
A pear has the same weight as 7 plums.

Method 2
Algebra:

| | | | | |
|---|---|---|---|---|
| Given | (1) | 13P | = | 2A + 1R |
| Given | (2) | 1R | = | 1A + 4P |
| Substitute for 1R in (1) from (2) | (3) | 13P | = | 2A + 1A + 4P |
| Simplify the right side of (3) | (4) | 13P | = | 3A + 4P |
| Subtract 4P from both sides of (4) | (5) | 9P | = | 3A |
| Divide both sides of (5) by 3 | (6) | 3P | = | 1A |
| Substitute 3P for 1A in right side of (2) | (7) | 1R | = | 3P + 4P or 7P |

Thus 1 pear has the same weight as 7 plums.

## Olympiad 12

**1)** Work backward. Since the 3s are separated by 3 digits, then 3 must be either the first or the last digit of the six-digit number, that is 3 * * * 3* or * 3 * * * 3. (Each asterisk (*) represents another digit). Since the 2s are separated by two digits, only the following placements can be made in the above arrangements of 3s: 3 * 2 * 3 2 or 2 3 * 2 * 3. The 1s fill the remaining spaces. Therefore, there are two answers:  3 1 2 1 3 2 or 2 3 1 2 1 3.

**2)** Make a diagram. Let Y = yesterday, T = today, W = tomorrow, and W+1 = day after tomorrow. Five days before the day after tomorrow was Wednesday. Count back 5 days from W+1 and place Wednesday on the diagram. Yesterday was two days after Wednesday. Yesterday was Friday.

**3)** The following diagrams show the different paths that can be taken in going from A to C. There are six different paths.

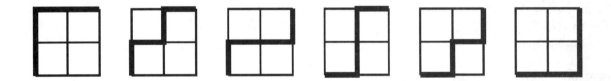

**(Olympiad 12)**

**4)** Method 1

Suppose all 16 coins were nickels, Then their total value would be 80¢. This is 20¢ short of the desired total value of $1. Exchange 4 of the nickels for 4 dimes and thus add 20¢ to the 80¢. Therefore the change consisted of 12 nickels and 4 dimes.

Method 2

Instead of nickels and dimes, think of nickelpeds (spiders which have 5 legs on the ground) and dimepeds (spiders which have 10 legs, 5 on the ground and 5 in the air at all times) Instead of 100¢, think of 100 legs. Now transform the problem into: There are 16 spiders consisting of nickelpeds and dimepeds with a total of 100 legs. How many spiders of each kind were there? Since each spider has 5 legs on the ground, there are 80 legs on the ground. Then there must be 20 legs in the air. Since each dimeped has 5 legs in the air, there must be 20/5 = 4 dimepeds. It follows that there are 12 nickelpeds and 4 dimepeds.

Method 3

Algebra: Let N represent the number of nickels and D the number of dimes.

| | | | | | | |
|---|---|---|---|---|---|---|
| Given | (1) | N | + | D | = | 16 |
| Given | (2) | 5N | + | 10D | = | 100 |
| Divide both sides of (2) by 5 | (3) | N | + | 2D | = | 20 |
| Subtract sides of (1) from (3) | (4) | | | D | = | 4 |
| Substitute 4 for D in (1) | (5) | N | + | 4 | = | 16 |
| Subtract 4 from both sides | (6) | | | N | = | 12 |

The number of nickels is 12, and the number of dimes is 4.

**5)** Let N be the required number. Notice that when N is divided by 4, 5, or 6, the remainder is 3 less than the divisor in each case. If N is increased by 3, this new number N + 3 will be divisible by 4, 5, and 6. The smallest number that N + 3 can be is the least common multiple of 4, 5, and 6 which is 60. Therefore the required number is 57.

## Olympiad 13

1) Make a table of the number of different squares that can be obtained for each of the following types of squares: 1 by 1, 2 by 2, 3 by 3.

| Size of Squares | Number |
|---|---|
| 1 by 1 | 15 |
| 2 by 2 | 6 |
| 3 by 3 | 1 |
| | Total 22 |

2) The product of the first multiplication, $C \times C$, has a units digit which is also C. Then C may have the values 1, 5, or 6.

*Case 1.* Suppose C = 1. Then the product will be ABC. However the product is DBC. Reject the assumption that C = 1.

*Case 2.* Suppose C = 5. Then A must be 1, otherwise the product would be a four-digit number. Notice that when the tens digit B of the multiplicand is multiplied by 5 and the "carry" of 2 is added, the result should have a units digit of B. This will occur when B = 2 or 7. If B = 2, then D = 6. If B = 7, then D = 8. Thus, A = 1, B = 2, C = 5, D = 6, or A = 1, B = 7, C = 5, D = 8. Therefore DBC is 625 or 875.

*Case 3.* Suppose C = 6. Then A must be 1, otherwise the product would be a four-digit number. When B in the multiplicand is multiplied by 6 and the "carry" of 3 is added, the result is an odd number with B being the odd digit. But B cannot be 1, 7, or 9 because A = 1, and each of 7 and 9 will produce a four-digit product. Futhermore, when B = 3 or 5, the condition that $1B6 \times 6 = DB6$ cannot be satisfied. Therefore C cannot be 6.

3) The average of the first and third numbers is the second number. Thus the average is $118 \div 2 = 59$. The three numbers are 58, 59, and 60.
*Comment:* For any 3 consecutive numbers, the average of the first and third numbers is the second number. We show this in the following way. Let the three numbers be N−1, N, and N+1. The average of the first and third numbers is $[(N−1) + (N+1)] \div 2 = 2N \div 2 = N$. In a similar manner, you can show that the average of the three consecutive numbers given in the preceding sentence is also N.

4) Let A, B, and C represent the respective amounts that Anne, Betty, and Cynthia have. Then the conditions of the problem are: (1) A+B = 12, (2) B+C = 18, and (3) A+C = 10.

Method 1
If we add the given conditions (1), (2) and (3), we get 2A+2B+2C = 40. Then A+B+C = 20. From the given condition (2), B+C = 18. Therefore A must be 2. From conditions (1) and (3), it follows that B and C are larger than A. Therefore, Anne had $2, the least amount.

Method 2
From conditions (1) and (2) it is clear that C = A+6. From (2) and (3), it is clear that B = A+8. From Method 1, A+B+C = 20. Substitute A+8 for B and A+6 for C. The following equation results:
A + (A+8) + (A+6) = 20. Simplifying, 3A+14 = 20 or 3A = 6. So A = 2.

## Solutions

### (Olympiad 13)

**4)** Method 3
Algebra:

| | | | | | | | | | |
|---|---|---|---|---|---|---|---|---|---|
| Given | (1) | A | + | B | | | | = | 12 |
| Given | (2) | | | B | + | C | | = | 18 |
| Given | (3) | A | | | + | C | | = | 10 |
| Add the sides of (1), (2), and (3) | (4) | 2A | + | 2B | + | 2C | | = | 40 |
| Divide both sides of (4) by 2 | (5) | A | + | B | + | C | | = | 20 |
| Subtract sides of (2) from those of (5) | (6) | | | | | A | | = | 2 |

Answer: Anne had the least amount which was $2.

**5)** Method 1
The different ways 15 pennies can be distributed into 4 piles are (1,2,3,9), (1,2,4,8), (1,2,5,7), (1,3,4,7), (1,3,5,6), (2,3,4,6). Thus, the number of pennies in the largest pile of each distribution may be 6, 7, 8, or 9. The smallest of these is 6.

Method 2
To find the smallest possible number of pennies in the largest pile, make the sum of the numbers of pennies in the other three piles as large as possible. This occurs when the first three piles contain 1, 3, and 5 pennies, or 2, 3, and 4 pennies. In either case the fourth pile will contain 6 pennies.

### Olympiad 14

**1)** The sum of the length and width is the semi-perimeter, 10 feet. The table at right gives all possible lengths and widths. There are five rectangles having different shapes, a perimeter of 20 feet, and sides whose foot-measure is a whole number. (Reminder: a square is a rectangle.)

| Length | 9 | 8 | 7 | 6 | 5 |
|---|---|---|---|---|---|
| Width | 1 | 2 | 3 | 4 | 5 |

**2)** Method 1
The maximum score of 50 occurs when all ten answers are correct. For each incorrect answer, one has to deduct 7 points from the maximum score; 5 points for the loss of the problem score and 2 points for the incorrect answer. Since Nancy scored 29 points, 21 points were deducted for incorrect answers. This represents 3 incorrect answers. Therefore Nancy had 7 correct answers.

Method 2
Make a table. Let C represent the number correct and I represent the number incorrect. When Nancy has 7 correct answers (and 3 incorrect answers), her total score is 29 points. Notice that the number of incorrect problems in the table is the same as the number of 7s subtracted from 50 on the same line under the Total Points column.

| C | I | Total Points |
|---|---|---|
| 10 | 0 | 50 |
| 9 | 1 | $43 = 50 - 1 \times 7$ |
| 8 | 2 | $36 = 50 - 2 \times 7$ |
| 7 | 3 | $29 = 50 - 3 \times 7$ |

**(Olympiad 14)**

**2)** Method 3

Algebra: Let C represent the number correct and I the number incorrect.

| | | | | | | |
|---|---|---|---|---|---|---|
| Given | (1) | C | + | I | = | 10 |
| Given | (2) | 5C | − | 2I | = | 29 |
| Multiply both sides of (1) by 2 | (3) | 2C | + | 2I | = | 20 |
| Add the sides of (2) and (3) | (4) | 7C | | | = | 49 |
| Divide both sides of (4) by 7 | (5) | | | C | = | 7 |

**3)** Method 1

Notice that the order of entries in the table is reversed on the even rows. Take the 3rd and 4th entries in the C column and divide each by 8. The remainders are 3 and 6 respectively. These remainders also happen to be the first two entries in column C. The same relationship occurs in each of the columns if we consider 8 in column A to be equivalent to a remainder of 0. When 101 is divided by 8, the remainder is 5. Therefore 101 will appear in column D.

| A | B | C | D |
|---|---|---|---|
| 1 | 2 | 3 | 4 |
| 8 | 7 | 6 | 5 |
| 9 | 10 | 11 | 12 |
| ... | ... | 14 | 13 |

Method 2

Each group of 8 consecutive numbers, beginning with 1, is arranged the same way in the table. If 101 is divided by 8, we get 12 and a remainder of 5. Interpret this as 12 groups of 8 ending with 96 in column A and 1 partial group of 5. The partial group will have 97 as its first number in column A. As shown at the right, the number 101 appears in column D.

| A | B | C | D |
|---|---|---|---|
| 97 | 98 | 99 | 100 |
| ... | ... | ... | 101 |

Method 3

Arrange each group of 8 consecutive numbers on one line by repeating the column headings in reverse order as shown at the right. The 12th group will end with 96 in the A-column. The next group will begin with 97; 101 will be in the D column.

| A | B | C | D | D | C | B | A |
|---|---|---|---|---|---|---|---|
| 1 | 2 | 3 | 4 | 5 | 6 | 7 | 8 |
| 9 | 10 | 11 | 12 | 13 | 14 | 15 | 16 |
| ... | ... | ... | ... | ... | ... | ... | ... |
| 97 | 98 | 99 | 100 | 101 | ... | ... | ... |

**4)** In one hour, the first pipe will fill $\frac{1}{8}$ of the pool, the second pipe $\frac{1}{12}$, and the third pipe $\frac{1}{24}$. Together, in one hour, they will fill $\frac{1}{8} + \frac{1}{12} + \frac{1}{24}$ or $\frac{3}{24} + \frac{2}{24} + \frac{1}{24} = \frac{6}{24} = \frac{1}{4}$ of the pool. Therefore the three pipes will fill the entire pool in 4 hours.

## (Olympiad 14)

**5)** The sum of the entries in the diagonal beginning at the lower left is 34. Therefore the entry in column 3, row 1 is 2, the entry in column 4, row 1 is 13, and the entry in column 4, row 3 is 6. The sum of the entries in row 3 is N+19. Therefore N is 15. (N can also be determined by finding the entry in column 1, row 2 which is 10, the entry in column 2, row 4 which is 14, and the entry in column 1, row 4 which is 1. The sum of the four entries in column 1 is N+19. N is therefore 15.)

| ROW | 1 | 2 | 3 | 4 |
|---|---|---|---|---|
| 4 | | | 7 | 12 |
| 3 | N | 4 | 9 | ⑥ |
| 2 | | 5 | 16 | 3 |
| 1 | 8 | 11 | ② | ⑬ |

COLUMN

## Olympiad 15

**1)** Method 1

Sum the consecutive counting numbers beginning with 1 until a total of 78 is reached. 1+2+3+4+5+6+7+8+9+10+11+12=78. Therefore, the train will be full after 12 stops.

Method 2

To find the sum (S) of consecutive numbers, multiply the average value (A) of the terms by the number of terms (N). The average value is obtained by dividing the sum of the first and last terms by 2.

| Series | A | × | N | = | S |
|---|---|---|---|---|---|
| $1+2+3+\cdots+10$ | $\frac{1+10}{2}$ | × | 10 | = | 55 |
| $1+2+3+\cdots+10+11$ | $\frac{1+11}{2}$ | × | 11 | = | 66 |
| $1+2+3+\cdots+10+11+12$ | $\frac{1+12}{2}$ | × | 12 | = | 78 |

**2)** Method 1

Each of the outer cubes of the 4-inch cube has paint on one or more faces. If these cubes are removed, the remaining figure is a 2-inch cube. A 2-inch cube contains 8 1-inch cubes. As required, each of these 8 inner cubes does not have paint on any of its faces.

Method 2

Those cubes marked by a circle have paint on one or more faces. The third layer is like the second layer; the fourth layer is like the first. The first layer has 16 cubes with paint on one or more faces; the second layer has 12 cubes with paint on one or more layer faces. Therefore there are 56 cubes with paint on one or more faces. Since the entire cube contains 64 1-inch cubes, there are 8 1-inch cubes which have no paint.

1st
layer

2nd
layer

## (Olympiad 15)

**3)** Method 1

A purchase of $10 can be paid for with 5 two-dollar bills or with 2 five-dollar bills. A $10 purchase paid for with two-dollar bills requires 3 more bills than a $10 purchase paid for with five-dollar bills. Since it is given that the number of two-dollar bills needed for a purchase is 9 more than the number of five-dollar bills needed, the value of the purchase must be equivalent to 3 purchases of $10 or a total of $30.

Method 2

Let T represent the number of two-dollar bills and F represent the number of five-dollar bills needed to make the purchase. We seek a purchase for which T – F = 9. Referring to the table, a $30 purchase is made when T – F = 9.

| Purchase | T | F | T – F |
|----------|----|----|------|
| $10 | 5 | 2 | 3 |
| $20 | 10 | 4 | 6 |
| *$30 | 15 | 6 | *9 |

Method 3

Algebra: Let N represent the number of five-dollar bills needed for the purchase. Then N+9 is the number of two-dollar bills needed for the same purchase. The value of the purchase is 5N or 2(N+9).

| | | | |
|---|---|---|---|
| Given | (1) | 5N | = 2(N + 9) |
| Expand the right side of (1) | (2) | 5N | = 2N + 18 |
| Subtract 2N from both sides of (2) | (3) | 3N | = 18 |
| Divide both sides of (3) by 3 | (4) | N | = 6 |

Since 6 five-dollar bills are needed, the value of the purchase is $30.

**4)** Method 1

If 3/4 of the tank contains 24 gallons, then 1/4 of the tank contains 1/3 of 24 or 8 gallons. Thus 4/4, being a full tank, contains 4×8 or 32 gallons.

Method 2

Let the tank be represented by the diagram at the right in which each box represents 1/4 of the tank's capacity. Observe that 3/4 of the tank contains 24 gallons. Then 1/4 of the tank contains 8 gallons. Therefore 4/4 or a full tank contains 32 gallons.

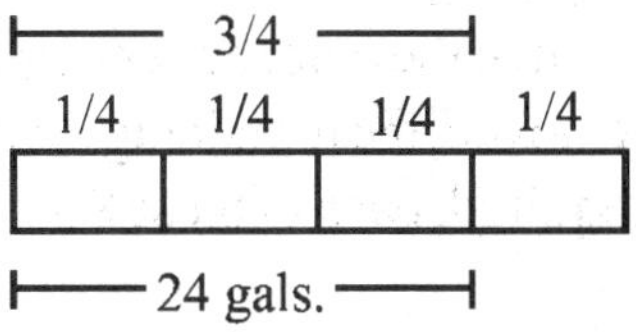

**(Olympiad 15)**

**4)** Method 3

Algebra: Let N represent the gallon-capacity of the tank.

| | | |
|---|---|---|
| Given | (1) | $\frac{3}{4} \times N = 24$ |
| Multiply both sides of (1) by 4/3 | (2) | $\frac{4}{3} \times \frac{3}{4} \times N = \frac{4}{3} \times 24$ |
| Simplify both sides of (2) | (3) | $N = 32$ |

The capacity of the tank is 32 gallons.

**5)** Make a table of the end-digits of completed multiplication strings. Notice that the end-digits repeat in groups of four. Since thirty-five 3s will appear on the 35th line of the table, and since thirty-five equals 8 groups of 4 plus 3, the end digit will be the same as end-digit of line 3 which happens to be 7. Observe that the end-digit of any line can be obtained by multiplying the end-digit of the preceding line by 3.

| String | End-Digit |
|---|---|
| 3 | 3 |
| 3×3 | 9 |
| 3×3×3 | 7 |
| 3×3×3×3 | 1 |
| 3×3×3×3×3 | 3 |
| 3×3×3×3×3×3 | 9 |
| 3×3×3×3×3×3×3 | 7 |

## Olympiad 16

**1)** Three weeks or 21 days before Friday the 25th is Friday the 4th. Count back to the first day. The first day of the month is Tuesday.

**2)** Method 1

Let AB and BA represent the respective ages of the man and his wife. The given conditions are shown at the right as (1) and (2). From (1), observe that the sum of A and B is 9. From the tens column of (2), observe that B is 1 less than A. In other words, A and B are consecutive numbers whose sum is 9. Then A = 5 and B = 4. The man is 54 years old.

$$
\begin{array}{c}
(1) \\
\begin{array}{r}
A\ B \\
+\ B\ A \\
\hline
9\ 9
\end{array}
\end{array}
\qquad
\begin{array}{c}
(2) \\
\begin{array}{r}
A\ B \\
-\ B\ A \\
\hline
9
\end{array}
\end{array}
$$

Method 2

The sum of the digits of the man's age must be 9. Since the man is older than his wife, A is greater than B. Test two-digit numbers whose digit-sum is 9. When the difference between the man's age and his wife's age is 9, the man's age is the required age.

| Man's Age | 81 | 72 | 63 | 54 |
|---|---|---|---|---|
| Wife's Age | 18 | 27 | 36 | 45 |
| Difference | 63 | 45 | 27 | 9 |

## (Olympiad 16)

**2)** Method 3

Algebra: Let M represent the man's age and W the wife's age.

| | | | | | | |
|---|---|---|---|---|---|---|
| Given | (1) | M | + | W | = | 99 |
| Given | (2) | M | − | W | = | 9 |
| Add sides of (1) and (2) | (3) | 2M | | | = | 108 |
| Divide both sides of (3) by 2 | (4) | | | M | = | 54 |

The man's age is 54.

**3)** Going to the fair, 12 people rode in the buggies. Since 3 people rode in each buggy, there were 4 buggies. On the return trip, 4 people rode in each buggy. Then 16 people rode in the buggies. Since the total number of people was 21, 5 rode in the coach.

**4)** From the first and third views, the letters on the faces adjacent to H are A, Y, X, N. Then the remaining letter E is opposite H. Similarly, from the second and third views, the letters on the faces adjacent to X are E, Y, H, N. Then the remaining letter A is opposite X. The letters which have not been paired are Y and N. They must be opposite each other. The required answer, therefore, is E, A, and N in that order.

**5)** Let D represent the sum of the odd numbers from 1 through 99, and N represent the sum of the even numbers from 2 through 98.

$$D = 1 + 3 + 5 + 7 + \cdots + 97 + 99$$
$$N = 0 + 2 + 4 + 6 + \cdots + 96 + 98$$
$$D - N = 1 + 1 + 1 + 1 + \cdots + 1 + 1$$

D − N is the sum of 50 ones. Answer: D is 50 more than N.
(Notice that the sum of the even numbers is not changed by adding zero to the series. Doing so, permits us to pair the numbers of both series one-to-one.)

## Olympiad 17

**1)** We have to find 7 coins whose value is 25¢. If the coins were nickels, their total value would be too large. There must be at least 5 pennies. Then we need two coins whose value is 20¢. The coins are dimes. Therefore the remaining coins are 5 pennies and 2 dimes.

**2)** Method 1

If 2 loaves and 4 rolls cost $2.40, then 1 loaf and 2 rolls cost $1.20. Since 1 loaf and 6 rolls cost $1.80, then 4 rolls cost 60¢ or 15¢ each. One loaf and 6 rolls cost $1.80, but the 6 rolls cost 6×15 or 90¢. Therefore the loaf must cost 90¢.

### (Olympiad 17)

**2)** Method 2

Algebra: Let L represent the cost of a loaf in cents and R represent the cost of a roll in cents.

| | | | | | | | |
|---|---|---|---|---|---|---|---|
| Given | (1) | L | + | 6R | = | 180 |
| Given | (2) | 2L | + | 4R | = | 240 |
| Divide the sides of (2) by 2 | (3) | L | + | 2R | = | 120 |
| Subtract the sides of (3) from (1) | (4) | | | 4R | = | 60 |
| Divide both sides of (4) by 4 | (5) | | | R | = | 15 |
| Replace R by 15 in (3) | (6) | L | + | 30 | = | 120 |
| Subtract 30 from both sides of (6) | (7) | | | L | = | 90 |

A loaf cost 90¢.

**3)** Let S represent the inch-length of one side of a small box. The perimeter of figure A is 16 times S which equals 48. This yields S = 3. Therefore the perimeter of B is 20S, or 20×3 = 60 (inches).

**4)** Since the number of children is 3 more than a multiple of 4, that number could be 7, 11, 15, 19, 23, 27, 31, 35, 39, 43, ... . Since the number of children is 2 less than a multiple of 5, the number could be 3, 8, 13, 18, 23, 28, 33, 38, 43, ... . The numbers satisfying both conditions are 23, 43, 63, 83, and so forth. The smallest of these numbers is 23. Thus, there are 23 children in the class.

**5)** In the units column, notice that the sum of A, B, and C ends in B. Then A+C = 10. Since A is also the tens digit of the sum, A must be 1. Therefore C = 9.

```
    A
    B
 +  C
 ----
  A B
```

## Olympiad 18

**1)** Method 1

The average of the two weights is 69. The heavier boy is 17 more than the average or 69 + 17 = 86, and the lighter boy is 17 less than the average or 69 – 17 = 52.

Method 2

Algebra: Let H represent the weight of the heavier boy and L represent the weight of the lighter boy.

| | | | | | | |
|---|---|---|---|---|---|---|
| Given | (1) | H | + | L | = | 138 |
| Given | (2) | H | – | L | = | 34 |
| Add (1) and (2) | (3) | | | 2H | = | 172 |
| Divide both sides of (3) by 2 | (4) | | | H | = | 86 |

The heavier boy weighs 86 lb.

## (Olympiad 18)

2) If page numbers are in the 40s, then the product is greater than 1,600. If the page numbers are in the 50s, then the product is greater than 2,500. Clearly the page numbers must be in the 40s. Since the two page numbers are consecutive numbers, the units digits must be 2 and 3, or 7 and 8. Try 42 and 43. They work! (Page numbers 47 and 48 don't work.)

3) Just the shaded cubes have 4 red faces.
   The other cubes have either 3 or 5 red faces.

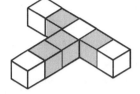

4) Since $13 \times 13 = 169$, the club had 13 members and each contributed 13¢ in 5 coins. The 5 coins had to consist of 3 pennies and 2 nickels. Thus a total of 26 nickels were contributed by the 13 members.

5) The average of the set of the consecutive numbers, 15, must also be equal to the middle number. Thus there are 7 consecutive numbers before 15 and 7 consecutive numbers after 15. The 7 numbers before 15 are 8, 9, 10, 11, 12, 13, 14. The average of the first 5 numbers, 8, 9, 10, 11, 12, is the middle number 10.

## Olympiad 19

1) Method 1
   The average cost of the camera and case is $50. Since the camera and case differ in cost by $90, they each differ from the average cost by $45. Therefore the camera will cost $50 + $45 or $95, and the case $50 − $45 or $5. Notice that these results satisfy the given conditions: the total cost is $100 and the difference in costs is $90. See the diagram at the right.

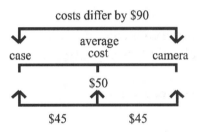

Method 2
Algebra: Let M represent the cost of the camera and S represent the cost of the case.

| | | | | | | |
|---|---|---|---|---|---|---|
| Given | (1) | M | + | S | = | 100 |
| Given | (2) | M | − | S | = | 90 |
| Add the sides of (1) and (2) | (3) | 2M | | | = | 190 |
| Divide both sides of (3) by (2) | (4) | | | M | = | 95 |
| Replace M in (1) by 95 | (5) | 95 | + | S | = | 100 |
| Subtract 95 from both sides of (5) | (6) | | | S | = | 5 |

The case cost $5.

2) From the second addition, B = 7. From the first addition C = 5. Therefore A must be 4. The required answer is A = 4, B = 7, and C = 5.

**(Olympiad 19)**

3) <u>Method 1</u>
The given conditions are: (1) K+L = 11, (2) L+M = 19, and (3) K+M = 16. From (1) and (2), *M = K+8; from (1) and (3), *M = L+5. If we add the two equations which are preceded by an *, we get 2M = K+8 + L+5, or 2M = K+L+13. Condition (1) tells us that K+L = 11. Replace K+L with 11 in the last equation to produce 2M = 11+13 = 24. The value of M is 12.

<u>Method 2</u>
If we add (1), (2), and (3) as given in Method 1, we get 2K+2L+2M = 46 which is equivalent to K+L+M = 23. From (1), we may replace K+L with 11. This produces 11+M = 23 or M = 12.

4) <u>Method 1</u>
Work backward. Mrs. Winthrop had $10 before her last purchase in the second store. This is half of what she had when she entered the store. Therefore she had $20 when she entered the second store. This is also what she had when she left the first store. Before she made her last purchase in the first store, she had $10 more than $20, or $30. But $30 is half of what she had when she entered the first store. She must have had $60 when she entered the first store.

<u>Method 2</u>
Make a diagram of what happened in the two stores working backward.

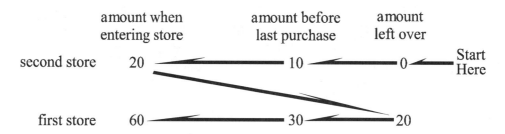

5) If a number is divisible by 72, it is also divisible by 8 and by 9. Rewrite the number A4273B as the following sum: A42000 + 73B.

A42000 is divisible by 8 (any multiple of 1000 is divisible by 8). Then 73B has to be divisible by 8 if the entire number is to be divisible by 8. Therefore B has to be 6. (See Appendix 4, section 3.)

If a number is divisible by 9, its digit-sum is also divisible by 9. Therefore, A+4+2+7+3+6 or A+22 is a multiple of 9. The smallest multiple of 9 which is greater than 22 is 27. So A+22 = 27, producing A = 5. (See Appendix 4, section 4.)

## Olympiad 20

**1)** Method 1

The train moves 3 miles in $3 \times (1\,\text{min}\ 20\,\text{sec}) = 4$ minutes. There are 15 groups of 4 minutes in 1 hour. Therefore the train moves $15 \times 3$ miles or 45 miles in 1 hour.

Method 2

Since $60 \div 1\frac{1}{3} = 60 \times \frac{3}{4} = 45$, the train travels 45 miles in 1 hour.

**2)** Since the remainder is 1 when the number is divided by 3 or 5, the remainder is also 1 when the number is divided by 15. Then the number has to be one of the following: 16, 31, 46, 61, 76, or 91. Among these, only 91 is divisible by 7.

**3)** Examine the following table of train lengths.

| Total train-length | No. of 6-inch trains | No. of 7-inch trains |
|---|---|---|
| 30 inches | 5 | 0 |
| 31 inches | 4 | 1 |
| 32 inches | 3 | 2 |
| 33 Inches | 2 | 3 |

Only the first train length, 29 inches, cannot be made by some hook-up.

**4)** In 10 minutes, A travels 7,000 yards, B travels 8,000 yards, and C travels 9,000 yards. At that time, each is at the starting point and together again for the first time since they started the race.

**5)** Method 1

Make a table of some of the costs the ruler might have. Let C = cost of the ruler, and A and B be the respective amounts that Alice and Betty have. If the ruler costs 25¢, together they will have enough to purchase the ruler. The most the ruler could cost if they together do not have enough money to purchase the ruler is 24¢.

| C | A | B | A+B |
|---|---|---|---|
| 22¢ | 0¢ | 19¢ | 19¢ |
| 23¢ | 1¢ | 20¢ | 21¢ |
| 24¢ | 2¢ | 21¢ | 23¢ |
| 25¢ | 3¢ | 22¢ | 25¢ |

Method 2

Suppose the ruler costs R¢. Then Alice has $(R-22)$¢, Betty has $(R-3)$¢, and together they have $(2R-25)$¢. But this sum is still not enough to pay for the ruler.

| Given | (1) | $2R - 25 < R$ |
|---|---|---|
| Subtract R from both sides of (1) | (2) | $R - 25 < 0$ |
| Add 25 to both sides of (2) | (3) | $R < 25$ |

Since R is less than 25¢, the most R could be is 24¢.

## Olympiad 21

**1)** <u>Method 1</u>
One nickel and one dime have a total value of 15¢. If $6.00 is divided by $.15, the result is 40. Therefore there are 40 nickels (and 40 dimes) in $6.00.

<u>Method 2</u>
A set of ten dimes and ten nickels is worth $1.50. Four such sets are worth $6.00. Therefore, there are 40 nickels in the $6.00.

<u>Method 3</u>
Algebra: Let N represent the number of nickels and also the number of dimes. The value in cents of the nickels and dimes is 5N and 10N respectively. The sum of both values is 600.

| | | | | | |
|---|---|---|---|---|---|
| Given | (1) | 5N | + 10N | = | 600 |
| Simplify (1) | (2) | | 15N | = | 600 |
| Divide both sides of (2) by 15 | (3) | | N | = | 40 |

**2)** When A is multiplied by 7, the result is a number whose unit's digit is A. The only digits which satisfy this condition are 0 and 5. If A = 0, then B = 0. But A and B are different digits. Our assumption that A = 0 is rejected. So A must be 5. Since B times 7 plus a "carry" of 3 also ends in 5, B is 6. Then the original multiplication BA×7 = HAA becomes 65×7 = 455. Thus A + B + H = 5 + 6 + 4 = 15.

$$\begin{array}{r} B\ A \\ \times\ 7 \\ \hline H\ A\ A \end{array}$$

**3)** The number of packages of cheese is $350 \div 1\frac{3}{4} = \dfrac{350}{1\frac{3}{4}}$.

The selling price is the number of packages times $1.75.

The selling price is $\dfrac{350}{1\frac{3}{4}} \times \$1.75 = \$350$. (Note that $1\frac{3}{4} = 1.75$).

**4)** Each of the 4 corner cubes has 4 red faces. Each of the 8 other cubes on the edges has 3 red faces. Each of the 4 central cubes has 2 red faces. Then, each of the corner cubes and each of the central cubes has an even number of red faces. There are 8 such cubes.

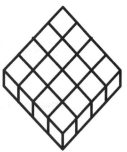

**5)** <u>Method 1</u>
Suppose the share of the youngest is Y. Then each of the other brothers, in order of age, get the following shares: Y+100, Y+200, and Y+300. Together the 4 brothers get Y+Y+100+ Y+200 + Y+300 or, simply, 4Y+600. But 4Y+600 = 1200, so 4Y = 600. Thus Y = 600 ÷ 4 or 150. The share of the youngest brother is $150.

## (Olympiad 21)

**5)** <u>Method 2</u>

If the money was divided equally among the brothers, they would each get $300, the average share. Since the oldest gets $300 more than the youngest, he gets $150 more than the average share, and the youngest gets $150 less than the average share. The share of the youngest is $300 − $150 or $150.

Note that in the graphic representation of the shares, 1 represents the smallest share and 4 the largest.

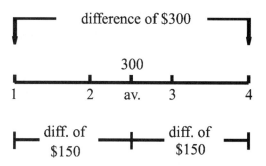

## Olympiad 22

**1)** Today is Tuesday. 365 days from now is equivalent to 52 weeks and 1 day. 52 weeks from today is also Tuesday. The 365th day is Wednesday.

**2)** Work backward.

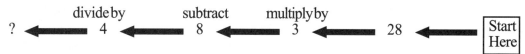

The result is $(28 \times 3 - 8) \div 4 = 19$. The starting number at the left end is 19.

**3)** <u>Method 1</u>

The square region has an area of 4 square feet or 576 square inches. A tile has an area of 6 square inches. Then $576 \div 6 = 96$. The least number of tiles needed to cover the square region is 96.

<u>Method 2</u>

Separate the square into twelve strips each 2 inches wide.

One Strip: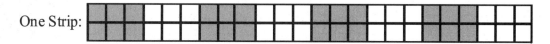

The number of 2 by 3 tiles in one strip is 8. Since there are twelve strips, there are $12 \times 8 = 96$ tiles in the twelve strips.

**4)** The total score has to be greater than or equal to $6 \times 3 = 18$, and less than or equal to $6 \times 7 = 42$. Therefore neither of the scores 16 and 44 can be obtained. Since the point-value assigned to each of the three regions is odd, the sum of any pair of the given point-values is even. Then the sum of any six scores (3 pairs of scores) is also even. It follows that the scores 19, 31, and 41 cannot be obtained. Only 26 is possible and can be obtained in any of the following ways: (3,3,3,3,7,7), (3,3,3,5,5,7) or (3,3,5,5,5,5).

**(Olympiad 22)**

5) <u>Method 1</u>
Let R be the remainder when 17 and 30 are each divided by N. Then N divides each of 30 – R and 17 – R exactly. N also divides their difference (30–R) – (17–R) exactly. Since (30–R) – (17–R) = 13, the largest value that N can have is 13. (See Appendix 5, section 7.)

<u>Method 2</u>
Test various divisors in decreasing order until the remainders for 17 and 30 are the same. Then that divisor will be the largest which satisfies the given conditions. The number 13 is the largest number which divides 17 and 30 with the same remainder.

| Divisor | Remainder for 17 | Remainder for 30 |
|---------|------------------|------------------|
| 16 | 1 | 14 |
| 15 | 2 | 0 |
| 14 | 3 | 2 |
| 13 | 4 | 4 |

**Olympiad 23**

1) The average increase is 3. The average of the set of increased numbers is 18+3 = 21.

2) <u>Method 1</u>
Slice the stairs vertically into 3 congruent figures. One figure is shown in the diagram at the right. Each slice contains 1+3+5+7 = 16 cubes. The staircase contains 3 × 16 = 48 cubes.

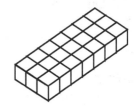

<u>Method 2</u>
Slice the stairs into 4 horizontal layers. The bottom layer has 21 cubes, the next layer has 15, the next layer has 9, and the top layer has 3. The stairs have 21+15+9+3 = 48 cubes.

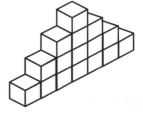

3) A number whose square is between 1000 and 2000 must be greater than 30 and less than 50 because 30×30 = 900 and 50×50 = 2,500. The smallest square between 1000 and 2000 is 32×32 = 1024; the largest square is 44×44 = 1,936. The square numbers are: 32×32, 33×33, 34×34, ... , 44×44; or $32^2$, $33^2$, $34^2$, ... , $44^2$. There are 13 square numbers between 1000 and 2000.

4) Since each cycle has two wheels, there are 25 cycles on sale. If each of the cycles on sale was a bicycle, there would be just 50 wheels. An additional 14 wheels are needed to make the given total of 64 wheels. Therefore there must be 14 tricycles.

5) The weight of the water poured out was 10 – 5¾ = 4¼ lb. This is ½ of the total weight of the water. The total weight of the water must be 2 × 4¼ = 8½ lb. Then the jar weighs 10 – 8½ = 1½ or 1.5 lb.

## Olympiad 24

1) Person A was 14 years old when person B was born in 1962. Fourteen years later, person A was 28 and person B was 14. Therefore person A was twice as old as person B in 1976.

2) <u>Method 1</u>
Let s be the length of one side of the square. Then the perimeter of one of the congruent rectangles is 3s. Since 3s = 18, s = 6 and 4s = 24. Therefore the perimeter of the square is 24.

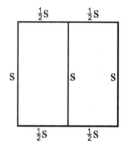

<u>Method 2</u>
To avoid the use of fractions, let the length of a side of the square be 2s. Then the perimeter of one of the congruent rectangles is 6s. Since 6s = 18, s = 3, and a side of the square is 2s = 6. Again, we conclude that the perimeter of the square is 24.

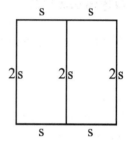

3) Since there is no remainder, the second partial product (spp) must end in 1. The only two distinct digits whose product ends in 1 are 7 and 3. The sum of 7 and 3 is 10.

$$A B \overline{) \begin{array}{r} B \, A \\ \underline{\phantom{---}} \\ \begin{array}{r} \underline{= = = -} \text{ fpp} \\ \underline{- - \ } 1 \\ \underline{= = = -} \text{ spp} \end{array} \end{array}}$$

4) <u>Method 1.</u>

$$10 = 2 \times 5$$
$$10{,}000 = (2{\times}5) \times (2{\times}5) \times (2{\times}5) \times (2{\times}5)$$
$$10{,}000 = (2{\times}2{\times}2{\times}2) \times (5{\times}5{\times}5{\times}5) \text{ (by regrouping)}$$
$$10{,}000 = 16 \times 625 \text{ (by simplifying)}$$

<u>Method 2</u>
$$10{,}000 = 10^4 = (2{\times}5)^4 = 2^4 \times 5^4 = 16 \times 625$$

**(Olympiad 24)**

**5)**

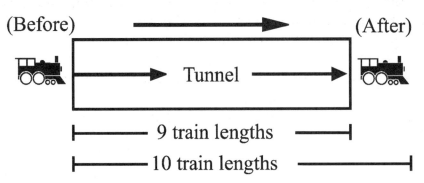

The train travels a distance equal to 10 times the train length (see diagram). The rate of 30 miles per hour is equivalent to $1/2$ mile per minute. Since the train takes 2 minutes to clear the tunnel, it will travel a distance of 1 mile in 2 minutes. One mile also happens to be 10 times the train's length. Therefore the length of the train is $1/10$ of a mile or 528 feet.

## Olympiad 25

**1)** Multiples of 7 which are between 20 and 80 are: 21, 28, 35, 42, 49, 56, 63, 70, and 77. If 1 is added to the desired multiple of 7, the sum is a multiple of 5. Then the multiple of 7 must end in 4 or 9. Only 49 satisfies this condition. Therefore, 6 years from now I will be 49 + 6 or 55 years old.

**2)** Method 1

Represent the people by A, B, C, D, E, and F.
Let AB represent a match between A and B.
The set of different matches which can be
arranged is shown at the right.
There are 15 different matches listed above.
Since each match occurs three times,
there will be 45 matches in the tournament.

|    |    |    |    |    |
|----|----|----|----|----|
| AB | AC | AD | AE | AF |
| BC | BD | BE | BF |    |
| CD | CE | CF |    |    |
| DE | DF |    |    |    |
| EF |    |    |    |    |

Method 2

Make a tree-diagram to show all possible pairings.

Each pairing is associated with a line segment joining two letters. There are 6×5 = 30 pairings. However each pairing is repeated. The pairing (B,F) in the second tree-diagram, also appears in the sixth tree-diagram as (F,B). Therefore we need to divide 30, the number of pairings, by 2. Thus there are 15 different matches. Since each match occurs three times, there are a total of 45 matches in the tournament.

## (Olympiad 25)

**3)** Since $20 \times 20 \times 20 = 8000$ and $30 \times 30 \times 30 = 27{,}000$, the three consecutive numbers are between 20 and 30. One of the three numbers must end in 5; otherwise the product cannot end in 0. The possibilities are: 23,24,25; 24,25,26; 25,26,27. Since $24 \times 25 \times 26 = 15{,}600$, the required numbers are 24, 25 and 26.

**4)** Let N be the third number. For the average to be 1, the sum of the three numbers must be 3.

| | | |
|---|---|---|
| Given: | (1) | $\frac{1}{2} + \frac{1}{3} + N = 3$ |
| Simplify (1) | (2) | $\frac{5}{6} + N = 3$ |
| Subtract 5/6 from both sides of (2) | (3) | $N = 3 - \frac{5}{6} = 2\frac{1}{6}$ |

**5)** If A 5 5 B is divisible by 36, then it is also divisible by any factor of 36 and, in particular, by 4 and 9. The number formed by the last two digits, 5B, must be divisible by 4. Therefore B is either 2 or 6. A+5+5+B must be 18. If B = 2, A = 6; if B = 6, A = 2. In either case, A+B = 8.
(See Appendix 4, sections 3 and 4.)

## Olympiad 26

**1)** Method 1
There are $31 + 22 = 53$ days in the interval from January 1 to February 22 inclusive. Mondays occur on days 1, 8, 15, 22, 29, 36, 43, and 50 of the interval. Then day 53 is on Thursday.

Method 2
February 22 occurs 52 days after January 1. Mondays occur 7 days, 14 days, 21 days, ... , and 49 days after January 1. Then 52 days after January 1 will be Thursday.

**2)** If the blank interior spaces were covered by Xs, the entire figure would contain $8 \times 18 = 144$ Xs, the blank rectangular region would then contain $3 \times 5 = 15$ Xs, and the blank triangular region would then contain $1+3+5 = 9$ Xs. Therefore, there are $144 - (9+15) = 120$ Xs.

**3)** Only the following triples of counting numbers have a product of 24: (1,1,24), (1,2,12), (1,3,8), (1,4,6), (2,2,6), (2,3,4). Answer: There are six triples which each have a product of 24.

**4)** There are $12 \times 8 = 96$ individual daily rations. If the number of scouts is increased to 16, the 96 individual daily rations will last for $96 \div 16 = 6$ days.

**5)** Each of the required numbers will divide $171 - 6 = 165$ without remainder. Since $165 = 3 \times 5 \times 11$, the required divisors are: 11, $3 \times 5$, $3 \times 11$, and $5 \times 11$, or 11, 15, 33, and 55.

## Solutions

### Olympiad 27

**1)** The total cost in cents of any number of 5¢-stamps will have a units digit of 0 or 5. Similarly, the cost of the 13¢-stamps must also have a units digit of 0 or 5. But 0 is not possible since there is no multiple of 13 less than 100 that has a units digit of 0. The only multiple of 13 less than 100 that has a units digit of 5 is 65. Therefore, Carol bought five 13¢-stamps for 65¢. The remaining 35¢ was spent for seven 5¢-stamps.

**2)** If the area of the square is 144 square inches, the length of a side is 12 inches. Then each of the congruent rectangles is 4 inches by 6 inches. The required perimeter is 20.

**3)** Since the sum of A, B, and C in the units column ends in C, A + B must be 10. In the tens column, the sum of A, B, C, and the carry of 1 (from the units column) ends in A. Thus B + C + 1 = 10 and A + B + C + 1 is less than 20. Therefore the hundreds digit of the sum BAC is 1. This produces B = 1, A = 9, and C = 8.

**4)** The 20th century contains the years 1901 through 2000 inclusive. Since $40^2 = 1600$ and $45^2 = 2025$, the year is between $41^2$ and $45^2$: $43^2 = 1649$, $44^2 = 1936$. The year was 1936.

**5)** Let T represent the tens digit and U the units digit of the largest number that satisfies the difference condition shown at the right, where T > U.

$$
\begin{array}{r}
T\ \ U \\
-\ U\ \ T \\
\hline
4\ \ 5
\end{array}
$$

**Method 1**
Since we seek the largest number that satisfies the difference condition, let T = 9 as shown at the right. Then U must be 4. The two-digit number TU is 94.

$$
\begin{array}{r}
9\ \ U \\
-\ U\ \ 9 \\
\hline
4\ \ 5
\end{array}
$$

**Method 2**
From the given difference condition with T > U in the units column, T = U + 5. Each of the four numbers in the table at the right satisfies the difference condition TU − UT = 45. The largest of the four numbers is 94.

| TU |
|----|
| 9 4 |
| 8 3 |
| 7 2 |
| 6 1 |

### Olympiad 28

**1)** The largest value occurs when A = 40 and B = 39, namely $\dfrac{40 \times 39}{40 - 39} = 1560$.

**2)** The slow clock must lose the equivalent of 12 hours or 720 minutes before it will again show the correct time. Since the clock loses 1 minute every hour, it will lose 720 minutes in 720 hours.

## Solutions

### (Olympiad 28)

**3)** <u>Method 1</u>

Since the number is divisible by 3 and 5, it is also divisible by 15. Examine the multiples of 15 which are 15, 30, 45, 60, 75, 90, and so on. Now find the smallest of these multiples which when divided by 7 will have a remainder of 4. That number is 60. (Other multiples of 15 which have this property are: 165, 270, 375, and so on.)

<u>Method 2</u>

The numbers which have a remainder of 4 when divided by 7 are 4, 11, 18, 25, 32, 39, 46, 53, 60, 67, and so on. The smallest of these numbers which is also divisible by 15 is 60.

**4)** The top face of each cube which has 3 red faces is marked with a star. There are 16 stars, therefore 16 cubes which have 3 red faces.

**5)** In 1 minute Alice can do 1/60 of the job and Betty can do 1/30 of the job. Working together, they can do $\frac{1}{60} + \frac{1}{30} = \frac{3}{60} = \frac{1}{20}$ of the job in one minute.
The entire job will require 20 minutes.

### Olympiad 29

**1)** The required multiples are:
12, 15, 18, 21, ... , 225, or 4×3, 5×3, 6×3, 7×3, ... , 75×3.
Notice then, that there are 72 multiples of 3 between 10 and 226.

**2)** <u>Method 1</u>

Partition ABCD into congruent right triangles as shown. The rectangle contains 8 triangles; triangle EFG contains 2 triangles. Then triangle EFG has 2/8 or 1/4 of the total area, or 1/4 of 36 = 9.

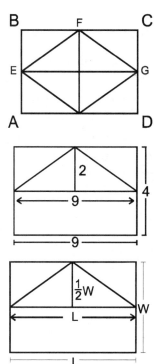

<u>Method 2</u>

Assign any measures to the dimensions of the rectangle which will result in an area of 36. Suppose we let the length and width be 9 and 4 respectively. Then the area of the triangle will be $1/2 \times 9 \times 2 = 9$.

*Comment:* If we let the length and width of the rectangle be L and W respectively, the area of the triangle is $\frac{1}{2}\left(L \times \frac{1}{2}W\right)$ which is equivalent to $\frac{1}{4}(L \times W)$. Therefore, the area of the triangle is always $\frac{1}{4}$ of the area of the rectangle, no matter what values are assigned to L and W.

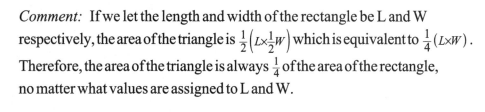

## (Olympiad 29)

3) 85 can be expressed as a product of two factors in two ways: 17×5 or 85×1. In each of the two ways, the larger factor represents the sum of the two whole numbers and the smaller factor represents the difference. Since the difference cannot be 1, 17 must be the sum.

4) The numbers which have 5 as a factor are: 5, 10, 15, 20, 25, 30. The prime factorization of the product of these numbers will have seven 5s. (Remember: 25 = 5×5.)

5)

| Pages | Pieces of Type | | |
|---|---|---|---|
| 1-9 | 9×1 | = | 9 |
| 10-99 | 90×2 | = | 180 |
| 100-150 | 51×3 | = | 153 |
| | Total | | 342 |

## Olympiad 30

1) From 1 to 1000, there are 100 groups of 10. These are 1–10, 11–20, 21–30, ... , 991–1000. Each group of 10 contains just two numbers which end in 2 or 7. Therefore, there are 100×2 = 200 numbers which end in 2 or 7. But the first group of 10 should not be included. Therefore, there are 200 – 2 = 198 numbers which end in 2 or 7.

2) Each time 4 coins are taken out of the pocket, just one coin remains. Thus, there are 5 different coins that can be the one coin that remains. For each of the five coins that remains, there is the sum of the other four coins which is different from other sums. Therefore there are 5 possible sums.

3) The front wheel makes $\frac{5280}{3} = 1760$ turns. The rear wheel makes $\frac{5280}{4} = 1320$ turns.

The front wheel makes 1760 – 1320 = 440 more turns than the rear wheel.

4) The 9 in the first partial product (fpp) is the units digit of the product C × C. Then C can be either 3 or 7. Suppose C = 3. Then, the 4 in the second partial product (spp) is the units digit of the product 3×B. So B = 8. Similarly the 1 in the third partial product (tpp) is the units digit of the product 3 × A. Thus A = 7, B = 8, and C = 3.

```
        A  B  C
     ×  A  B  C
     ─────────────
     *  *  *  9   fpp
  *  *  *  4       spp
*  *  *  1         tpp
─────────────
```

If C = 7, it can be shown that B = 2 and A = 3. But the second and third partial products will then each have just three digits. Therefore C cannot be 7.

## (Olympiad 30)

**5)** Work backward.

| CONDITION | ANNE | BETTY | TOTAL |
|---|---|---|---|
| 1. End Situation | 12 | 12 | 24 |
| 2. Betty gave Ann as many cents as Ann had. (Ann must have had 6.) | 6 | 18 | 24 |
| 3. Ann gave Betty as many cents as Betty had. (Betty must have had 9.) | 15 | 9 | 24 |
| 4. Answer: Ann had 15¢ at the beginning. | | | |

## Olympiad 31

**1)** From the given information we conclude that 2/3 of the brick weighs 4 pounds. So 1/3 of the brick weighs 2 pounds. It follows then, that 3/3 or the entire brick weighs 6 pounds.

**2)** The "middle" number of any set of consecutive numbers also is the average of the set. Try this out on sets like: 5, 7, 9, and 8, 9, 10, 11, 12. (If the set has an even number of elements like: 9, 11, 13, 15, there is no "middle" number unless you consider it to be the number halfway between 11 and 13 which happens to be 12.) In our problem, 41 is the "middle" number: *, *, *, 41, *, *, *.
Counting backward by 2s gives 35 as the first number.

**3)** Method 1
Any number of the form ABA will be the same when the order of the digits is reversed. Clearly, A may be any digit except zero; B may be any of the ten digits. Since there are nine choices for A and ten for B, there are 90 counting numbers which satisfy the given conditions.

Method 2
A partial listing follows.

```
101  111  121  131  141  151  161  171  181  191
202  212  222  232  242  .....  .....  .....  .....  292
.....  .....  .....  .....  .....  .....  .....  .....  .....  .....
909  919  929  939  949  .....  .....  .....  .....  999
```

There are a total of 90 numbers in the complete listing.

**Solutions**

### (Olympiad 31)

4) When the wheel makes one complete turn, it has rolled a distance of 88 inches. The number of turns equals 1 mile divided by 88 inches (1 mile = 5280 feet = 5280×12 inches).

Dividing yields $\dfrac{5280 \times 12 \text{ inches}}{88 \text{ inches}} = 720$.

5) D in the sum DEER must be 1. The R in the second addend must be 9. It follows that E must be 0 and DEER represents 1009.

$$\begin{array}{r} I\,N \\ +\ R\,I\,D \\ \hline D\,E\,E\,R \end{array}$$

### Olympiad 32

1) What number multiplied by 2½ gives 50 as an answer? This question is equivalent to finding what number is equal to 50 divided by 2½? That number is 20. To get the correct answer, divide 20 by 2½ producing 8.

2) $40^2 = 1600$, $45^2 = 2025$. Since 2025 is "close" to 1985, try $44^2 = 1936$. Then 1985 is between the consecutive squares $44^2$ and $45^2$: $44^2 = 1936 < 1985 < 2025 = 45^2$. The difference between 1936 and 1985 is 49; the difference between 1985 and 2025 is 40. Therefore 1985 is closer to 2025.
The number whose square is closest to 1985 is 45.

3) <u>Method 1</u>
Algebra: Let A, B, and C represent the respective ages of Al, Bill, and Carl.

| | | | | | | | | |
|---|---|---|---|---|---|---|---|---|
| Given | (1) | A | + | B | | | = | 25 |
| Given | (2) | A | | | + | C | = | 20 |
| Given | (3) | | | B | + | C | = | 31 |
| Subtract (2) from (1) | (4) | | | B | − | C | = | 5 |
| Add (3) and (4) | (5) | | | | 2B | | = | 36 |
| Divide both sides of (5) by 2 | (6) | | | | B | | = | 18 |

From (1) and (2), B is older than C. From (1) and (3), C is older than A.
Therefore Bill is the oldest and he is 18 years old.

<u>Method 2</u>
Add conditions (1), (2), and (3) given in Method 1. The sum should be 2A + 2B + 2C = 76. Divide both sides by 2. The result should be (*) A + B + C = 38. Condition (2) states that A + C = 20. Replace A + C in (*) by 20. The result is B + 20 = 38. Clearly B = 18. Therefore Bill is the oldest and he is 18 years old.

4) Let 3S represent the length of a side of the square as shown in the diagram. Then the perimeter of one of the congruent rectangles is 8S or 16. It follows that S = 2, and 3S, the length of a side of the square, is 6. Therefore the perimeter of the square is 24 meters.

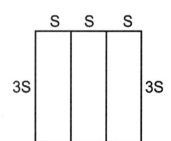

### (Olympiad 32)

**5)** List the possible amounts.
1 coin: produces 1, 2, 4, 8
2 coins: produces 1+2, 1+4, 1+8, 2+4, 2+8, 4+8
3 coins: produces 1+2+4, 1+2+8, 1+4+8, 2+4+8
4 coins: produces 1+2+4+8
There are 15 different amounts that can be made. Notice that the amounts are the counting numbers from 1 to 15 inclusive.

### Olympiad 33

**1)** Method 1
Since the weight of one bowl and the marbles it contains is 50 ounces, the weight of two bowls and twice as many marbles is 100 ounces. It is given that the weight of one bowl and twice as many marbles is 92 ounces. Then the difference of weights between 100 ounces and 92 ounces is the weight of the bowl, or 8 ounces.

Method 2
The increase in weight from 50 ounces to 92 ounces occurs because the weight of the marbles is doubled. That increase therefore is the weight of the original set of marbles, 42 ounces. It follows that the bowl weighs 8 ounces.

**2)** We want 1 less than the number to be a multiple of 5 and also of 7. Therefore 1 less than the number is a multiple of 35. Then the number is 1 more than a multiple of 35. These numbers are 36, 71, 106, 141, and so on. The smallest odd number in this set is 71.

**3)** Method 1
Count the number of cubes in each horizontal layer starting at the top.

| Layer | Number of cubes |
|:-----:|:---------------:|
| 1 | 1 |
| 2 | 3 |
| 3 | 6 |
| 4 | 10 |
| 5 | 15 |
| Total | 35 |

**(Olympiad 33)**

**3)** Method 2
Count the number of cubes in each vertical column.

| Column Height | Number of Columns | Total Number of Cubes |
|---|---|---|
| 5 | 1 | $5 \times 1 = 5$ |
| 4 | 2 | $4 \times 2 = 8$ |
| 3 | 3 | $3 \times 3 = 9$ |
| 2 | 4 | $2 \times 4 = 8$ |
| 1 | 5 | $1 \times 5 = 5$ |
| | | Total = 35 |

**4)** Method 1

| | | Time elapsed on slow clock (min) | Time elapsed on normal clock (min) |
|---|---|---|---|
| | (1) | 45 | 60 |
| Divide (1) by 3: | (2) | 15 | 20 |
| Add (1) and (2): | (3) | 60 | 80 |

Observe that 60 minutes on the slow clock is equivalent to 80 minutes on the normal clock.
The correct time will be 80 minutes after 9 or at 10:20.

Method 2
Determine what 1 minute on the slow clock is equivalent to on the normal clock. This is obtained by dividing each the entries on line (1) of Method 1 by 45. Then 45/45 or 1 minute on the slow clock is equivalent to 60/45 or 4/3 minutes on the normal clock. Then 60 minutes on the slow clock is equivalent to 60×4/3 or 80 minutes on the normal clock.

**5)** Method 1
Let A and B represent the number of marbles Anne and Betty each had at the outset, respectively. Make a table of values for A and B at the outset using the information that B is 2 more than A. Make a second table showing what happens when Anne gives 1 marble to Betty. The second table shows that Betty will have twice as many if, at the outset, Anne had 5 and Betty had 7.

| Outset | | Anne Gives 1 to Betty | |
|---|---|---|---|
| A | B | A–1 | B+1 |
| 1 | 3 | 0 | 4 |
| 2 | 4 | 1 | 5 |
| 3 | 5 | 2 | 6 |
| 4 | 6 | 3 | 7 |
| 5 | 7 | 4 | 8 |

**(Olympiad 33)**

**5)** Method 2

At the outset, let Betty have $N + 1$ marbles and Anne $N - 1$ marbles. When Anne gives Betty 1 marble, Anne will then have $N - 2$ marbles and Betty will then have $N + 2$ marbles. But Betty will then also have twice as many marbles as Anne then has.

| | | |
|---|---|---|
| Given | (1) | $N + 2 = 2 \times (N - 2)$ |
| Expand the right side of (1) | (2) | $N + 2 = 2N - 4$ |
| Add 4 to both sides of (2) | (3) | $N + 6 = 2N$ |
| Subtract N from both sides of (3) | (4) | $6 = N$ |

Betty had $N + 1$ or 7 marbles, and Anne had $N - 1$ or 5 marbles.

Method 3

Use a diagram to show what happens.
At the outset, let Anne have $N + 1$ marbles and Betty $N + 1 + 2$ as shown. When Anne gives 1 to Betty, Anne then will have $N$ and Betty will have $N + 1 + 2 + 1$ or $N + 4$.

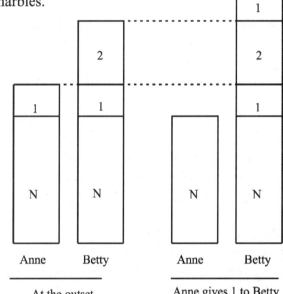

After Anne gives 1 marble to Betty, Anne has $N$ marbles and Betty has $N + 4$ marbles. But what Betty now has is twice what Anne now has. Then $N = 4$. Therefore, at the outset, Anne had 5 marbles and Betty had 7 marbles.

**Olympiad 34**

**1)** Method 1

| | | |
|---|---|---|
| Given: | (1) | $1 + 2 + 3 + 4 + \cdots + 25 = 325$ |
| Find: | (2) | $26 + 27 + 28 + 29 + \cdots + 50 = ?$ |

Each term of series (2) is 25 more than each corresponding term of series (1) which is located directly above. Since there are twenty-five addends in each of series (1) and (2), the sum of series (2) is $25 \times 25$ or 625 greater than the sum of series (1). The sum of series (2) is $625 + 325 = 950$.

Method 2

Since the average of 1, 2, 3, 4, ... , 25 is the "middle" number which is 13, then the average of 26, 27, 28, ... , 50 is also its "middle" number which is $13 + 25$ or 38.
The sum of 26, 27, 28, ... , 50 is $38 \times 25$ or 950.

**(Olympiad 34)**

**1)** Method 3

The sum of the second series can be found without using the first series. Let S represent the sum of the second series.

| | | | | |
|---|---|---|---|---|
| Given | (1) | S | = | $26 + 27 + 28 + \cdots + 49 + 50$ |
| Rewrite (1) in reverse order | (2) | S | = | $50 + 49 + 48 + \cdots + 27 + 26$ |
| Add (1) and (2) | (3) | 2S | = | $76 + 76 + 76 + \cdots + 76 + 76$ |
| 76 appears 25 times in (3) | (4) | 2S | = | $25 \times 76$ |
| Divide both members of (4) by 2 | (5) | S | = | $25 \times 38$ or $950$ |

**2)** Let N represent the number of nickels, D the number of dimes, and Q the number of quarters that Eric has where Q < D and N < Q, or N < Q < D. If N = 2, then Q ≥ 3 and D ≥ 4. This produces 9 or more coins which is too many. Therefore N = 1. If Q = 3, then D has to be at least 4. Again this produces too many coins. Therefore Q = 2 and D must be 4 so that the total number of coins is 7. The total value of the 7 coins is 95¢.

**3)** The length of a side of the square is 6m. The dimensions of rectangle AEFG are 3m and 12m. The perimeter of the rectangle is 2×(3m + 12m) which is equivalent to 30m.

**4)** The given information can be represented by the following: $\frac{a}{b} = \frac{3}{4}$ and $\frac{b}{c} = \frac{5}{6}$. When the left sides of both equations are multiplied, the result is $\frac{a}{b} \times \frac{b}{c} = \frac{a}{c}$. When the right sides of both equations are multiplied, the result is $\frac{3}{4} \times \frac{5}{6} = \frac{5}{8}$. Thus $\frac{a}{c} = \frac{5}{8}$. So we can read this equation as: the result of dividing a by c is equal to $\frac{5}{8}$.

**5)** Let D divide each of 364, 414, and 539 with the same remainder R. Then D divides each of the following exactly: 364 – R, 414 – R, and 539 – R. D also divides each of the following exactly: (414–R) – (364–R) = 50, (539–R) – (414–R) = 125, and (539–R) – (364–R) = 175. (See Appendix 4, Section 2.) Therefore D will have its greatest value when D = GCF(50,125,175) = 25.

## Olympiad 35

1) Suppose as many schools as possible entered 4 teams. The multiple of 4 that is closest to and less than 347 is 344. In this case, it would take 86 schools to enter 344 teams. The remaining 3 teams could be entered by 1 school. Then the smallest number of schools that could enter 347 teams is 87.

2) $4 \times 21 + 15 = 99$.

3) Method 1

$$\frac{1}{2+\frac{1}{2}} + \frac{1}{3+\frac{1}{3}} = \frac{1}{\frac{5}{2}} + \frac{1}{\frac{10}{3}} = \frac{2}{5} + \frac{3}{10} = \frac{7}{10}.$$

Method 2

$$\frac{1}{2\frac{1}{2}} = \frac{1+1}{2\frac{1}{2}+2\frac{1}{2}} = \frac{2}{5} \quad \text{and} \quad \frac{1}{3\frac{1}{3}} = \frac{1+1+1}{3\frac{1}{3}+3\frac{1}{3}+3\frac{1}{3}} = \frac{3}{10}. \quad \text{Then:} \quad \frac{2}{5} + \frac{3}{10} = \frac{7}{10}.$$

4)
Total of new members: $1+2+4+8+16 = 31$.

| number of week: | 1 | 2 | 3 | 4 | 5 |
|---|---|---|---|---|---|
| number of new members: | 1 | 2 | 4 | 8 | 16 |

5) Method 1
The graphs shown below display the number of minutes after noon when the two lights flash. Noon is represented by 0 on the graphs. Both lights flash together every 14 minutes. Then both lights will flash together $5 \times 14$ or 70 minutes after noon or 1:10 PM.

Method 2

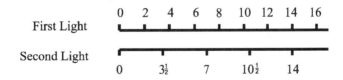

Since both lights flash together every 14 minutes, they will flash together at the following times:
noon, 12:14, 12:28, 12:42, 12:56, 1:10, 1:24, 1:38, and so on.
The first time after 1 PM that the lights will flash together will be 1:10 PM.

## Solutions

### Olympiad 36

**1)** It is clear that B = 0 and A = 1. Substitute those numbers for letters as shown at the right. Therefore C is 9.

$$
\begin{array}{r}
1\;0\;1 \\
-\;C\;1 \\
\hline
1\;0
\end{array}
$$

**2)** The "steps" have 4 vertical segments. The sum of the lengths of these 4 segments is equivalent to the length of side $\overline{AD}$. In a similar way, we can show that the sum of the lengths of the 4 horizontal segments of the "steps" is equivalent to the length of side $\overline{AB}$. Therefore the perimeter of the step-like figure is the same as the perimeter of the square ABCD which is 36 cm.

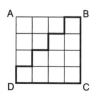

**3)** Since 10×10×10 = 1000 and 20×20×20 = 8000, the number we seek is between 10 and 20. Consider the following products: 11×11×11, 12×12×12, 13×13×13, ... , 19×19×19. Of these nine products, only 17×17×17 ends in 3. When the multiplication is carried out, we get 17×17×17 = 4913.

**4)** Let A be the point-score of the A-ring, and B the point-score of the B-circle.

(1) 2A + 1B = 17
(2) 1A + 2B = 22

#### Method 1
Compare (1) and (2) above. Observe that the B-value is 5 more than the A-value. Make a table of values for A and B in which the B-value is 5 more than the A-value. Then check to see whether 2A + 1B = 17.

| A | B | 2A + 1B |
|---|---|---------|
| 1 | 6 | 8 |
| 2 | 7 | 11 |
| 3 | 8 | 14 |
| *4 | 9 | 17 |

*If A = 4 and B = 9, 2A + 1B = 17

#### Method 2
Algebra:

| | | | | | | |
|---|---|---|---|---|---|---|
| Given | (1) | 2A | + | 1B | = | 17 |
| Given | (2) | 1A | + | 2B | = | 22 |
| Add (1) and (2) | (3) | 3A | + | 3B | = | 39 |
| Divide both sides of (3) by 3 | (4) | A | + | B | = | 13 |
| Subtract (4) from (2) | (5) | | | B | = | 9 |

The value of B is 9 points.

**(Olympiad 36)**

**5)** The ones column of the 30 numbers contains 30 ones making a sum of 30. Thus, the ones digit of the sum is 0, carry 3. The tens column contains 29 ones. Its sum is 29 plus the 3 from the "carry", making 32. Therefore the tens digit of the sum is 2.

**Olympiad 37**

**1)**

| Type of Box | Large | Small | Smaller | Total |
|---|---|---|---|---|
| Number | 4 | 12 | 24 | 40 |

**2)** The number of coins must be a multiple of 30. The multiples of 30 are 30, 60, 90, 120, 150, and so on. The smallest of these multiples that leaves a remainder of 1 when divided by 7 is 120.

**3)** Method 1

There are 3 choices for the first move starting from A. Having made the first move, then there are 2 choices for the second move. Then there is just 1 choice for the third move. Thus, there are 3×2×1 or 6 paths from A to B.

Method 2

Make a diagram for each of the different paths.

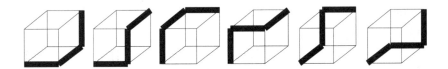

**(Olympiad 37)**

4) Method 1

Consider the numbers: 01, 02, 03, ... , 99. Of these 99 numbers, 9 have repeated digits, namely: 11, 22, 33, ... , and 99. Thus there are 90 two-digit numbers whose digits are not repeated. Among these, 45 have a tens digit greater than the units digit. (The other 45 have a tens digit smaller than the units digit.) The required answer is 45.

Method 2

| List of Numbers | | | | | Number of Numbers |
|---|---|---|---|---|---|
| 10 | | | | | 1 |
| 20 | 21 | | | | 2 |
| 30 | 31 | 32 | | | 3 |
| ... | ... | ... | ... | ... | ... |
| 90 | 91 | 92 | ... | 98 | 9 |
| | | | | | Total  45 |

5) Method 1

Alice runs 50m in the same time that Betty runs 40m. Thus Alice runs 5m for every 4m Betty runs. Therefore in the 60m race, Alice will run $12 \times 5m$ or 60m, and Betty will run $12 \times 4$ or 48m.
So Alice wins by 12m.

Method 2

Since Alice wins the 50m race by 10m, Alice must gain 2m over Betty for every 10m that Alice runs. Therefore, in a 60m race, Alice will gain $6 \times 2m$ or 12m.

# Solutions

## Olympiad 38

**1)** The largest value of the sum occurs when 3 and 5 are assigned to B and C. Thus the required answer is 848.

$$\begin{array}{r} 3\;2\;5 \\ +\;5\;2\;3 \\ \hline 8\;4\;8 \end{array}$$

**2)** $(5273)^6$ and $(3)^6$ have the same units digit.

Method 1

| Number | $3^1$ | $3^2$ | $3^3$ | $3^4$ | $3^5$ | $3^6$ |
|---|---|---|---|---|---|---|
| Units digit | 3 | 9 | 7 | 1 | 3 | 9 |

Observe that the units digit can be obtained by multiplying the preceding units digit by 3 and that the first four units digits thus obtained will repeat if the table is extended. The required answer is 9.

Method 2

$$3^6 = 3^2 \times 3^4 = 9 \times 81 = 729$$

The units digit of $(5273)^6$ is 9.

**3)** Suppose each team played just one game with each of the remaining teams. Then each of the nine teams plays eight games. This makes a total of $9 \times 8$ or 72 games. However each game has been counted twice in this total. For example, the game between Team A and Team B appears in A's 8 games and also B's 8 games. Therefore there are $9 \times 8/2 = 36$ different games played. Since each game is played three times, the total number of games played is $3 \times 36 = 108$.

**4)** If June 1 is a Sunday, so are June 8, 15, 22, and 29. But that gives five Sundays in the month. Therefore June 1 and June 29 cannot be Sundays, and June 30 cannot be a Monday. Similarly, if June 2 is a Sunday, so are June 9, 16, 23, and 30. Again, this gives five Sundays. Therefore June 30 could not have been a Sunday or Monday.

**5)** Method 1

| Number of red faces | Number of one-inch cubes |
|---|---|
| *3 | 8 |
| *2 | 12 |
| 1 | 6 |
| 0 | 1 |
| | Total = 27 |

* Number of cubes with 2 or 3 red faces is $8 + 12 = 20$.

Method 2

The square in the center of each face is the outside face of a one-inch cube having just one red face. There are six such cubes, one for each face. There is one cube in the center of the three-inch cube which has no paint on any face. All the other cubes have paint on two or three faces. Their number is $27 - (6 + 1) = 20$.

## Olympiad 39

1) We build up the conditions using a table.

| Statement | Possible order of digits |
|---|---|
| "3" is next to "8" | 38 or 83 |
| "2" is not next to "3" | 382, 283, 38*2, or 2*83 |
| "5" is not next to "2" | 5382 or 2835 |

Since the number is less than 5000, the answer is 2835.

2) <u>Method 1</u>

Consider the case of six apples. Six apples cost 50¢ and sell for 75¢. Thus a profit of 25¢ is made on a sale of 6 apples. If four such sales are made, a profit of 4×25¢ or $1 will result. So she sold 24 apples.

<u>Method 2</u>

The profit on one apple in cents is $\frac{25}{2} - \frac{25}{3} = \frac{25}{6}$ ¢.

3) <u>Method 1</u>

$$\frac{\text{Total Profit}}{\text{Profit per apple}} = \text{Number of apples}$$

$$100¢ \div \frac{25}{6}¢ = 24$$

Rotate region I about point D (see figure 2) until it falls in place as shown in figure 3.

Area I + Area II = Area square ADEF = 100 sq. cm.

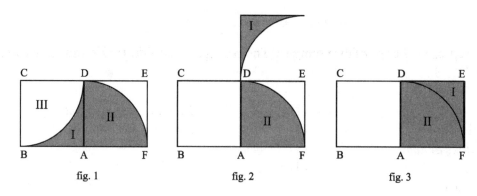

fig. 1                    fig. 2                    fig. 3

*Note:* This "neat" method was found in the notebooks of Leonardo DaVinci.

### (Olympiad 39)

Method 2
Area II = Area III.
Therefore Area I + Area II = Area I + Area III = Area ABCD = 100 sq.cm.

**4)** Method 1

Consider fractions equivalent to $\frac{2}{3}$: $\frac{4}{6}, \frac{6}{9}, \frac{8}{12}, \frac{10}{15}, \cdots$ .

Of these fractions, $\frac{6}{9} = \frac{2+4}{5+4}$. Therefore 4 was the number added to 2 and 5.

Method 2
Algebra: Let N represent the number that is added to the numerator and to the denominator.

| | | | | |
|---|---|---|---|---|
| Given | (1) | $\frac{2+N}{5+N}$ | $=$ | $\frac{2}{3}$ |
| Multiply both sides of (1) by $3(5+N)$ | (2) | $3(2+N)$ | $=$ | $2(5+N)$ |
| Expand both sides of (2) | (3) | $6+3N$ | $=$ | $10+2N$ |
| Subtract 2N from both sides of (3) | (4) | $6+N$ | $=$ | $10$ |
| Subtract 6 from both sides of (4) | (5) | $N$ | $=$ | $4$ |

The number that should be added to the numerator and denominator is 4.

**5)** Method 1

Make a table of ages for the three children beginning with the youngest and then the oldest. The third line of the table satisfies the condition that the sum of the three ages is 32. Therefore, the age of the youngest child is 7.

| Youngest | Oldest | Middle | Sum of the ages |
|----------|--------|--------|-----------------|
| 5 | 10 | 7 | 22 |
| 6 | 12 | 9 | 27 |
| 7 | 14 | 11 | 32 |

Method 2
Algebra: Let Y represent the age of the youngest. Then the age of the oldest is 2Y and the age of the middle child is $2Y-3$.

| | | | | |
|---|---|---|---|---|
| Given | (1) | $Y+2Y+(2Y-3)$ | $=$ | $32$ |
| Simplify the left side of (1) | (2) | $5Y-3$ | $=$ | $32$ |
| Add 3 to both sides of (2) | (3) | $5Y$ | $=$ | $35$ |
| Divide both sides of (3) by 5 | (4) | $Y$ | $=$ | $7$ |

The youngest child is 7.

## Olympiad 40

1) There are 13 hours between 9 AM and 10 PM. Thus the slow clock will lose 13 × 3 or 39 minutes and show 9:21 or 21:21 on a 24-hour clock.

2) The sum of the 4 entries on the major diagonal is 34. Then the missing entry at the bottom of the third column should be 2. Calculating B produces B = 13. Similarly, A+4+16+13 = 34 or A + 33 = 34. Therefore A = 1 and B = 13.

3) Suppose XY represents the original two-digit number. Then Y must be 1 in the units column and also in the tens column. So X must be 4. Therefore the original number XY is 41.

$$
\begin{array}{ccc}
X & Y & 3 \\
- & X & Y \\
\hline
3 & 7 & 2
\end{array}
$$

4) Method 1

Area trapezoid AEFC = Area triangle ABC – Area triangle EBF

$$\text{Area } \triangle ABC = \frac{1}{2} \times 4 \times 4 = 8$$

$$\text{Area } \triangle EBF = \frac{1}{2} \times 2 \times 2 = 2$$

$$\text{Area } AEFC = 8 - 2 = 6$$

Method 2

Let G be the midpoint of AC. Draw EG and GF. Then △ABC is divided into four small congruent triangles. Since the area of △ABC = 8, the area of each small triangle is 2. Trapezoid AEFC has area 3×2 or 6, or 6 sq. meters.

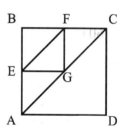

5) When Peter worked 3 fewer weeks than the agreed period of 8 weeks, he received $60 less than the original amount. Therefore each week's work yielded $20. At this rate, he was entitled to $160 for 8 weeks. Since he was to receive $85 and a bicycle, the bicycle was worth 160 – 85 = $75.

## Olympiad 41

1) The time 2 o'clock is repeated every twelve hours. There are 83 twelves in 1000 plus a remainder of 4. Therefore the clock will show a time of 6 o'clock 1000 hours from now.

2) The sum of the five numbers is 5×6 = 30. After the number is removed, the sum of the remaining numbers is 4×7 = 28. The number removed is 30 – 28 = 2.

**(Olympiad 41)**

**3)**

| Order of terms | 1 | 2 | 3 | . . . | ? |
|---|---|---|---|---|---|
| Terms of sequence | 3 | 10 | 17 | . . . | 528 |
| Multiples of 7 | 7 | 14 | 21 | . . . | (532) |

Compare each term of the sequence with its corresponding multiple of 7. Notice that each multiple of 7 is 4 more than the corresponding term of the sequence. The multiple of 7 that corresponds to 528 is $528 + 4 = 532$. Since $532 = 7 \times 76$, 528 is the 76th term of the sequence.

**4)** Since $10,000 = 100 \times 100$, each of the perfect squares $1 \times 1, 2 \times 2, 3 \times 3, \ldots, 99 \times 99$ is less than $100 \times 100$. There are 99 numbers in the above sequence.

**5)** Method 1
Suppose just 2 people were seated at each of the 30 tables. Then a total of 60 people would be seated. Since the seating capacity is 81, there would be 21 vacant seats. Each of the tables for 5 people has 3 vacant seats. There must be 7 tables that seat 5 people. Thus there must be 23 tables that seat 2 people.

Method 2
Make a table and look for a pattern.
In the right column, observe that the number of 3s added to 60 is the same as the number of tables for 5. Since $81 = 60 + 7 \times 3$, there must be 7 tables for 5 people and 23 tables for 2 people.

| Number of Tables for 2 | Number of Tables for 5 | Total Number of People Seated |
|---|---|---|
| 30 | 0 | 60 |
| 29 | 1 | $63 = 60 + 1 \times 3$ |
| 28 | 2 | $66 = 60 + 2 \times 3$ |
| . . . | . . . | . . . . . . . . . |
| 23 | 7 | $81 = 60 + 7 \times 3$ |

Method 3
Algebra: Let T represent the number of tables for 2 and F the number of tables for 5.

| | | | | | |
|---|---|---|---|---|---|
| Given | (1) | T | + F | = | 30 |
| Given | (2) | 2T | + 5F | = | 81 |
| Multiply both sides of (1) by 5 | (3) | 5T | + 5F | = | 150 |
| Subtract (2) from (3) | (4) | | 3T | = | 69 |
| Divide both sides of (4) by 3 | (5) | | T | = | 23 |

There are 23 tables for two.

## Olympiad 42

**1)** Since $\$8.00 \div 6 = \$1.33+$, the most a book could cost is $\$1.33$.
Since $\$8.00 \div 7 = \$1.14+$, the least a book could cost is $\$1.15$.
Notice that the first condition is not needed for the answer. The least a book could cost is $\$1.15$.

**2)**

The sum of all digits is 127.

|  | Numbers | Digit-sum |
|---|---|---|
| 1- 9: | 1, 2  3,  4, . . . , 9 | 45 |
| 10-19: | 10, 11, 12, 13, . . . , 19 | 45 (sum of units digits)<br>10 (sum of tens digits} |
| 20-25: | 20, 21, 22, 23, 24, 25 | 15 (sum of units digits)<br>12 (sum of tens digits) |

**3)** <u>Method 1</u>
The average amount earned was $\$65/5 = \$13$ which is the amount earned for the third (or middle) day. (Note: the third number of any five consecutive (also even or odd) numbers is the average of the five numbers). Therefore she earned $\$9$ the first day.

<u>Method 2</u>
Let F represent how much she earned the first day:

| Day | 1 | 2 | 3 | 4 | 5 |
|---|---|---|---|---|---|
| Earnings | F | F+2 | F+4 | F+6 | F+8 |

Alice's total earnings was $5F+20$ or five times what she earned the first day plus $\$20$. If we subtract $\$20$ from the total earned, the remainder $\$45$ represents five times what she earned the first day. Then she earned $\$45/5 = \$9$ the first day.

**4)** There are 13 small squares in the figure, each with an area of 52/13 or 4 square units. Then each side of a small square has length of 2 units. Since there are 20 sides in the perimeter, the perimeter is $20\times2$ units or 40 units.

**5)** Four people working 15 days is equivalent to one person working 60 days. To complete the other half of the job, ten people would have to work 6 days which is also equivalent to one person working 60 days.

## Olympiad 43

**1)** Each register had $\$150$ after the transfer. So, before the transfer, one register had $150+15$, while the other had $150-15$. The larger amount was $\$165$.

## Solutions

**(Olympiad 43)**

**2)** Method 1

List pairs of factors of 128 and their quotients.
The factors 32 and 4 have a quotient of 8.

| Factors | 128 1 | 64 2 | 32 4 | 16 8 |
|---|---|---|---|---|
| Quotient | 128 | 32 | 8 | 2 |

Method 2

One number is 8 times the other. Call the numbers B and 8B.
Then 8B×B = 128. So B×B = 16, or B = 4. The other number, 8B, is 8×4 or 32.

**3)** There are many ways to partition the region. Here are two.

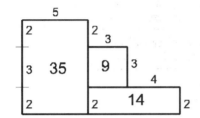  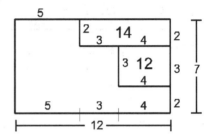

By addition:                By subtraction:
Area = 35 + 9 + 14 = 58     Area = 7 × 12 – 14 – 12 = 58

**4)** The value of H must be 1. In order to get the carry from the tens column to the
hundreds column, A must be 9. Then E = 0. So HEE is 100.

$$\begin{array}{ccc} & A & H \\ + & & A \\ \hline H & E & E \end{array}$$

**5)** Method 1

To gain 30¢ in the exchange, the number of nickels (N) must be 6 more
than the number of dimes (D) before the exchange is made. Since N is
greater than D and N + D = 20, make a table for N and D beginning
with N = 11 and D = 9. We seek a pair of values for which N – D = 6.
This occurs when N = 13 and D = 7. From the table, we see that
Barbara had 7 dimes to begin with.

| N | 11 | 12 | 13 |
|---|---|---|---|
| D | 9 | 8 | 7 |
| N – D | 2 | 4 | 6* |

Method 2
Algebra:

| Given | (1) | N + D | = 20 |
|---|---|---|---|
| Given | (2) | N – D | = 6 |
| Subtract (2) from (1) | (3) | 2D | = 14 |
| Divide both sides of (3) by 2 | (4) | D | = 7 |

Barbara had 7 dimes to begin with.

## Olympiad 44

1)  List multiples of 7 greater than 24 and less than 72. Also list that multiple of 6 which is less than and closest to each of the corresponding multiples of 7.

| Multiples of 7: | 28 | 35 | 42 | 49 | 56 | 63 | 70 |
|---|---|---|---|---|---|---|---|
| Multiples of 6: | 24 | 30 | 36 | 48 | 54 | 60 | 66 |

Notice that 56 is the desired multiple of 7 which is 2 more than a multiple of 6. The required answer is 56 inches.

2)  Method 1
BBB is divisible by 111 which equals 3×37. Then AB is either 37 or a multiple of 37 which, in this case, can only be 74. Test 37×6. It fails the given conditions. However 74×6 = 444 does satisfy the given conditions. So the answer is 74.

Method 2
AB × 6 is an even number. Therefore B = 2, 4, 6, 8. Test each of these values for B in the given problem. Only 4 works, producing the answer 74 for AB.

3)  Method 1  Work backward.

|  | **had** | **spent 1/3** | **left 2/3** |
|---|---|---|---|
| **store 1:** | 27 ⟵ | 9 ⟵ | 18 |
| **store 2:** | 18 ⟵ | 6 ⟵ | 12 ⟵ **Start Here** |

Method 2
Tom spent 1/3 of his money in store 1 and had 2/3 left. In store 2 he spent 1/3 of 2/3 of his original amount. In both stores he spent 1/3+1/3×2/3, or 3/9+2/9 = 5/9 of his money. Clearly he had 4/9 of his money left which was equal to $12. Then 1/9 of his money was $3. He originally had 9×3 or $27.

4)  In the front view, all shaded cubes have 3 red faces. However there is one cube with 3 red faces that is not visible. See bottom view for this cube. There are eleven cubes which each have red paint on just three faces.

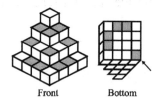

Front          Bottom

5)  Since the number is divisible by 8 (which equals 2×2×2 or $2^3$), the number 43B formed by the last three digits of the given number is divisible by 8. Digit B must be 2. (See Appendix 4, section 3.)

Since A95432 is divisible by 11, the difference between the sum of its odd-place digits and the sum of its even-place digits is 0 or a multiple of 11. In this case, the difference is 0. Then (A+5+3) − (9+4+2) = 0 is equivalent to A + 8 = 15 or A = 7. (See Appendix 4, section 5.)

## Olympiad 45

1) Since OC = 8, OCTA = 8x8 = 64, and OCTIL = 8×64 = 512, then OCTILLA = 8×512 = 4096.

2) Since the sum of the three numbers in each diagonal is the same, and since they have the same middle number, the sum of each pair of numbers in opposite corners must be the same: 9 + 13 = 5 + ?. Clearly ? = 17. The bottom row now has a sum of 33. The middle number must be 11.

| 5 | | 13 |
|---|---|----|
| | | |
| 9 | 7 | ? |

3) Method 1

Since the number of FGs (Field Goals) is 6 more than the number of FSs (Foul Shots), subtract 12 points for 6 FGs from the total points producing 72 − 12 = 60. Then 60 points represent the total points for equal numbers of FGs and FSs. One FG and one FS have a total point value of 3. Twenty FGs and twenty FSs have a total point value of 60. Therefore, there must be twenty FSs and twenty-six FGs.

Method 2

Make a table and look for a pattern. Notice that the number of 3s added to 12 in the Total Points column is the same as the number in the FS column. Since 72 = 12 + 20×3, then FS = 20. However FG is 6 more than FS. So FG is 26.

| FG | FS | Total Points |
|----|----|--------------|
| 6 | 0 | 12 |
| 7 | 1 | 15 = 12 + **1**×3 |
| 8 | 2 | 18 = 12 + **2**×3 |
| ... | ... | ... ... |
| 26 | **20** | 72 = 12 + **20**×3 |

4) Each of the four congruent rectangles has a perimeter equivalent to 2½ sides of the square. Since the length of 2½ sides = 25 units, then, by doubling, we get the length of 5 sides = 50 units. Clearly, the length of one side is 10 units. Therefore the perimeter of the square is 40 units.

5) Notice that each term of the second series is 4 times as large as the corresponding term of the first series.

$$1 + 4 + 9 + \cdots + 625$$
$$4 + 16 + 36 + \cdots + 2500$$

Then $4 + 16 + 36 + \cdots + 2500 = 4 \times (1 + 4 + 9 + \cdots + 625) = 4 \times 5525 = 22,100$.

## Olympiad 46

1) The largest amount that can be made is 49¢. Using the given set of coins, any amount from 1¢ to 49¢ can be made. Therefore there are 49 different amounts that can be made.

2) Method 1
Suppose the 30 people consisted solely of children. Then they would have paid 30×$2 or $60 for their tickets. Since $87 was paid for the 30 tickets, the difference of $27 was paid by adults. Each adult paid $3 more than a child. There must have been 27/3 = 9 adults.

Method 2
Make a table. Let C represent the number of children and A the number of adults. In the Cost column, observe that the number of 3s added to 60 is the same number that appears in the A column. Since 87 = 60 + 9×3, there must be 9 adults in the group.

| C | A | Cost of Tickets |
|---|---|---|
| 30 | 0 | 60 |
| 29 | 1 | 63 = 60 + **1**×3 |
| 28 | 2 | 66 = 60 + **2**×3 |
| 27 | 3 | 69 = 60 + **3**×3 |
| .... | .... | .... |
| 21 | **9** | 87 = 60 + **9**×3 |

Method 3
Algebra: Let C represent the number of children and A the number of adults.

| | | | | | | |
|---|---|---|---|---|---|---|
| Given | (1) | C | + | A | = | 30 |
| Given | (2) | 2C | + | 5A | = | 87 |
| Multiply both sides of (1) by 2 | (3) | 2C | + | 2A | = | 60 |
| Subtract (3) from (2) | (4) | | | 3A | = | 27 |
| Divide both sides of (4) by 3 | (5) | | | A | = | 9 |

There are 9 adults in the group.

3) Method 1
Determine the number of cubes in each layer from the top layer down.

| Layer | Number of Cubes |
|---|---|
| 1 | 1×2 = 2 |
| 2 | 2×3 = 6 |
| 3 | 3×4 = 12 |
| 4 | 4×5 = 20 |
| Total = 70 | |

Method 2
Add the number of visible cubes in each layer to the number of cubes in the preceding layer.

| Layer | Number of Cubes | |
|---|---|---|
| 1 | 2 | = 2 |
| 2 | 2+4 | = 6 |
| 3 | 2+4+6 | = 12 |
| 4 | 2+4+6+8 | = 20 |
| 5 | 2+4+6+8+10 | = 30 |
| | Total | = 70 |

## (Olympiad 46)

3) Method 3
   Each of the visible cubes is the top of a vertical column of cubes. For example, each of the top two cubes is the top of a column of five cubes, and each of the four visible cubes in the next layer is the top of a column of four cubes. The table at the right shows the number of cubes in columns of different sizes.

| Number of Cubes in Column | Number of Columns | Total Number of Cubes |
|---|---|---|
| 5 | 2 | 10 |
| 4 | 4 | 16 |
| 3 | 6 | 18 |
| 2 | 8 | 16 |
| 1 | 10 | 10 |
| | Total = | 70 |

4) If the average of five numbers is 16, then the sum of these numbers is 80. When the sixth number, 10, is added to the other five numbers, the sum of these six numbers is 90. Therefore the average of the six numbers is 90/6 = 15.

5) (1) AB must be less than 15 because AB×7 is the first partial product (fpp) which is a two-digit number.
   (2) The greatest value that C could have is 9. Since AB×C is the second partial product (spp) which is a three-digit number, AB must be greater than 11.
   (3) Clearly AB is between 11 and 15. Candidates for AB are 12, 13 and 14.
   (4) If AB = 14 and C = 9, then the tens digit of the spp will be 2.
   (5) The other possibilities, AB = 12 or 13 and C = 8 or 9, do not yield a tens digit of 2 in the spp. Therefore A = 1, B = 4, and C = 9.

$$\begin{array}{r} 7C \\ AB{\overline{\smash{\big)}\,\_\_\_\_}} \\ \underline{\_\_} \quad \text{(fpp)} \\ \_\_\_ \\ \underline{\_2\_} \quad \text{(spp)} \\ 0 \end{array}$$

## Olympiad 47

1) The cost of 12 cans at the old rate was 4×$2 or $8. The cost of 12 cans at the new rate was 3×$2.50 or $7.50. The new price for 12 cans is $.50 less than the old price for 12 cans.

2) Method 1
   condition a: 40 < N < 80
   condition b: N could be 42, 47, 52, 57, 62, 67, 72, 77
   condition c: N could be 46, 53, 60, 67, 74
   The number that satisfies all three conditions is 67.

   Method 2
   The number N must end in 2 or 7. Begin with 6×7+4 = 46 and count by 7s to the first number ending in 2 or 7. This yields 46, 53, 60, 67. The required number is 67.

3) Method 1
   The average of the five consecutive numbers is 100/5 or 20 which also happens to be the middle number. The smallest of the five consecutive numbers is 18.

**(Olympiad 47)**

3) <u>Method 2</u>
Algebra: Let the five numbers be N, N+1, N+2, N+3, and N+4. Their sum is 5N+10.

| | | | | | |
|---|---|---|---|---|---|
| Given | (1) | 5N | + | 10 = | 100 |
| Subtract 10 from both sides of (1) | (2) | | 5N | = | 90 |
| Divide both sides of (2) by 5 | (3) | | N | = | 18 |

The smallest number is 18.

4) For each 4 steps the cat takes, the dog takes 3. Therefore when the cat takes 3×4 = 12 steps, the dog takes 3×3 = 9 steps which covers a distance of 9 feet. Therefore the cat covers 9 feet.

5)   (1)   S must be 3 or 8.

(2)   Since there must be a carry of 1 from the 100s column, H = 9 and E = 0. Then I = 5.

```
  T  H  I  S
+       I  S
-----------
  K  E  E  6
```

(3)   If S = 8, the carry of 1 to the tens column would make E an odd number. But this is impossible because E = 0. Therefore, S = 3.
Place the known numbers in the example.

(4)   T cannot be 1, 3, 5, 6, 9.
If T = 2, K = 3. But S = 3.
If T = 4, K = 5. But I = 5.
If T = 7, K = 8. This does not violate any of the given conditions.

```
  T  9  5  3
+       5  3
-----------
  K  0  0  6
```

(5)   The required number is 7953.

## Olympiad 48

1) Remember that a number may be repeated in a triple. List the triples so that the numbers in each triple are arranged according to size to prevent duplication.
     (1,1,8), (1,2,7), (1,3,6), (1,4,5), (2,2,6), (2,3,5,), (2,4,4), (3,3,4).
There are eight triples which each have a sum of 10.

2) <u>Method 1</u>
If we add $12 to what Rhoda has, she will have as much as Patricia. If we add $15 to what Sarah has, she will also have as much as Patricia. Since all three together have $87, then $87 + $12 + $15 or $114 represents three times what Patricia has. Thus Patricia has $114/3 or $38.

## Solutions

**(Olympiad 48)**

**2)** <u>Method 2</u>
Algebra: Let P, R, S represent the dollar amounts Patricia, Rhoda, and Sarah each has, respectively.

| Given | (1) | | P | = | R + 12 |
|---|---|---|---|---|---|
| Given | (2) | | P | = | S + 15 |
| Given | (3) | P + R + S | | = | 87 |
| Add 12 and 15 to both sides of (3) | (4) | P + (R+12) + (S+15) | | = | 87 + 12 + 15 |
| Substitute from (1) and (2) into (4) | (5) | P + P + P | | = | 114 |
| Simplify (5) | (6) | 3P | | = | 114 |
| Divide both sides of (6) by 3 | (7) | | P | = | 38 |

Patricia has $38.

**3)** <u>Method 1</u>
Let S be the sum of the numbers from 1 to 12.

| Given | (1) | S | = | $1 + 2 + 3 + \cdots + 10 + 11 + 12$ |
|---|---|---|---|---|
| Reverse the order of (1) | (2) | S | = | $12 + 11 + 10 + \cdots + 3 + 2 + 1$ |
| Add (1) and (2) | (3) | 2S | = | $13 + 13 + 13 + \cdots + 13 + 13 + 13$ |
| Simplify (3) | (4) | 2S | = | $12 \times 13$ |
| Divide both sides of (4) by 2 | (5) | S | = | $6 \times 13$ or 78 |

<u>Method 2</u>
Extend the given staircase until it is 12 units tall. Notice that it contains 3 of the original staircases 4 units tall and also 3 4×4 squares. Then the total number of unit squares contained is $3 \times 10 + 3 \times 16 = 78$.

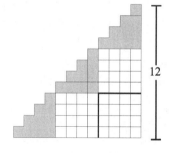

**4)** <u>Method 1</u>

| numbers: | | | 8 | | 17 | | | | | ? |
|---|---|---|---|---|---|---|---|---|---|---|
| order: | 1 | 2 | 3 | 4 | 5 | 6 | 7 | 8 | 9 | 10 |

It takes 3 uniform increases to get from 8 to 17. Since the difference of 8 and 17 is 9, each increase must be 3. It takes 5 increases of 3 to get from 17 to the 10th number. Thus the 10th number is 17 + 15 or 32.

<u>Method 2</u>
Let the difference between successive numbers be D. Then the numbers that follow 8 are 8+D, 8+2D, and 8+3D. But 8+3D = 17; 3D = 9 and D = 3. Since the 10th number is 15 more than the 5th number, the 10th number is 17 + 15 = 32.

**(Olympiad 48)**

**5)** List some of the possible share values and the corresponding number of members (M) for each share value. Examine the table for a place where the value of a share increases by $1 as M decreases by 1. That occurs

| Share ($) | $1 | $2 | $3 | $4 | $5 | $6 | $8 | $10 | $12 | $15 | $16 |
|---|---|---|---|---|---|---|---|---|---|---|---|
| M | 240 | 120 | 80 | 60 | 48 | 40 | 30 | 24 | 20 | 16 | 15 |

when the value of the original share is $15 for 16 members. Notice that the value of a share becomes $16 when there is 1 less member, or when there are 15 members. Therefore 15 members got a share of the $240.

**Olympiad 49**

**1)** If the number is divisible by both 7 and 8, it is also divisible by 56.
Divide 56 into 999, the largest three-digit number as shown at the right
Then $999 - 47 = 952$ (or $56 \times 17 = 952$) is the required number.

$$
\begin{array}{r}
17 \\
56\overline{)999} \\
56 \\
\hline
439 \\
392 \\
\hline
47
\end{array}
$$

**2)** Method 1
The semiperimeter of the rectangle is 12 meters. Use a table to show some possible dimensions in meters and the corresponding areas in square meters. According to the dimensions shown the largest area is 36. See Method 2 for a demonstration that 36 is the largest area that a rectangle with semiperimeter 12 meters can have.

| dimension 1: | 1 | 2 | 3 | 4 | 5 | 6 |
|---|---|---|---|---|---|---|
| dimension 2: | 11 | 10 | 9 | 8 | 7 | 6 |
| area: | 11 | 20 | 27 | 32 | 35 | 36 |

Method 2
If one dimension of the rectangle is more than 6, say
$6 + x$, the other dimension must be $6 - x$. Otherwise the
semiperimeter will not be 12. Compare the 6 by 6 square
in fig. 1 with the $(6+x)$ by $(6-x)$ in fig. 2.
In fig. 3, the shaded area of fig. 2 is moved to a new
position. Now compare fig. 3 with fig. 1. Notice that the
difference in areas is equal to the area of the small missing
square in the upper right corner of fig. 3.
The area of the small missing square in fig. 3 in the upper right corner is $x^2$.
Therefore the area of fig. 2 is $36 - x^2$ which is always smaller than 36, the area of the square.
Rule: For a given perimeter, the rectangle of largest area is always a square.

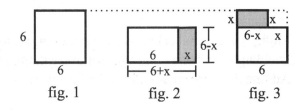

fig. 1          fig. 2          fig. 3

**3)** Method 1
1/3 of the number is the same as decreasing the number by 2/3 of itself. Then 2/3 of the number must be 8. It follows that 1/3 of the number must be 4. Then the number must be 12.

## (Olympiad 49)

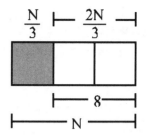

**3)** Method 2

The diagram at the right shows that N/3 is obtained by subtracting 2/3 of N or 8 from N itself. If 8 is the value of 2 of the three boxes, then each box has value 4. N must be 12.

**4)**

|  |  |
|---|---|
| Total Charge: | $3.45 |
| Charge for first five pounds: | $1.65 |
| Charge for remaining pounds: | $1.80 |

Since the charge for each of the remaining pounds is 12¢ per pound, the number of remaining pounds is $180/12 = 15$. The total number of pounds in the package is $15 + 5$ or 20.

**5)** Method 1

Change each fraction to a decimal equivalent.

$$\frac{1}{2} = 2\overline{)1.0}^{\;.5} \;\; ; \;\; \frac{1}{2} = 2\overline{)\;.10}^{\;.05} \;\; ; \;\; \frac{1}{.2} = .2\overline{)1.0}^{\;5} \;\; ; \;\; A.BC = 5.55$$

Method 2

Find equivalent fractions which do not have a decimal point.

$$\frac{1}{2}, \;\; \frac{.1}{2} = \frac{.1\times10}{2\times10} = \frac{1}{20}, \;\; \frac{1}{.2} = \frac{1\times10}{.2\times10} = \frac{10}{2}$$

$$\frac{1}{2} + \frac{1}{20} + \frac{10}{2} = \frac{10}{20} + \frac{1}{20} + \frac{100}{20} = \frac{111}{20} = 5.55$$

Method 3

Multiplying a number by .1 results in moving the number's decimal point one place to the left. Dividing a number by .1 results in moving the number's decimal point one place to the right. Adding the three values, $.5 + .05 + 5$, yields 5.55.

$$\text{Begin with } \frac{1}{2} = .5; \;\; \frac{.1}{2} = .1\times\frac{1}{2} = .1\times.5 = .05; \;\; \frac{1}{.2} = \frac{1}{.1\times2} = \frac{1/2}{.1} = \frac{.5}{.1} = 5$$

## Olympiad 50

**1)** Only the following symbols have the same meaning in the USA and England: 1/1, 2/2, 3/3, ... , 12/12. This set of symbols corresponds to 12 different days of the year.

**(Olympiad 50)**

**2)** Let 6A and 6B represent the numbers. The product (6A)(6B) is equal to 36AB. Since 36AB = 504, AB = 504/36 = 14. If A = 1, then 6A = 6 which violates the condition that neither of the numbers is 6. So A = 2 and B = 7, or A = 7 and B = 2. In either case, the larger number is 6×7 or 42.

**3)** <u>Method 1</u>
Find the dimensions of the large rectangle containing the walk and garden.

(1) Area of the large rectangle is 20×27 or 540 sq ft.

(2) Area of the garden is 14×21 or 294 sq ft.

(3) Area of the walk is 540 – 294 or 246 sq ft.

<u>Method 2</u>
Let A, B, C represent the areas as shown in the diagram.

(1) The area of the walk = 4A + 2B + 2C.

(2) A = 3×3 sq ft, B = 14×3 sq ft, C = 21×3 sq ft.

(3) Then the area of the walk = (4×9 + 2×42 + 2×63) or 246 sq ft.

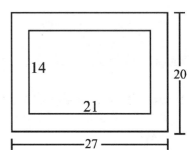

**4)** <u>Method 1</u>
Divide the difference between 1/2 and 1/3 by 3 since it takes three increases to go from 1/3 to 1/2. The result is 1/18.

$$\frac{\frac{1}{2}-\frac{1}{3}}{3}=\frac{1}{18}$$

The two missing numbers are

$$\frac{1}{3}+\frac{1}{18} \text{ and } \frac{1}{3}+\frac{2}{18}, \text{ or } \frac{7}{18} \text{ and } \frac{8}{18}.$$

**4)** <u>Method 2</u>
Given

(1) $\frac{1}{3}$ , ? , ? , $\frac{1}{2}$

Change (1) to equivalent fractions with the same denominator

(2) $\frac{2}{6}$ , ? , ? , $\frac{3}{6}$

Since we need three increases to go from the first to the fourth term and the numerators of (2) differ by only 1, multiply each fraction by 3/3

(3) $\frac{6}{18}$ , ? , ? , $\frac{9}{18}$

The missing terms are given in (4): $\frac{7}{18}, \frac{8}{18}$

(4) $\frac{6}{18}, \frac{7}{18}, \frac{8}{18}, \frac{9}{18}$

## (Olympiad 50)

**5)** Denote the three given weighings in the given order as W1, W2, and W3.

| | | |
|---|---|---|
| W1 is given | (1) | $\bigcirc = \triangle\ \square\ \square$ |
| Add $\square$ to both sides of (1) | (2) | $\bigcirc\ \square = \triangle\ \square\ \square\ \square$ |
| W2 is given | (3) | $\bigcirc\ \square = \triangle\ \trapezoid$ |
| Then the right sides of (2) and (3) are equal | (4) | $\triangle\ \square\ \square\ \square = \triangle\ \trapezoid$ |
| Remove $\triangle$ from both sides of (4) | (5) | $\square\ \square\ \square = \trapezoid$ |
| W3 is given | (6) | $\triangle = \trapezoid\ \square$ |
| Substitute from (5) into (6) | (7) | $\triangle = \square\ \square\ \square\ \square$ |
| Substitute from (7) into (1) | (8) | $\bigcirc = \square\ \square\ \square\ \square\ \square\ \square$ |

Thus, the required number is 6.

## Olympiad 51

**1)** Method 1

Count the number of Xs in each row: $3+5+7+9+6+10+14+17=71$

Method 2

Suppose the missing Xs in the "triangular" region were filled in. Then there is a total of::
$3+5+7+9+11+13+15+17=80$ Xs. (Notice that the average of the 8 addends is 10, that the addends can be paired 3 and 17, 5 and 15, 7 and 13, 9 and 11, and that the sum of each pair is 20.) Since the triangular region was filled with $5+3+1=9$ Xs, then there are $80-9=71$ Xs in the diagram.

**2)** Find the least common multiple (LCM) of the numbers. Factor each of the numbers into primes:
$2$, $3$, $2^2$, $5$, $2 \times 3$, $7$, $2^3$. The LCM of these numbers is $2^3 \times 3 \times 5 \times 7 = 840$.

**3)** The two squares are between $30 \times 30 = 900$ and $40 \times 40 = 1600$. Since 1000 is closer to 900, try $31 \times 31 = 961$ and $32 \times 32 = 1024$. Notice that $31 \times 31$ and $32 \times 32$ are consecutive perfect squares and that 1000 is between them. Clearly, 1000 is closer to 1024 than it is to 961, so the answer is 1024 or $32 \times 32$ or $32^2$.

**4)** Method 1

Work backward. The $4 that remained when I left store B was 2/3 of what I had when I entered store B. Since 2/3 of what I had was $4, then 1/3 of what I had was $2, and 3/3 of what I had was $6. This $6 is 1/3 of what I had when I entered store A, so I had $18 when I entered store A.

Method 2

I had 1/3 of my money when I left store A. I spent 1/3 of that, or 1/3 of 1/3 = 1/9 of my money, in store B. I spent 2/3 in store A and 1/9 in store B, or a total of 2/3 + 1/9 = 6/9 + 1/9 = 7/9 of my money. I had 2/9 of my money, or $4, left over. Then 1/9 of my money was $2 and 9/9, or all of my money, was 9×$2, or $18. I had $18 when I entered store A.

Method 3

Let 9M represent the amount of money I had when I entered store A. The following table shows the transactions that occurred. (If the original amount upon entering store A is M, each of the remaining representations in the table will be in fractional form. It is simpler to begin with 9M as the amount.)

| Amount in A | Amount Spent | Amount Left | Amount in B | Amount Spent | Amount Left |
|---|---|---|---|---|---|
| 9M | 6M | 3M | 3M | 1M | 2M |

Since 2M = 4, M = 2 and 9M = 18. Then I had $18 when I entered store A.

## (Olympiad 51)

**5)** Method 1

Let AB represent the original two-digit number. Then AB6 is the three-digit number which results when 6 is placed at the right end of AB. It is given that AB6 is 294 more than AB. In the units column, it is clear that B = 2. It then follows that A = 3.

$$
\begin{array}{rcc}
 & \text{A} & \text{B} \\
+\ 2 & 9 & 4 \\
\hline
\text{A} & \text{B} & 6 \\
\end{array}
$$

Method 2

The information can also be expressed by saying that the difference between AB6 and AB is 294. This leads to the same solution: A = 3, B = 2.

$$
\begin{array}{ccc}
\text{A} & \text{B} & 6 \\
- & \text{A} & \text{B} \\
\hline
2 & 9 & 4 \\
\end{array}
$$

## Olympiad 52

**1)** Method 1

Since the sum of the number and 24 is equal to three times the number, 24 must be equal to twice the number. The number must be 12.

Method 2

Represent the given information in a diagram. Clearly, 2N is 24. Then N = 12.

| N | 24 | |
|---|---|---|
| N | N | N |

Method 3

Algebra: Let N represent the number.

| | | |
|---|---|---|
| Given: | (1) | $N + 24 = 3N$ |
| Subtract N from both sides of (1): | (2) | $24 = 2N$ |
| Divide both sides of (2) by 2: | (3) | $12 = N$ |

The required number is 12.

**2)** If each of the numbers shown is divided by 7, the numbers which have a remainder of 1 appear in column A, those with remainder 2 appear in column C, those with remainder 3 in column E, and so forth. Divide 300 by 7. The quotient is 42 and the remainder is 6, so 300 will appear in column D.

**3)** Method 1

A quarter and a nickel differ in value by 20¢, 2 quarters and 2 nickels differ in value by 2×20¢ or 40¢, 3 quarters and 3 nickels differ in value by 3×20¢ or 60¢, and so forth. Since the total difference 180¢ equals 9×20¢, there must be 9 quarters and 9 nickels. Their total value is 9×30¢ or $2.70.

# Solutions

## (Olympiad 52)

**3)** <u>Method 2</u>
Make a table of equal numbers of quarters and nickels and the difference in values. Let Q and N denote the number of quarters and nickels respectively, and D the difference in values. In the table we observe that the number of quarters or the number of nickels is the same as the number multiplying 20¢ in the D column. Since 180¢ = 9×20¢, there must be 9 quarters and 9 nickels, which have a total value of $2.70.

| Q | N | DIFFERENCE |
|---|---|---|
| 1 | 1 | 20¢ or **1**×20¢ |
| 2 | 2 | 40¢ or **2**×20¢ |
| 3 | 3 | 60¢ or **3**×20¢ |
| ... | ... | ... |
| ? | ? | 180¢ or **9**×20¢ |

**4)** From the units column, B must equal 5. Then there is a carry of 1 in the tens column, so 1+5+A+A must equal 10+A. Therefore 1+5+A must equal 10, so A must be 4.

```
    5  A
    A  5
 +  A  5
 -------
 C  A  A
```

**5)** Count the number of 3s that appear in the units, tens, and hundreds places, separately.

<u>Units Place.</u> In each group of 10 consecutive numbers (1–10, 11–20, 21–30, ... , 291–300), 3 appears in the units place once: 3, 13, 23, 33, 43, ... , 293. There are 30 groups of 10 consecutive numbers in 1 through 300. Therefore, 3 appears 30 times in the units place.

<u>Tens Place.</u> In each group of 100 consecutive numbers (1–100, 101–200, 201–300), 3 appears in the tens place 10 times for a total of 30 times in the entire group:

$$30, \ 31, \ 32, \ 33, ... , \ 39$$
$$130, 131, 132, 133, ... , 139$$
$$230, 231, 232, 233, ... , 239$$

But half of the above 30 numbers are even and half are odd. Therefore, 3 appears in the tens place of the odd numbers 15 times.

<u>Hundreds Place.</u> 301 is the only number to consider. It is odd and 3 appears in the hundreds place just 1 time.

Answer: The digit 3 appears 30+15+1 = 46 times in the set of odd numbers from 1 through 301.

## Olympiad 53

**1)** If I pick 6 disks blindfolded, there could be 3 disks of the same color among them. However, it is possible that I picked 2 disks of each color. Therefore I cannot be absolutely certain there are at least 3 disks of the same color among the 6 disks I picked. If I now pick a 7th disk, it must result in having 3 disks of the same color.

**(Olympiad 53)**

2)  Method 1
    Algebra: Let a, b, and c represent the point values of A, B, and C, respectively. Find a+b+c.

    | | | |
    |---|---|---|
    | Given | (1) | $a + b \phantom{+ c} = 23$ |
    | Given | (2) | $\phantom{a +} b + c = 33$ |
    | Given | (3) | $\underline{a \phantom{+ b} + c = 30}$ |
    | Add (1), (2), and (3) | (4) | $2a + 2b + 2c = 86$ |
    | Divide both sides of (4) by 2 | (5) | $a + b + c = 43$ |

    The sum of the point values is 43.

    Method 2
    Since a+b = 23 and b+c = 33, it follows that c is 10 more than a. Since a+c = 30, a = 10 and c = 20. Then, from either of the first two conditions, b = 13. Then a+b+c = 10+13+20 = 43. The sum of the point values is 43.

3)  Since the four-digit number is divisible by 88, it is also divisible by 8 and by 11. But when a number is divisible by $8 = 2^3$, the number formed by its last three digits, in this case 37V, must be divisible by 8. (See Appendix 4, section 3.) Therefore V must be 6. The number T376 is also divisible by 11. We could try different values for T but it is easier to use the theorem for divisibility by 11: If a number is divisible by 11, the sum of the digits in the odd places (3+6) and the sum of the digits in the even places (T+7) must be equal or differ by a multiple of 11. Then T+7 = 3+6 = 9, or T = 2.
    (See Appendix 4, section 5.)

4)  Make a diagram for each path. It will be easier if you use a rule like "make the path go to the right as far as possible without repeating a previous path."

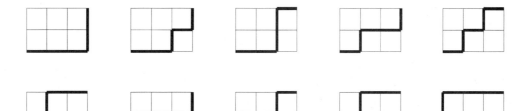

    There are 10 different paths.

---

## (Olympiad 53)

**5)** <u>Method 1</u>

Work backward.

Since there were twice as many liters in the larger container at the start, the condition is satisfied if X = 8 liters. Therefore the containers had 16 liters and 32 liters to begin with. The smaller container had 16 liters to begin with.

<u>Method 2</u>

Let the smaller container have X + 8 liters to begin with.

Since the larger had three times as many liters at the end, 8 must be X. The containers had 16 and 32 liters of water to begin with, so the smaller had 16 liters of water.

## Olympiad 54

**1)** <u>Method 1</u>

If the quotient of the two numbers is 4, the larger must be 4 times the smaller, and the difference of the two numbers must be 3 times the smaller. Since the difference is 39, 3 times the smaller is 39. The smaller number must be 13. (The larger number will then be 52.)

<u>Method 2</u>

Algebra: Let n represent the smaller number and 4n the larger number.

| | |
|---|---|
| Given | (1) $4n - n = 39$ |
| Simplify the left side of (1) | (2) $\quad 3n = 39$ |
| Divide both sides of (2) by 3 | (3) $\quad\quad n = 13$ |

The smaller number is 13.

**2)** This is an "extended unit fraction"; work from the bottom up.

$$\cfrac{1}{3+\cfrac{1}{3+\cfrac{1}{3}}} = \cfrac{1}{3+\cfrac{1}{\frac{10}{3}}} = \cfrac{1}{3+\frac{3}{10}} = \cfrac{1}{\frac{33}{10}} = \frac{10}{33}$$

## Solutions

### (Olympiad 54)

**3)** <u>Method 1</u>

Consider the structure as a collection of vertical columns of cubes. Count the number of columns having the same height and determine the number of cubes contained in those columns. The tallest vertical column contains 6 cubes; the smallest vertical column has just 1 cube. See table at the right. T represents the total number of cubes in the structure.

| Cubes in Column | No. of Columns | Total Cubes |
|---|---|---|
| 6 | 1 | 6 |
| 5 | 1 | 5 |
| 4 | 1 | 4 |
| 3 | 3 | 9 |
| 2 | 5 | 10 |
| 1 | 4 | 4 |
| | | Total = 38 |

<u>Method 2</u>

"Slice" the structure mentally as shown. Count the number of cubes in each slice. See diagram and table at the right.

| Slice | Total Cubes |
|---|---|
| 1 | 16 |
| 2 | 9 |
| 3 | 5 |
| 4 | 7 |
| 5 | 1 |
| | T=38 |

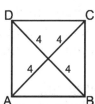

**4)** List the six three-digit numbers each of which contains the digits 4, 5, and 6. Notice that each of the digits 4, 5, and 6 appears twice in each column. Therefore the sum of the digits in each column (without carrys) is 30. The sum is 3330.

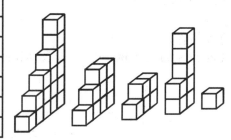

```
  4 5 6
  4 6 5
  5 4 6
  5 6 4
  6 4 5
  6 5 4
 ───────
  3 3 3 0
```

**5)** <u>Method 1</u>

Draw diagonal BD. Four congruent right triangles are created, each with area (1/2)×4×4 = 8. Therefore the area of the square is 4×8 = 32 square units.

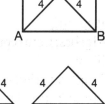

<u>Method 2</u>

Regroup the 4 congruent squares as shown in Method 1 to form 2 squares. Each of the two squares has area 16, for a total of 32.

<u>Method 3</u>

Rearrange the two triangles given in the statement of the problem as shown and add two dotted lines to complete a square. The sum of the areas of the two given triangles is half of the area of the square obtained by adding the dotted lines. The area of that square is 8×8 = 64, so the sum of the areas of the two given triangles is 32.

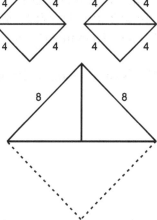

## Olympiad 55

**1)** Find D first, and then find ABC by dividing 1673 by D. Possible values for D are 1, 2, 3, 4, 5, 6, 7, 8, or 9. Clearly D can't be 1; otherwise the product would be the three-digit number ABC. D can't be 2, 4, 6, or 8; otherwise the product would be an even number. D can't be 5; otherwise the product would have to end in 5 or 0. D can't be 3; otherwise, the sum of the digits of the product 1673 would have to be a multiple of 3. Similarly, D can't be a 9; otherwise, the sum of the digits of the product would have to be a multiple of 9. The only digit that remains is 7. Then D = 7 and ABC = 1673/7 = 239.

$$\begin{array}{r} A\ \ B\ \ C \\ \times\ \ \ \ \ D \\ \hline 1\ \ 6\ \ 7\ \ 3 \end{array}$$

**2)** Notice that the rectangle contains 8 separate regions: a, b, c, d, e, f, g, and h. Some of these regions are rectangles. Other rectangles can be formed by combining two or more regions.

| regions which form a rectangle | | number of rectangles |
|---|---|---|
| 1 region: | (a),(b),(c),(d) | 4 |
| 2 regions: | (a,b),(b,c),(c,d),(d,a), (a,f),(b,g),(c,h),(d,e) | 8 |
| 4 regions: | (f,a,b,g),(e,d,c,h),(f,a,d,e), (g,b,c,h),(a,b,c,d) | 5 |
| 8 regions: | (a,b,c,d,e,f,g,h) | 1 |
| | total | 18 |

**3)** The answer to this problem is the number of different pairs that can be formed with the four students. Denote the different students by A, B, C, and D. Then the different pairs are: AB, AC, AD, BC, BD, and CD. Since there are 6 different pairs, then there are 6 days when it can be arranged that the same pair of students do not work together. (Note that AB and BA stand for the same pair; AB and BC are different pairs.)

**4)** The sum of the width and length (together they form the "semiperimeter") is 18. We need to find two primes to represent the width (W) and the length (L) with sum 18. The largest area the rectangle could have is 77 sq. units.

| W | L | Area |
|---|---|---|
| 5 | 13 | 65 |
| 7 | 11 | 77 |

**5)**

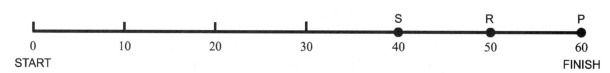

When Paul finished the 60 meter race, Robert was at the 50-meter mark and Sam was at the 40-meter mark. This means that for every 5 meters that Robert runs, Sam runs 4 meters; or, for every 10 meters that Robert runs, Sam runs 8 meters. So when Robert ran 10 meters to complete the race, Sam ran 8 meters to be at the 48-meter mark. Robert beats Sam by 12 meters.

## Olympiad 56

1) The four digits whose product is 70 must be 1, 2, 5, and 7. The largest number that can be formed from these four digits is 7521.

2) Method 1

A mixed number such as $5\frac{1}{3}$ represents the sum $5 + \frac{1}{3}$. Similarly, if $2\frac{1}{2}$ is to be subtracted, it is equivalent

to subtracting 2 and subtracting $\frac{1}{2}$; that is, $-2\frac{1}{2} = -2 - \frac{1}{2}$.

Then $(5\frac{1}{3} - 2\frac{1}{2}) + (5\frac{1}{2} - 3\frac{1}{3}) = 5 + \frac{1}{3} - 2 - \frac{1}{2} + 5 + \frac{1}{2} - 3 - \frac{1}{3} = 5 + 5 - 2 - 3 + \frac{1}{3} - \frac{1}{3} + \frac{1}{2} - \frac{1}{2} = 5$.

Method 2

$$(5\frac{1}{3} - 2\frac{1}{2}) + (5\frac{1}{2} - 3\frac{1}{3}) = (5\frac{1}{3} + 5\frac{1}{2}) - (2\frac{1}{2} + 3\frac{1}{3}) = 10\frac{5}{6} - 5\frac{5}{6} = 5$$

3) Only the 2 by 2 by 2 cubes at the eight vertices (corners) of the 3 by 3 by 3 cube have exactly three red faces. The diagram at the right shows the location of one of the eight cubes.

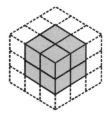

4) Method 1
In one minute, the water faucet fills 1/15 of the tub and the drain empties 1/20 of the tub. Together, the faucet and drain "fill" 1/15 – 1/20 of the tub each minute. This is equivalent to 4/60 – 3/60 or 1/60 of the tub. Therefore, in 60 minutes the faucet and drain working together will fill 60/60 or the entire tub.

Method 2
In 15 minutes, the faucet fills the tub but the drain empties 15/20 or 3/4 of the tub. Therefore, in 15 minutes the faucet and drain working together "fill" 1 – 3/4 or 1/4 of the tub. In 4×15 or 60 minutes, the faucet and drain together will fill 4/4 or the entire tub.

5) When the first partial product (fpp) and the second partial product (spp) are added, T in WHAT equals 6. Replace T by 6 as shown. The 8 in the spp comes from multiplying 6 by U. Then U must be 3 or 8. If U = 3, then WHAT = 36×36 or 1296. If U = 8, then WHAT = 86×86 or 7396. But WHAT is less than 5000. Therefore WHAT = 1296.

```
        U 6
        U 6
      _____
      _ _ 6   (fpp)
      _ _ 8   (spp)
      _____
      W H A 6
```

## Olympiad 57

**1)** The stamp collector spent $30 + $50 or $80, and received $42 + $48 or $90. The stamp collector made $10.

**2)** Method 1
Make the denominator as large as possible. This will occur when M = 25 and N = 1.
Then $\dfrac{M \times N}{M - N} = \dfrac{25 \times 1}{25 - 1} = \dfrac{25}{24}$. Any other substitution for M and N, with M greater than N, will yield a value larger than 25/24. See Method 2 for a complete mathematical proof.

Method 2
A fraction will have its smallest value when its numerator is as small as possible and its denominator is as large as possible. Divide the numerator and denominator of the given fraction by M to obtain an equivalent fraction:
The numerator $1 \times N$ will be as small as possible when N = 1. The denominator will be as large as possible when N/M is as small as possible. This occurs when N = 1 and M = 25.
$$\frac{M \times N}{M - N} = \frac{(M/M) \times N}{(M/M) - (N/M)} = \frac{1 \times N}{1 - (N/M)}$$

**3)** Method 1

Area $\triangle ACE = \dfrac{1}{2}$ (base $\times$ height) $= \dfrac{1}{2}$ (AE $\times$ CD) $= \dfrac{1}{2}$ (4 $\times$ 6) = 12.

Method 2

Area $\triangle ACE$ = Area $\triangle ACD$ – Area $\triangle ECD = \dfrac{1}{2}$ (6 $\times$ 6) $- \dfrac{1}{2}$ (2 $\times$ 6) = 18 – 6 = 12.

**4)** Method 1

Divide 400 by 9: $\dfrac{400}{9} = 44^+$. The largest prime number less than 44 is 43.

Method 2
Since 9×40 is less than 400 and 9×50 is greater than 400, check the prime numbers between 40 and 50. These prime numbers are: 41, 43, and 47. Since 9×41 = 369, 9×43 = 387, and 9×47 = 423, 43 is the largest prime such that its product with 9 is less than 400.

**(Olympiad 57)**

**5)** To find the incorrect charge, subtract $4.88 from $20.

$20.00
$\underline{-4.88}$ incorrect change
$15.12 incorrect charge

The incorrect charge, $15.12, represents C dollars and D cents. Therefore the correct charge is $12.15. To get the correct change, subtract $12.15 from $20.

$20.00
$\underline{-12.15}$ correct charge
$ 7.85  correct change

**Olympiad 58**

**1)** (a) 3 occurs in the units place once in each group of ten consecutive numbers. Therefore 3 will appear 10 times in the units place.
(b) 3 occurs in the tens place ten times in 100 consecutive numbers: 30, 31, 32, 33, ... , 38, 39.
(c) Statements (a) and (b) are also true for occurrences of 8. Therefore there will be a total of 40 occurrences of 3s and 8s in the numbers from 1 through 100.

**2)** Use the distributive principle: $A \times B - A \times C = A \times (B-C)$. Example: $5 \times 7 - 5 \times 3 = 5 \times (7-3) = 5 \times 4 = 20$. Thus we have: $1990 \times 1991 - 1989 \times 1990 = 1990 \times (1991-1989) = 1990 \times 2 = 3980$.

**3)** <u>Method 1</u>
Numerator: $\quad 8! = 8 \times 7 \times 6 \times 5 \times 4 \times 3 \times 2 \times 1 = 8 \times 7 \times 6! = 56 \times 6!$
$\quad\quad\quad\quad\quad\quad 8! - 6! = 56 \times 6! - 6! = 6!(56-1) = 6! \times 55$
Denominator: $\quad 3! = 3 \times 2 \times 1 = 6$
$\quad\quad\quad\quad\quad\quad 3! \times 5! = 6 \times 5! = 6!$

Then: $\quad \dfrac{8! - 6!}{3! \times 5!} = \dfrac{6! \times 55}{6!} = 55$

<u>Method 2</u>
We have: $5! = 5 \times 4 \times 3 \times 2 \times 1 = 120$; $\quad 6! = 6 \times 5! = 6 \times 120 = 720$; $\quad 8! = 8 \times 7 \times 6! = 56 \times 720$

Then: $\quad \dfrac{8! - 6!}{3! \times 5!} = \dfrac{(56 \times 720) - (720)}{6 \times 120} = \dfrac{720(56-1)}{720} = 55$.

## (Olympiad 58)

**4)** <u>Method 1</u>

Connect the midpoints of the sides of ABCD as shown.
ABCD is now partitioned into 16 congruent right triangles.
EFGH contains 4 of those triangles. Then:

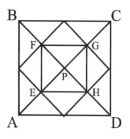

$$\frac{\text{Area(EFGH)}}{\text{Area(ABCD)}} = \frac{4}{16} = \frac{1}{4}.$$

<u>Method 2</u>

Notice that BP and FH are equal. "Slide" EFGH along the diagonal so that
F coincides with B as shown. The area of EFGH is 1/4 the area of ABCD.

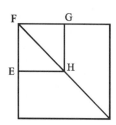

**5)** 30 people saved $2 each for a total of $60. Since the cost of the bus was fixed, the saving of $60 meant that the 10 new people had to pay a total of $60, or each of the 10 had to pay $6. Since each person in the group paid the same amount, each of the 40 people paid $6 for a total of $240.

## Olympiad 59

**1)**

From the diagram, yesterday (Y) was Friday and today (T) is Saturday. Saturdays occur 7, 14, 21, ... days after today. Find the largest multiple of 7 that is less than 100. That number is 98. Then 98 days from today is Saturday. It follows that 100 days from today is Monday.

**2)** <u>Method 1</u>

The average of the 15 multiples of 6 is the middle number, which is the 8th number. The eighth number is $8 \times 6 = 48$. Then the sum of the 15 multiplies is $15 \times 48 = 720$.

<u>Method 2</u>

| | | |
|---|---|---|
| Let S equal the sum | (1) | $S = 6 + 12 + 18 + 24 + \cdots + 84 + 90$ |
| Reverse (1) | (2) | $S = 90 + 84 + 78 + 72 + \cdots + 12 + 6$ |
| Add (1) and (2) | (3) | $2S = 96 + 96 + 96 + 96 + \cdots + 96 + 96$ |
| Simplify (3) | (4) | $2S = 15 \times 96$ |
| Divide both sides of (4) by 2 | (5) | $S = 15 \times 48 = 720.$ |

The sum is 720.

**(Olympiad 59)**

3) The first partial product (fpp) is equal to the product AB×B. Since the product ends in 4, B must be either 2 or 8. In either case, C must be 5 for the second partial product (spp) to end in 0. Since the spp is a two-digit number obtained from AB×C and C = 5, A must be 1. Otherwise the spp will be a three-digit number. If B = 2, the fpp is 12×2 or 24, a two-digit number. Therefore B = 8, A = 1, and C = 5.

```
              B C
       A B )‾‾‾‾‾‾
          _ _  4   fpp
            _ _
          _ 0   spp
          ‾‾‾‾
            0
```

4) Method 1
Rewrite 2520 as a product of prime factors: 2520 = 20×126 = 2×2×5×2×3×3×7 = 2×2×2×3×3×5×7. The largest factor not divisible by 6 cannot contain a 2 and a 3 as factors. Therefore the largest factor either has no 2s or no 3s. Since 3×3 = 9 and 2×2×2 = 8, eliminate 2×2×2. The largest factor not divisible by 6 is 3×3×5×7 = 315.

Method 2
We can either divide out as many 2s as possible from 2520 or as many 3s as possible.
Then, 2520 ÷ 2 = 1260, 1260 ÷ 2 = 630, 630 ÷ 2 = 315; and 2520 ÷ 3 = 840, 840 ÷ 3 = 280.
Therefore the largest factor not divisible by 6 is 315.

5) Method 1
The following are the possible values of the three selected disks:
    (1,2,4), (1,2,8), (1,2,16), (1,4,8), (1,4,16), (1,8,16), (2,4,8), (2,4,16), (2,8,16), (4,8,16)
Each triple has a different sum. Therefore there are 10 different sums possible.

Method 2
Each time 3 disks are selected, 2 are left over. Instead of counting triples, we can count doubles knowing that for each double there is a triple left over. The doubles are:
    (1,2), (1,4), (1,8), (1,16), (2,4), (2,8), (2,16), (4,8), (4,16), (8,16)
Each of these 10 doubles has a different sum. Thus there are 10 triples each having a different sum.

**Olympiad 60**

1) Method 1
If the sum of 5 consecutive odd numbers is 85, the average of the numbers is 85/5 = 17. The middle number or 3rd number of the five is 17: * * 17 * *. The five number are 13, 15, 17, 19, 21. The largest of the five numbers is 21.

Method 2
Suppose the middle number of the 5 consecutive odd numbers is N. Then the numbers can be represented by N–4, N–2, N, N+2, N+4. The sum of the 5 numbers is 85. Then N = 85/5 = 17. The largest number, N+4, is 17+4 = 21.

**(Olympiad 60)**

2) List, in increasing order, the three-digit numbers with a digit-sum of 5. Begin with those having a hundreds digit of 1.
   (a) hundreds digit of 1: 104, 113, 122, 131, 140
   (b) hundreds digit of 2: 203, 212, 221, 230
   (c) hundreds digit of 3: 302, 311, 320
   (d) hundreds digit of 4: 401, 410
   (e) hundreds digit of 5: 500
   Answer: There are 15 three-digit numbers which each have a digit-sum of 5.

3) Lights 1 and 2 flash together every 10 minutes after 9 AM. Light 3 flashes every 3 minutes after 9 AM. Since all 3 lights flash together at 9 AM and LCM(10,3) = 30, all 3 lights will again flash together at 9:30 AM.

4) Method 1

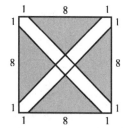 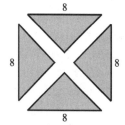 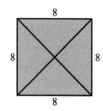

The sum of the areas of the shaded regions is 64 square units.

Method 2
Move two adjacent shaded regions to form an isosceles right triangle with each leg 8 units. The area of the triangle is 32. The area of the other two shaded regions together is also 32. The total area is 64.

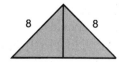

Method 3
Consider just one of the triangular shaded regions. It is a triangle with base 8 units and height 4 units. Its area is (1/2)(8×4) = 16 square units. Then the total area is 4×16 = 64 square units.

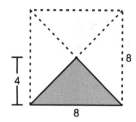

5) After one true hour, the two clocks are 3 minutes apart. After two true hours, the clocks are 6 minutes apart. For every true hour after that, the number of minutes the clocks are apart increases by 3 minutes. Since the times of the two clocks finally differ by 1 hour (or 60 minutes), they have been running for 20 hours since they were set at the correct time. Therefore the fast clock has gained 20 minutes and the slow clock has lost 40 minutes. The correct time is 20 minutes before 9 o'clock, or 40 minutes after 8 o'clock (8:40).

## Olympiad 61

**1)** <u>Method 1</u>

| | | | | | | |
|---|---|---|---|---|---|---|
| Given: | Enter at (?) | up 6 | down 4 | | up 3 | = Floor 7 |
| Work backward: | Start at Floor 7 → down 3 → | up 4 | → down 6 | | | = Floor 2 |

<u>Method 2</u>
The elevator moved a total of 6 + 3 = 9 floors up and 4 floors down. The overall change was 5 floors up. Since you ended at floor 7, you must have started at floor 2.

<u>Method 3</u>
Use a diagram.

```
Start      # → # → # → # → # → # → #   [up 6]
                 # ← # ← # ← # ← #      [down 4]
                 # → # → # → #          [up 3]
          2 — 3 — 4 — 5 — 6 — 7         floor
```

**2)** <u>Method 1</u>
The bottom layer contains 3 complete boards. Since the cube has 6 layers, all the boards can be arranged into 6 layers with 3 boards in each layer. The total number of boards is 18.

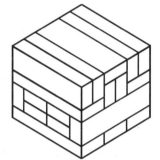

<u>Method 2</u>
The top half of the cube contains 9 boards. Then the lower half also contains 9 boards. The total number of boards is 18.

**3)** <u>Method 1</u>
If all questions were answered correctly, David's score would be 120 points. For each incorrect answer, David loses 10 points for the answer plus a deduction of 5 points; that is, he loses a total of 15 points for each incorrect answer. Since his score was 75, he lost 120–75 = 45 points.
Answer: David had 3 incorrect answers.

<u>Method 2</u>
Make a table.

| Number Correct | Number Wrong | Deduction | Total Score |
|---|---|---|---|
| 12 | 0 | 0 | 120 – 0 = 120 |
| 11 | 1 | 5 | 110 – 5 = 105 |
| 10 | 2 | 10 | 100 – 10 = 90 |
| 9 | 3 | 15 | 90 – 15 = 75 |

David had 3 incorrect answers.

**(Olympiad 61)**

4) Make a list of the different combinations. Clearly there must be either 4 or 9 pennies. There can't be 14 pennies since the total number of coins is 10. If there are 4 pennies, the remaining 6 coins must have a value of 55¢. If there are 9 pennies, the remaining 1 coin must have a value of 50¢. There are three different ways for 10 coins to have a value of 59¢.

| P | N | D | Q | H |
|---|---|---|---|---|
| 4 | 1 | 5 | 0 | 0 |
| 4 | 4 | 1 | 1 | 0 |
| 9 | 0 | 0 | 0 | 1 |

5) Method 1
Find the sum of groups of 5 consecutive odd numbers:

$$\begin{aligned}
\text{First 5 odd numbers: } & 1 + 3 + 5 + 7 + 9 = 25 \\
\text{Next 5 odd numbers: } & 11 + 13 + 15 + 17 + 19 = 75 \\
\text{Next 5 odd numbers: } & 21 + 23 + 25 + 27 + 29 = 125 \\
\text{Next 5 odd numbers: } & 31 + 33 + 35 + 37 + 39 = \underline{175} \\
& \text{total} = 400
\end{aligned}$$

Notice that each addend of the second set of odd numbers is 10 more than the corresponding addend in the first set of odd numbers. Then the second set is 50 more than the first, the third set is 50 more than the second, and the fourth set is 50 more than the third. The total of all four sets is 400. There are 20 numbers in the set.

Method 2
Form a sequence of partial sums as shown at the right and look for a pattern. Notice that each of the partial sums can be represented as a perfect square. Observe that a partial sum of 2 terms has a sum of $2^2$, 3 terms has a sum of $3^2$, 4 terms has a sum of $4^2$, and so forth. Since $400 = 20^2$, the partial sum must have 20 terms.

$$\begin{aligned}
1 &= 1 = 1^2 \\
1 + 3 &= 4 = 2^2 \\
1 + 3 + 5 &= 9 = 3^2 \\
1 + 3 + 5 + 7 &= 16 = 4^2 \\
&\cdots \\
1 + 3 + 5 + \cdots + N &= 400 = 20^2
\end{aligned}$$

**Olympiad 62**

1) Method 1
The LCM of a set of numbers is the smallest number N which each number of the set will divide exactly. LMC(6,14,15) = 210.

Method 2
List the prime factors of each of the given factors of N: $6 = 2 \times 3$; $14 = 2 \times 7$; $15 = 3 \times 5$. N must have 2, 3, 5, and 7 as factors. Then $N = 2 \times 3 \times 5 \times 7 = 210$.

## (Olympiad 62)

**2)** Use a line-diagram and show the following below the line: yesterday(YY), today(TY), and tomorrow(TW) as shown at the right. Let the day before yesterday(YY) be denoted by 0 above the line and number the five days after 0, also above the line. Five days after the day before yesterday(YY) is Friday. Then tomorrow (TW) will be two days before Friday, or Wednesday.

```
0    1    2    3    4    5
#----#----#----#----#----#
    YY   TY   TW        F
```

**3)** For each big fish sold for $4, two small fish were sold for $1 each. One big fish and two small fish were sold for a total of $6. Since the total received for big and little fish was $72, there were 72/6 = 12 sets of 1 big fish and 2 little fish sold. Therefore 12 big fish were sold.

**4)** Method 1
The sum of the entries in the top row is 9+N+17; the sum of entries in the 2nd column is 15+?+N. Since the sum of the three entries in each row, column, and diagonal are equal, 15+?+N and 9+N+17 are equal. Then 15+? = 9+17 = 26. The value of ? is 11.

| 9 | N | 17 |
|---|---|----|
| 19 | ? | 3 |
| | 15 | |

Method 2
The sums of the entries in the 2nd column and 2nd row are equal: 15+?+N = 19+?+3. Then 15+N = 19+3 = 22; N = 7. The sum of the entries in the top row is 9+7+17 = 33. The value of ? is 11.

**5)** Method 1
Since dog 1 and dog 2 are at the starting point every 20 and 25 seconds after starting, the smallest amount of time needed for them to be together again is the LCM(20,25), which is 100 seconds.

Method 2
Make a diagram which shows both dogs at the starting point.

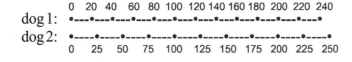

Both dogs are at the starting point every 100 seconds. Therefore the dogs are together again at the starting point 100 seconds after they start.

## Olympiad 63

**1)** Count the number of squares of different sizes in an organized manner.

| Size | # Squares |
|------|-----------|
| 1×1 | 21 |
| 2×2 | 8 |
| 3×3 | 1 |
| | Total 30 |

**(Olympiad 63)**

**2)** Use a simpler problem. Instead of one marble being left over each time, assume that no marbles were left over each time. Then the least number of marbles is the LCM(6,7,8) which is equal to $3 \times 7 \times 8 =$ 168. However, since one marble should be left over each time, the least number of marbles in the box is $168 + 1$ or 169.

**3)** Work backward.

Store 2:

Mr. Chin spent 1/3 of his money and had 2/3 left. He then spent $14 and had nothing left. Then 2/3 of the initial amount had to be $14, or 1/3 of the inital amount had to be $7. So the initial amount when he entered Store 2 was $21. Enter $21 in the last column of the table for Store 1.

| Initial Amount | Amount Spent: 1/3 | Amount Left: 2/3 | Amount Spent:$14 | Final Amount |
|---|---|---|---|---|
| ? | ? | ? | $14 | $0 |

Store 1:

Mr. Chin had $21 left when he left store 1. Prior to leaving the store, he had spent $14. Then he must have had $35 before spending the $14. But $35 is what he had remaining after he spent 1/2 of his money. Therefore $35 was 1/2 of the amount he had when he entered store 1.

Answer: Mr. Chin had $70 when he entered store 1.

| Initial Amount | Amount Spent: 1/2 | Amount Left: 1/2 | Amount Spent:$14 | Final Amount |
|---|---|---|---|---|
| ? | ? | ? | $14 | $21 |

**4)** Method 1

Use a diagram in which the number N is represented by a rectangle divided into 3 congruent parts. The triple of the number is represented by 3 rectangles.

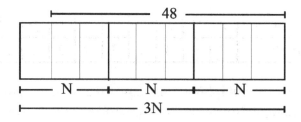

Eight small boxes represent 48. Then each small box represents a value of 6. Since the number is represented by three small boxes, the value of the number is $3 \times 6 = 18$.

Method 2

Since the triple of the number is 3 times or 9/3 of the number, 8/3 of the number is 48 and 1/3 of the number is 48/8 = 6. The number is 18.

### (Olympiad 63)

5) Notice that B cannot be 0 since it is the lead digit of the product BEDB. B cannot be 1 since the first partial product (fpp) is not AB. Observe that the B of the fpp is the units digit of the product B×B. Then B is 5 or 6. Suppose B = 5. Then the second partial product BDB is greater than 500 and less than 600. Since BDB = AB×A, A must be 7. Thus AB represents 75. (If B = 6, a contradiction results: 76×76 is too small and 86×86 is too big.)

```
            A   5
      x     A   5
      ─────────────
      C     A   5    (fpp)
  5   D     5        (spp)
  ─────────────────
  5   E     D   5    (prod)
```

## Olympiad 64

1) (Use the principle: the sum of n numbers = n times the average of the n numbers.) If the average of 6 numbers is 7, their sum is 6×7 = 42. If the average of 4 numbers is 8, their sum is 4×8 = 32. The sum of the two numbers which were removed is 42–32 = 10.

2) Method 1
Make a table and look for a pattern. Since the terms of the sequence increase by 3s, compare the terms of the sequence with the multiples of 3. Notice that each of the given terms is 1 more than the corresponding multiple of 3. Then N is 1 more than 150. N is 151.

| Order: | 1 | 2 | 3 | 4 | ... | 50 |
|---|---|---|---|---|---|---|
| Given terms: | 4 | 7 | 10 | 13 | ... | N |
| Multiples of 3: | 3 | 6 | 9 | 12 | ... | 150 |

Method 2
After the first term 4, there are 49 increases of 3 needed to reach the 50th term. Then the 50th term is 4+49×3 = 4+147 = 151.

3) Make a table and look for a pattern.

| Powers of 7: | $7^1$ | $7^2$ | $7^3$ | $7^4$ | $7^5$ | $7^6$ | $7^7$ | $7^8$ | ... |
|---|---|---|---|---|---|---|---|---|---|
| Units digit: | 7 | 9 | 3 | 1 | 7 | 9 | 3 | 1 | ... |

To get the units digit of a power of 7, multiply the units digit of the preceding power by 7. The units digit of this product is the desired units digit. Notice that the pattern of units digits, 7, 9, 3, 1 repeats in groups of 4. Then $7^{20}$ will have the same units digit as $7^4, 7^8, 7^{12}, ...$ . The units digit of $7^{20}$ is 1.

4) Use the divisibility principle for 9: If a number is divisible by 9, its digit-sum is a multiple of 9. The digit-sum is A+6+A+4+1 = 2A+11. Then the candidates for 2A+11 are 9, 18, 27, 36, ... . But 2A+11 has to be greater than 9. If 2A+11 = 18, then 2A = 7 and A = 3.5. But A has to be a digit. If 2A+11 = 27, then 2A = 16 and A = 8. No other digit will work.

## Solutions

### (Olympiad 64)

**5)** Since the game-time is 48 minutes, the total playing time for the five active players is $5 \times 48 = 240$ minutes. If eight players share the total playing time, each player will play $240/8 = 30$ minutes.

### Olympiad 65

**1)** Method 1

Rearrange the product of factors as follows so that the result is a perfect square.
$32 \times 162 = 32 \times 2 \times 81 = 64 \times 81 = 8 \times 8 \times 9 \times 9 = (8 \times 9) \times (8 \times 9) = 72 \times 72$. The number 72 when multiplied by itself is equal to $32 \times 162$.

Method 2

Multiply the given numbers: $32 \times 162 = 5184$. Since $70 \times 70 = 4900$ and $80 \times 80 = 6400$, the number we seek is between 70 and 80. Since the units digit of the product is 4, the only possibilities are 72 and 78. Since 5184 is much closer to 4900 than to 6400, we choose 72 and check it: $72 \times 72 = 5184$. The required number is 72.

**2)** Method 1

Find the area of one triangle. The four triangular regions I, II, III, IV are congruent and have equal areas.

Since Area of $\Delta I = \dfrac{5 \times 5}{2} = \dfrac{25}{2}$, the area of square ABCD is $4 \times \dfrac{25}{2} = 50$.

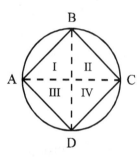

Method 2

Rearrange triangles I, II, III, and IV into two squares as shown. Each square has area of 25. The total area is 50.

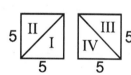

Method 3

Rearrange triangles I, II, III, and IV into a rectangle as shown. The area of the rectangle is $5 \times 10 = 50$.

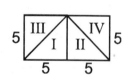

**3)** Method 1

A has to be 5 or more. Otherwise the sum will not be a three-digit number. In the second column, $A+A+1$ ends in A. Then A is odd, so $A = 5, 7,$ or 9. The only value that checks is 9. Therefore A is 9.

$$\begin{array}{r} A \quad A \\ + \quad A \quad A \\ \hline C \quad A \quad B \end{array}$$

Method 2

Use expanded notation: $AA = 10A + A = 11A$. Then $AA + AA = 22A$. Therefore C must be 1 and CAB $= 100 + 10A + B$. Then $22A = 100 + 10A + B$. If we subtract 10A from both sides of the equality, the result is $12A = 100 + B$. Since 12A has to be greater than 100, A has to be 9.

## (Olympiad 65)

4) Work from the bottom up. (See Appendix 4, section 3.)

$$F = \cfrac{1}{1+\cfrac{1}{2+\cfrac{1}{3}}} = \cfrac{1}{1+\cfrac{1}{\frac{7}{3}}} = \cfrac{1}{1+\cfrac{3}{7}} = \cfrac{1}{\frac{10}{7}} = \frac{7}{10}$$

5) <u>Method 1</u>
Look for a pattern when corresponding terms of both sets of multiples are subtracted.

$$A = 4 + 8 + 12 + 16 + \cdots + 100$$
$$\underline{B = 3 + 6 + \ 9 + 12 + \cdots + \ 75}$$
$$A-B = 1 + 2 + \ 3 + \ 4 + \cdots + \ 25$$

*Approach 1. Find the average of A–B. A–B has 25 addends; the 13th addend is the middle number 13, which is the average of all 25 numbers. Then A–B = 13×25 = 325.

*Approach 2. Use the Method of reversing the order of the addends to find the sum of A–B.

$$A-B = \ 1 + \ 2 + \ 3 + \ 4 + \cdots + 24 + 25$$
$$\underline{A-B = 25 + 24 + 23 + 22 + \cdots + \ 2 + \ 1}$$
$$2(A-B) = 26 + 26 + 26 + 26 + \cdots + 26 + 26$$

Then 2(A–B) = 25×26. So A–B = 25×26/2 = 325.

---

*Nota Bene: Approaches 1 and 2 may be applied only to an *Arithmetic Series* (a series in which the difference between successive terms is constant.)

<u>Method 2</u>
Use either Approach 1 or Approach 2 to find the sum of each of the A series and the B series. Subtracting these sums will give the difference of 325.

## Olympiad 66

1) The average of the two consecutive page numbers is 317/2 = 158.5 . Then the page numbers are 158 and 159, with 159 being the number of the right-hand page. The next page number is 160.

2) <u>Method 1</u>
Make a table and look for a pattern. Since the average age is less than 10, start with A = 9. Observe that a decrease of 1 in A's age will result in a decrease of 3 in the sum of the 3 ages. Since the desired sum of 29 is 9 less than the second sum of 38, three more decreases in A's age will decrease the second sum 38 by 9. A will then be 5 years old.

| A | B | C | A+B+C |
|---|---|---|---|
| 9 | 13 | 19 | 9+13+19 = 41 |
| 8 | 12 | 18 | 8+12+18 = 38 |
| ... | ... | ... | ... |
| 5 | 9 | 15 | 5+9+15 = 29 |

**(Olympiad 66)**

**2)** Method 2

Algebra: Let A, B, and C represent the respective ages of Alice, Betty, and Clara.

| Given | (1) | $A+B+C = 29$ |
|---|---|---|
| Given | (2) | $B = A+4$ |
| Given | (3) | $C = B+6$ |
| Replace B in (3) with A+4 | (4) | $C = A+4+6 = A+10$ |
| Add (2) and (4) | (5) | $B+C = A+4+A+10 = 2A+14$ |
| Replace B+C in (1) with 2A+14 | (6) | $A+2A+14 = 29$ |
| Subtract 14 from both sides of (6) | (7) | $3A = 15$ |
| Divide both sides of (7) by 3 | (8) | $A = 5$ |

Alice is 5 years old.

**3)** Method 1

1 mile requires 1 minute 12 seconds, or 72 seconds. Since 1 hour = 60 minutes = 3600 seconds, the car travels 1 mile for every 72 seconds that are in 3600 seconds. Since $3600/72 = 36 \times 100/72 = 50$, the car will travel 50 miles in 1 hour.

Method 2

1 mile requires 1 minute 12 seconds = 1 12/60 minutes = 1 1/5 minutes; 5 miles require $5 \times 6/5$ minutes = 6 minutes. For every 6 minutes that are in 1 hour, the car travels 5 miles. Since 1 hour divided by 6 minutes is 10, the car will travel $10 \times 5$ miles or 50 miles in 1 hour.

Method 3

Make a table in which 1 min 12 sec = 1.2 min.

| Time (minutes): | 0 | 1.2 | 2.4 | 3.6 | 4.8 | 6.0 |
|---|---|---|---|---|---|---|
| Distance (miles): | 0 | 1 | 2 | 3 | 4 | 5 |

Since the car travels 5 miles in 6 minutes, then the car will travel $10 \times 5$ miles or 50 miles in $10 \times 6$ minutes or 1 hour.

**4)** The number of cents spent for 15¢-stamps must end in 0 or 5. Since $2.50 ends in 0, the number of cents spent for 23¢-stamps must also end in 0 or 5. If Henry buys 10 23¢-stamps, he will spend 230¢ and thus leave 20¢ for 15¢-stamps. But this does not satisfy the given conditions. If Henry buys 5 23¢-stamps, he will spend 115¢ and thus leave 135¢ for 15¢-stamps. Since $9 \times 15$¢ = 135¢, Henry bought 9 15¢-stamps.

**5)** Method 1

Partition the figure into rectangles as shown. The area of each rectangle is shown by the circled number in it.

Total area = $30+12+20 = 62$.

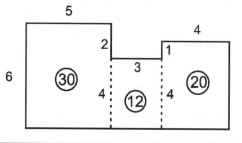

## Solutions

### (Olympiad 66)

5) <u>Method 2</u>
Complete the 6×12 rectangles as shown. The area of the large completed rectangle is $6 \times 12 = 72$ square units. We have to subtract the sum of the areas of the two rectangles added to the original figure: area $= 72 - (6+4) = 62$.

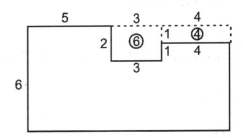

### Olympiad 67

1) The number must be divisible by 13 and by the least common multiple of 4 and 6. LCM(4,6) = 12. The number we seek is $13 \times 12 = 156$.

2) <u>Method 1</u>
List multiples of 5, each increased by 2: A = 7, 12, 17, 22, 27, 32, 37, 42, 47, 52, 57, ...
List multiples of 6, each increased by 3: B = 9, 15, 21, 27, 33, 39, 45, 51, 57, 63, 69, ...
List A and list B have 27, 57, 87, ... in common. The smallest number of children in the class is 27.

<u>Method 2</u>
Each multiple of 5, increased by 2, ends either in 2 or 7. Each multiple of 6, increased by 3, must be an odd number. Then the only possibilities for the class size are: 7, 17, 27, 37, ... . Divide each by 6. The first number that has a remainder of 3 is the required number. That number is 27.

<u>Method 3</u>
Algebra: Let A and B be numbers such that 5A+2 = 6B+3. Subtract 2 from each member of the equation. Then 5A = 6B+1. Since 6B+1 is an odd number, 5A is also odd. 5A may be 5, 15, 25, 35, 45, ... . Divide each of these numbers by 6. The first number that has a remainder of 1 is 25: 25/6 = 4 R1. So B = 4. Since 6B+3 is the class size, and B = 4, the class size is $6 \times 4 + 3 = 27$.

3) Find the largest square number less than 500: $20^2 = 400$; $21^2 = 441$; $22^2 = 484$; $23^2 = 529$. The largest square number less than 500 is $22^2$. The following square numbers are less than 500: $1^2, 2^2, 3^2, 4^2, ... , 20^2, 21^2, 22^2$. There are 22 square numbers less than 500.

4) <u>Method 1</u>

| | | (1) | A | B | 8 | | (2) | A | 2 | 8 |
|---|---|---|---|---|---|---|---|---|---|---|
| | | | − | A | B | | | − | A | 2 |
| | | | 2 | 9 | 6 | | | 2 | 9 | 6 |

Conclusion: in case (1), B must be 2; in case (2), A must be 3.

- - - - - - - - - - - - - - - - - - - - - - - - - - - - - - - - - - - - - - - - - - - - - - -

<u>Method 2</u>

| | | (1) | 2 | 9 | 6 | | (2) | 2 | 9 | 6 |
|---|---|---|---|---|---|---|---|---|---|---|
| | | | + | A | B | | | + | A | 2 |
| | | | A | B | 8 | | | A | 2 | 8 |

Same conclusion as in Method 1.

**(Olympiad 67)**

**4)** Method 3

```
(1)     A   B   8          (2)     A   B   8
      - 2   9   6                - 2   9   6
      ─────────────              ─────────────
            A   B                      A   B
```

Same conclusion as in Method 1.
Answer: AB = 32.

------------------------------------------------------------------------

**5)** Method 1

The tallest column has 5 cubes. The next tallest column has 4 cubes; the next tallest has 3 cubes, and so forth. Make a table showing the different numbers of cubes a column could contain and the number of columns having each of these numbers.

| Number of Cubes in Column | Number of Columns | Total Number of Cubes |
|---|---|---|
| 5 | 1 | 5×1 = 5 |
| 4 | 1 | 4×1 = 4 |
| 3 | 2 | 3×2 = 6 |
| 2 | 4 | 2×4 = 8 |
| 1 | 4 | 1×4 = 4 |
| | | Total = 27 |

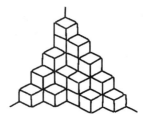

Method 2

Slice the tower vertically as shown. Count the number of cubes in each slice and add the numbers: 1+3+8+15 = 27.

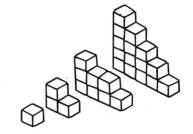

**Olympiad 68**

**1)** Method 1

The average height of the two people is 94/2 = 47 inches. Since the people differ in height by 8 inches, each differs from the average height by 4 inches. Then Rachel is 47+4 = 51 inches tall, and Paul is 47−4 = 43 inches tall. (Note: This method can be used whenever the sum and difference of two numbers is known.)

Method 2

Algebra: Let R and P represent the respective heights of Rachel and Paul.

| | | | | | | |
|---|---|---|---|---|---|---|
| Given | (1) | R | + | P | = | 94 |
| Given | (2) | R | − | P | = | 8 |
| Add (1) and (2) | (3) | 2R | | | = | 102 |
| Divide members of (3) by 2 | (4) | | | R | = | 51 |

The respective heights of Rachel and Paul are 51 inches and 43 inches.

**(Olympiad 68)**

**2)** No matter which two wheels are actually used at any time during the 600-mile trip, the total miles traveled by those wheels together is 1200 miles. Since three wheels are to share that total equally, each will travel 400 miles.

**3)**

| Type of numbers | Number of digits written |
|---|---|
| one-digit: 1-9 | $9 \times 1 = \phantom{00}9$ |
| two-digit: 10-99 | $90 \times 2 = 180$ |
| three-digit: 100-150 | $\underline{51 \times 3 = 153}$ |
| | total:  342 |

**4)** Method 1

Partition the figure by extending the sides of the "middle" square as shown at the right. Each original square contains four 3×3 small squares. The shaded figure consists of ten 3×3 squares, so its area is $10 \times 9 = 90$ square units.

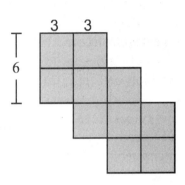

Method 2

Partition the shaded figure into a square and two L-shaped figures as shown at the right. Each of the L-shaped figures has an area equal to 3/4 of one of the original squares. Then the area of the shaded figure is $(1 + .75 + .75)$ or 2.5 times the area of one of the original squares: $2.5 \times 36 = 90$ square units.

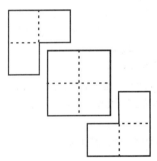

**5)** Method 1

Make a list of the six numbers that can be formed from the digits 4, 5, and 6. Add and divide the sum by 6. Note that each digit appears twice in each column and that the sum of the digits in each column is 30. The required average is $3330 \div 6 = 555$.

$$
\begin{array}{rrr}
4 & 5 & 6 \\
4 & 6 & 5 \\
5 & 4 & 6 \\
5 & 6 & 4 \\
6 & 4 & 5 \\
6 & 5 & 4 \\
\hline
3 \quad 3 & 3 & 0 \\
\end{array}
$$

Method 2

The average of the six digits that appear in each of the columns shown in Method 1 is 5. Then the average of all 6 three-digit numbers that can be formed by using the digits 4, 5, and 6 in each number must be: $5 \times 100 + 5 \times 10 + 5 \times 1 = 555$.

## Solutions

### Olympiad 69

1) $A = 2\times2\times2\times2\times2 = 32$; $B = 3\times3\times3\times3 = 81$; $C = 4\times4\times4 = 64$; $D = 5\times5 = 25$.
Answer: D, A, C, B; or $5^2$, $2^5$, $4^3$, $3^4$; or 25, 32, 64, 81.

2) Since the cost of the first ounce was 29¢, the total cost of the remaining ounces was 161¢.
Since the cost of each of the remaining ounces was 23¢ per ounce, the number of remaining ounces was $161¢ \div 23¢ = 7$. The total number of ounces in the letter was 8.

3) <u>Method 1</u>
Compare the two rates

|  |  | Fast | Normal |
|---|---|---|---|
| The fast clock goes 72 min. in 1 normal hr. | (1) | 72 min. | 60 min. |
| Divide both times in (1) by 12 | (2) | 6 min. | 5 min. |
| Multiply both times in (2) by 10 | (3) | 60 min. | 50 min. |

Both clocks registered the correct time at 1 PM. When the fast clock registered 2 PM, it had advanced 60 minutes. According to the table, the normal clock had advanced 50 minutes and registered 1:50 PM.

<u>Method 2</u>
In a normal hour of 60 minutes, the fast clock goes 72 minutes and a normal clock goes 60 minutes. The ratio of their times is:

fast clock/slow clock = 72 minutes/60 minutes = 6 minutes/5 minutes.

Notice that ratios can be reduced like ordinary fractions. The last ratio tells us that every 6 minutes on the fast clock is equivalent to 5 minutes on the normal clock. Then $10\times6$ minutes or 60 minutes on the fast clock is equivalent to $10\times5$ minutes or 50 minutes on the normal clock. The time on the normal clock is 1:50 PM when the fast clock registers 2 PM.

4) Since each of the 8 men works 6 days, they work a total of 48 individual-work-days. Another way of saying this is that one person will have to work 48 days alone to build the concrete wall. A crew of 12 people must also work a total of 48 individual-work-days to build the wall. If each of the 12 people works 4 days, the crew will have a total of 48 individual-work-days.

5)

| (1)ABCD | (2)1BCD | (3)1BC9 | (4)10C9 |
|---|---|---|---|
| $\times9$ | $\times9$ | $\times9$ | $\times9$ |
| DCBA | DCB1 | 9CB1 | 9C01 |

| A in ABCD must be 1. Otherwise, the product will have 5 digits. | D in 1BCD must be 9 to produce 1 in the product. | B in 1BC9 must be 0. Otherwise the product will have 5 digits. | $9\times C$ plus a carry of 8 must end in 0 in the product; $9\times C$ must end in 2. C must be 8. |
|---|---|---|---|

ABCD = 1089.

## Olympiad 70

1) The even multiples of 3 are 6, 12, 18, ... . The largest multiple of 6 less than 101 is $16 \times 6 = 96$. Multiples of 6 less than 101 are: $1 \times 6, 2 \times 6, 3 \times 6, 4 \times 6, ..., 16 \times 6$. There are 16 even multiples of 3 between 1 and 101.

2) Method 1

   Use a simpler problem. Consider the following set of coins: 1 quarter, 2 dimes, 4 nickels. The numbers 1, 2, 4 are in the same ratio as the numbers in the exchange set. The value of the small set is 65¢. Since the value of the exchange set is 390¢, we will need $390/65 = 6$ small sets to obtain the value of the exchange set. Since each small set contains 1 quarter, the exchange set contained 6 quarters.

   Method 2

   Make a table in which N represents the number of quarters, 2N the number of dimes, and 4N the number of nickels. The total value in terms of N is 65N, which is also equal to 390¢. Then 65 times what number (N) is equal to 390? N must be 6, which is also the number of quarters.

   | Coin type | Number | Value in ¢ |
   |-----------|--------|------------|
   | 25¢ | N | $25 \times N = 25N$ |
   | 10¢ | 2N | $10 \times 2N = 20N$ |
   | 5¢ | 4N | $5 \times 4N = 20N$ |
   | | | Total = 65N |

3) Method 1

   Change the times between flashes to seconds. Find the least common multiple (LCM) of the time for the first light and the time for the second light.

   (1 minute 15 seconds = 75 seconds; 1 minute 40 seconds = 100 seconds)

   The shortest amount of time before both lights again flash together is 300 seconds, or 5 minutes.

   $$LCM(75,100) = \frac{75 \times 100}{GCF(75,100)} = \frac{75 \times 100}{25} = 300$$

   Method 2

   Make a graph which shows when each light flashes. (Each space denotes 5 seconds.)

   Answer: The shortest amount of time before both lights again flash together is 5 minutes.

**(Olympiad 70)**

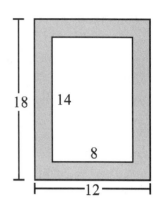

4) <u>Method 1</u>
The area of the border is equal to the difference between the areas of the outer and inner rectangles. Area = 18×12 – 14×8 = 216 – 112 = 104 (square units).

<u>Method 2</u>
Partition the border so that it contains 4 squares, one at each of the corners, and four rectangles as shown. Area = 4×(2×2) + 2×(14×2) + 2×(8×2) = 16 + 56 + 32 = 104 (square units).

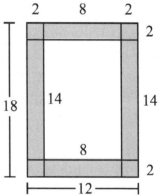

5) Use divisibility theorems. Since N is divisible by 24, it is also divisible by 8 and by 3. The number formed by the last three digits of N, namely 65B, must be divisible by 8. B has to be 6.
(See Appendix 4, Section 3.)

If a number is divisible by 3, the sum of its digits must be a multiple of 3.
Since 8+A+6+5+6 = A+25, A must be 2, 5, or 8. Since N is to be as small as possible, A is 2.
(See Appendix 4, Section 4.)

The number N must be 82656.

## Olympiad 71

1) Make the 3-digit number as small as possible and the 2-digit number as large as possible, as shown at the right. The smallest possible difference is 259.

$$\begin{array}{r} 3\;\;5\;\;6 \\ -\;\;\;9\;\;7 \\ \hline 2\;\;5\;\;9 \end{array}$$

2) <u>Method 1</u>
The average amount received by the 5 boys is $20. In order of age, the third boy receives the average amount of $20. The youngest receives $10 less than the third boy. Therefore, the youngest receives $10.

<u>Method 2</u>
Let Y represent the amount received by the youngest boy. Then the amounts received are Y, Y+5, Y+10, Y+15, and Y+20. These amounts can be regrouped and totaled as Y+Y+Y+Y+Y + 5+10+15+20, or more simply as 5Y+50.
Then 5Y+50 = 100, 5Y = 50 and Y = 10. The youngest receives $10.

3) Change each of the original operations to its opposite and work backward.
Since $(40 - 8) \div 4 + 3 = 11$, the starting number is 11.

4) Make an organized list of the triples with the elements of each triple in order of magnitude as shown at the right. There are 9 triples other than (1,1,9) which have a sum of 11.

| (1,2,8) | (1,3,7) | (1,4,6) | (1,5,5) |
|---------|---------|---------|---------|
| (2,2,7) | (2,3,6) | (2,4,5) |         |
| (3,3,5) | (3,4,4) |         |         |

5) Analyze just one face of the cube as shown in the diagram at the right. The number given on the front face of each of the 16 cubes shown indicates the total number of red faces that particular cube has. Only two cubes on each edge of the cube have just 2 red faces. Since the cube has 12 distinct edges, the number of cubes having just 2 red faces is $12 \times 2 = 24$.

| 3 | 2 | 2 | 3 |
|---|---|---|---|
| 2 | 1 | 1 | 2 |
| 2 | 1 | 1 | 2 |
| 3 | 2 | 2 | 3 |

## Olympiad 72

1) <u>Method 1</u>
Numbers which leave a remainder of 4 when divided by 5 must end in either 4 or 9. Start with 3 and count by 7s. The first number which ends in a 4 or 9 is the required number: 3, 10, 17, 24, .... The smallest number satisfying the given conditions is 24.

**(Olympiad 72)**

**1)** <u>Method 2</u>
Numbers which leave a remainder of 3 when divided by 7:
$$3, 10, 17, 24, 31, 38, 45, 52, 59, \ldots$$
Numbers which leave a remainder of 4 when divided by 5:
$$4, 9, 14, 19, 24, 29, 34, 39, 44, 49, 54, 59, \ldots$$
The numbers which satisfy both conditions are 24, 59, 94, .... The smallest of these is 24.

**2)** <u>Method 1</u>
Find the areas of square ABCD and triangle AEF. Let L be the length of a side of the square. Then the area of the square is $L \times L$ or $L^2$.

The legs of the right triangle are each L/2.

Area of $\triangle AEF$ is $\dfrac{1}{2} \times \dfrac{L}{2} \times \dfrac{L}{2} = \dfrac{1}{8} \times L^2$ .

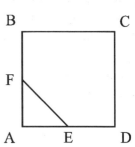

Area of $\triangle AEF$ is 1/8 of the area of square ABCD.
Note: This will always be true no matter what value is assigned to L.

<u>Method 2</u>
Partition the square as shown at the right. The interior of the square has 8 congruent triangles. The area of each triangle is 1/8 of the area of the square. Then the area of $\triangle AEF$ is 1/8 of the area of square ABCD.

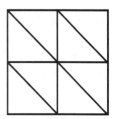

**3)** The sum of N grades = N × the average of those grades. Use this principle to find the total scored on any of the tests.
$$\text{The total scored on 5 tests: } 5 \times 88 = 440$$
$$\text{The total scored on 4 tests: } 4 \times 90 = 360$$
The difference between these two totals, 80, must be the test grade that was removed.

**4)** <u>Method 1</u>
Suppose all 72 coins were nickels. The value of these coins would then be $72 \times 5 = 360¢$, which is 140¢ short of being $5 or 500¢. For each nickel of the 72 exchanged for a dime, the 360¢ value goes up 5¢. Since the value is 140¢ short of 500¢, we need to exchange 140/5 = 28 nickels for dimes. Therefore 28 dimes were in the exchange.

**(Olympiad 72)**

4) Method 2
Make a table and look for a pattern. Let the number of nickels and the number of dimes be N and D respectively, and let the sum of N and D be 72, beginning with N = 72 and D = 0. Notice that each exchange of 1N for 1D increases the preceding value by 5¢. Also notice that the number of 5s by which 360 increases is the same number that appears in the dimes (D) column. Since 500 = 360+28 × 5, 28 should also appear in the D column. Then the number of dimes in the change was 28.

| N | D | ¢-VALUE |
|---|---|---|
| 72 | 0 | 360 |
| 71 | 1 | 360 + 1×5 |
| 70 | 2 | 360 + 2×5 |
| 69 | 3 | 360 + 3×5 |
| ... | ... | .................. |
| 44 | 28 | 360 + 28×5 |

5) List the given numbers in columnar form as shown at the right.
Units column sum = $10 \times 2 = 20$
[enter 0, carry 2]
Tens column sum = $9 \times 2 = 18$
[18+carry 2 = 20;
enter 0, carry 2]
Hundreds column sum = $8 \times 2 = 16$
[16+carry 2 = 18:
enter 8, (carry 1)]

```
          2
        2 2
      2 2 2
    2 2 2 2
    ................
    .....................
2 2 2 2 2 2 2 2 2 2
.....................5 8 0 0
```

The hundreds digit of the sum is 8.

## Olympiad 73

1) Since the number is divisible by 2, 5, and 9, it is also divisible by the product 2×5×9 = 90. The multiple of 90 between 200 and 300 is 270.

2) For every leap the kangaroo and rabbit make, the kangaroo gains 5 feet on the rabbit. Since the rabbit has a head start of 150 feet, the kangaroo has to make 150/5 = 30 leaps to catch up to the rabbit.

3) Make a list $L_1$ which contains the prime numbers less than or equal to 1/2 of 36. Make another list $L_2$ of the numbers which need to be added to each of the primes in $L_1$ to yield a sum of 36. Since 34, 33, and 25 in the $L_2$ list are not primes, cross out the three lines in the list which contain them. The remaining pairs satisfy the given condition. There are 4 pairs of prime numbers such that the sum of each pair is 36.

| $L_1$ | $L_2$ |
|---|---|
| ~~2~~ | ~~34~~ |
| ~~3~~ | ~~33~~ |
| 5 | 31 |
| 7 | 29 |
| ~~11~~ | ~~25~~ |
| 13 | 23 |
| 17 | 19 |

**(Olympiad 73)**

4) Find the length of a side of a small square. The interior of the figure has 8 small squares which are congruent to each other. Each small square has an area which is 1/8 of the total area of 72 square units, or 9 square units. Then the length of a side of a small square is 3 units. The length of the darkened border of the figure is equal to 16 times the length of a side of a small square, or $16 \times 3 = 48$ units.

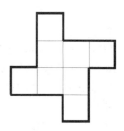

5) At 40 miles per hour, a car will travel 60 miles in 1½ hours. Since Peter arrived at 12:15, he must have left 1½ hours before 12:15, which is equivalent to 10:45 AM.

## Olympiad 74

1) If there were no tandems on the trip, only 23 people could have gone on the trip. Then 7 people of the 30 would have been left out. There must have been 7 tandems for the 7 extra people.

2) Make a table and look for a pattern. The table should show the order of the numbers of the sequence as well as the numbers. Since successive numbers of the sequence increase by 3, show the associated multiples of 3, M(3), in the table. Notice that the 100th

| Order: | 1 | 2 | 3 | 4 | 5 | ... | 100 |
|---|---|---|---|---|---|---|---|
| Sequence: | 7 | 10 | 13 | 16 | 19 | ... | ? |
| M(3): | 3 | 6 | 9 | 12 | 15 | ... | (300) |

multiple of 3 corresponds to the missing term of the sequence. Enter (300) on the bottom line of the table under the missimg term. Also notice that each number of the sequence is 4 more than the corresponding multiple of 3. The required number is 304.

3) Method 1
Use symbolic representation. Suppose the cost of the case is C dollars. Then the cost of the sunglasses is C+9 dollars. Together the cost is C+C+9 dollars, which has to be $10. Clearly C+C is $1, so C must be a half-dollar or 50¢.

Method 2
If the total cost of two objects is $10, the average cost of each is $5. (See diagram) Since the costs of the sunglasses and the case differ by $9, each must differ from the average by $4.50.

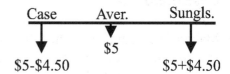

Case     Aver.     Sungls.

$5

$5-$4.50     $5+$4.50

4) Method 1
Make a table of the number of cubes hidden from view in each layer from the top down. The sum of the numbers of hidden cubes in each layer is 20.

| Layer | Number of cubes hidden |
|---|---|
| 1 | 0 |
| 2 | 1 = 1 |
| 3 | 1+2 = 3 |
| 4 | 1+2+3 = 6 |
| 5 | 1+2+3+4 = 10 |
| | Total = 20 |

### (Olympiad 74)

4) <u>Method 2</u>
Calculate the total number of cubes in the tower. Count the number of visible cubes. The difference between the two numbers is the number of cubes which are not visible. The number of cubes which are not visible is 20.

| Layer | Total number of cubes |
|-------|----------------------|
| 1 | 1 = 1 |
| 2 | 1+2 = 3 |
| 3 | 1+2+3 = 6 |
| 4 | 1+2+3+4 = 10 |
| 5 | 1+2+3+4+5 = 15 |
| | Total No. Cubes = 35 |
| | Total No. Visible = 15 |
| | Total not Visible = 20 |

5) <u>Method 1</u>
Make a diagram. Two geometric figures intersect if they have one or more points in common. Draw two circles which intersect in 2 points. Draw a line which intersects the two circles in 4 points. Draw another line which intersects the two circles in 4 points and also intersects the first line. There are 11 points of intersection.

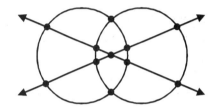

<u>Method 2</u>
Make a table of the maximum number of points of intersection.

| Geometric Figures | Number of Common Points |
|-------------------|------------------------|
| 2 Circles | 2 |
| Line (1) and 2 circles | 4 |
| Line (2) and 2 circles | 4 |
| 2 lines | 1 |
| Total = 11 | |

### Olympiad 75

1) Make a line-diagram with the following shown on the diagram: N representing now or today, T for tomorrow and T+1 for the day after tomorrow, Y for yesterday and Y−1 for the day before yesterday. Count 6 days to the right of Y−1 (the day before yesterday). Mark that day in the diagram as H for Thursday. Count back 2 days to T+1 (the day after tomorrow). That day is Tuesday.

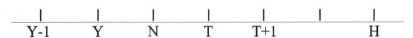

**(Olympiad 75)**

**2)** Method 1

The average of the terms of the arithmetic series is the middle or 13th term, which is $13 \times 2 = 26$. Since there are 25 terms, the sum $= 26 \times 25 = 650$. Notice that the average of the terms of an arithmetic series can also be obtained by taking one-half of the sum of the first and last terms. This is helpful when there are an even number of terms and therefore no middle term.

Method 2

| | | |
|---|---|---|
| Given | (1) | $S = 2+ 4+ 6+ \cdots +46+48+50$ |
| Reverse (1) | (2) | $S = 50+48+46+ \cdots + 6+ 4+ 2$ |
| Add (1) and (2) | (3) | $2S = 52+52+52+ \cdots +52+52+52$ |
| Simplify (3) | (4) | $2S = 25 \times 52$ |
| Divide both sides of (4) by 2 | (5) | $S = 25 \times 52/2 = 650$ |

**3)** Find the values of S, V, and E in that order: $S = 1$, $V = 9$, $E = 0$. Substitute those values in the cryptogram.

$$\begin{array}{ccccc} & & V & C & R \\ + & V & C & C & T \\ \hline S & E & R & V & E \end{array}$$

Clearly R+T in the units column must equal 10 which will yield a carry of 1 in the tens column. So C+C+1 must end in 9. C can be 9 or 4. But $V = 9$. So C must be 4. Substitute 4 for C.

$$\begin{array}{ccccc} & & 9 & C & R \\ + & 9 & C & C & T \\ \hline 1 & 0 & R & 9 & 0 \end{array}$$

Since there is no carry from the tens column, R in the hundreds column must be 3 (and T in the units column must be 7). SERVE is the number 10390.

$$\begin{array}{ccccc} & & 9 & 4 & R \\ + & 9 & 4 & 4 & T \\ \hline 1 & 0 & R & 9 & 0 \end{array}$$

**4)** Calculate the total number of classes during the school day. The 90 children can be separated into 6 classes of 15. Since each child has 4 classes during the day, a total of $4 \times 6 = 24$ classes meet during the day. Since each teacher teaches 3 classes during the day, there must be $24/3 = 8$ teachers.

**5)** Method 1

Let A* and B* be the points for 1 arrow in the A-region and B-region, respectively. Then:

(1) David's point-score is $4A*+2B* = 18$ points, and

(2) Eric's point-score is $3A*+3B* = 21$ points.

If David could exchange 1A* for 1B*, he would then have Eric's point-score and thus gain 3 points. This tells us that B* is worth 3 more points than A*. If Eric's point score in (2) is divided by 3, the result is $1A*+1B* = 7$ points. So we need to find two numbers A* and B* which have a sum of 7 points and a difference of 3 points. Clearly $A* = 2$ points and $B* = 5$ points.

## (Olympiad 75)

**5)** Method 2

Divide equation (1) in Method 1 by 2, and equation (2) by 3. The results are:

$$(1) \quad 2A^* + 1B^* = 9 \text{ points}$$
$$(2) \quad 1A^* + 1B^* = 7 \text{ points}$$

Subtract (2) from (1) $\qquad$ (3) $\qquad 1A^* = 2 \text{ points}$

Subtract (3) from (2) $\qquad$ (4) $\qquad 1B^* = 5 \text{ points}$

## Olympiad 76

**1)** Method 1

If we replace the missing Xs in the diagram, we get a 7 by 7 square of Xs or 49 Xs. Since there are 13 Xs missing, the figure has $49 - 13 = 36$ Xs.

Method 2

Count the number of Xs in each row starting with the top row: 7, 6, 4, 2, 4, 6, 7. (Notice the symmetry.) The sum of the counted Xs is 36.

**2)** H has to be less than or equal to 3. Otherwise the sum would be a three-digit number. Try H = 3, 2, and 1 as shown at the right. In case 1, E = 1 and A = 9; in case 2, E = 4 and A = 7; in case 3, E = 7 and A = 5. Only case 2 satisfies the condition that E = 2H. The required sum is 72.

| CASE 1 | CASE 2 | CASE 3 |
|--------|--------|--------|
| 3 E | 2 E | 1 E |
| 3 E | 2 E | 1 E |
| + 3 E | + 2 E | + 1 E |
| A 3 | A 2 | A 1 |

**3)** The counting numbers which each divide 83 with a remainder of 2 also divide 81 with a remainder of 0. Therefore, the required counting numbers are factors of 81 other than 1. Answer: 3, 9, 27, and 81.

**4)** Use a Venn diagram with two overlapping circles. One circle represents ng the number of Bio students and the other circle represents the number of Chem students. The diagram has three parts which we name I, II, and III. I denotes the number of students taking Bio but not Chem; II denotes the number of students taking both Bio and Chem; and III denotes the number of students taking Chem but not Bio. The sum of I, II, and III is 13+12+8 = 33 which is the number taking Bio or Chem (and includes those taking both Bio and Chem). Then there are 50 – 33 = 17 students who took neither Bio nor Chem.

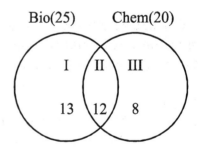

**5)** Since $40^2 = 1600$ and $50^2 = 2500$, the number whose square we seek is between 40 and 50 (and closer to 40 because the years 1701 through 1800 are closer to 1600 than to 2500). $41^2 = 1681$, which is not in the 18th century; $42^2 = 1764$ and thus satisfies the given condition; and $43^2 = 1849$, which is not in the 18th century. The required year is 1764.

# Solutions

## Olympiad 77

**1)** Method 1

Use: Average Weight × Total Number = Total Weight. The total weight of the 5 children is 5 × 72 = 360 pounds. The total weight of the 6 children is 6 × 73 = 438 pounds. The sixth child weighs 438 − 360 = 78 pounds.

Method 2

When the sixth child joined the original group, the average weight of each child increased from 72 pounds to 73 pounds. The total weight of the original group of 5 children was 5 pounds short of a 73 pound average weight for each child. The weight of the sixth child had to be 73+5 = 78 pounds.

**2)** Let N, D, and Q represent the respective numbers of nickels, dimes and quarters. Assume Q = 1 and N = 9. Their total ¢-value (TV) is 70. See line 1) of the table at the right. Since the TV of line 1) is 30¢ short of the required 100¢ and we do not have a different nonzero number for each type of coin, we need to alter line 1). If we replace 6 of the 9 nickels by dimes, we gain 30¢ in total value (TV), and have a total of 10 coins with a different nonzero number for each type. See line 2) of the table This satisfies the conditions of the problem.

| | N | D | Q | TV |
|---|---|---|---|---|
| 1) | 9 | 0 | 1 | 70 |
| 2) | 3 | 6 | 1 | 100 |
| 3) | 8 | 0 | 2 | 90 |
| 4) | 6 | 2 | 2 | 100 |

Now suppose Q = 2 and N = 8. See line 3) of the table. The TV is 10¢ short of the required 100¢. If we replace 2 of the nickels by dimes, we gain 10¢ in TV and have a nonzero number for each type of coin. But these numbers are not all different. See line 4) of the table. We therefore reject this solution. Answer: N = 3, D = 6, and Q = 1, or 3, 6, 1.

**3)** An asterisk (*) in the diagram at the right represents a nonzero digit. The first partial product (fpp) has a units digit of 3. Only 1 and 3, or 7 and 9 have a product which has a units digit of 3. But the product of 13 and 31 is a 3-digit number and therefore does not satisfy the given conditions of the problem. The given conditions are satisfied by the product of 79 and 97 which is 7663.

$$\begin{array}{r}
\text{A} \quad \text{B} \\
\times \quad \text{B} \quad \text{A} \\
\hline
* \quad * \quad 3 \quad \text{(fpp)} \\
* \quad * \quad * \qquad \text{(spp)} \\
\hline
* \quad * \quad * \quad * \quad \text{(prod)}
\end{array}$$

**4)** Method 1

It is given that Betty and Claire together have exactly enough to buy the bicycle. Since Betty is $23 short, Claire must have $23 so that together they can buy the bike. Similarly, since Claire is $25 short, Betty must have $25. Together, they have $25+$23 = $48, the cost of the bike.

Method 2

Algebra: Let B represent the bicycle's cost. Then Betty has B − 23 and Clair has B − 25.

| | | | | |
|---|---|---|---|---|
| Given | (1) | $(B − 23) + (B − 25)$ | = | B |
| Simplify left side of (1) | (2) | $2B − 48$ | = | B |
| Subtract B from both sides of (2) | (3) | $B − 48$ | = | 0 |
| Add 48 to both sides of (3) | (4) | $B$ | = | 48 |

The cost of the bicycle is $48.

### (Olympiad 77)

**5)** Let s represent the length of a side of the shaded square. Then $s + 7 = 12$. Then s must be 5 units. The area of the shaded square is 25 square units.

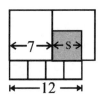

## Olympiad 78

**1)** The cents-value of the 29¢-stamps must have a units digit of 5 or 0. Otherwise the remainder of the 200¢ that is available for 5¢-stamps will not be divisible by 5. If five 29¢-stamps are purchased, the cost is 145¢, and 55¢ will be left over from the 200¢. Then eleven 5¢-stamps can be purchased. (200¢ is not enough to buy ten 29¢-stamps.)

**2)** If the smaller dimension of each of the congruent rectangles is 5 units, the other dimension is 10 units. Rectangle ABCD has dimensions 10 units by 15 units, and area of 150 square units.

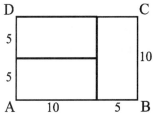

**3)** The total number of students in the 5th and 6th grades, $7 + 11 = 18$, must be 2/3 of the team. Then 1/3 of the team is 9, and 3/3 or the entire team has $3 \times 9 = 27$ students.

**4)** Method 1

The shortest amount of time after 8 o'clock for the three lights to flash together is the LCM of 4, 5, and 6. LCM(4,5,6) = 60 (seconds). The next time the lights flash together is 8:01 or 1 minute after 8.

Method 2

The two lights that flash every 4 and 5 seconds respectively will flash together every 20 seconds after 8 o'clock. Then the LCM(20,6) will tell us how frequently all three lights will flash together after 8 o'clock. The LCM(20,6) = 60 (seconds). The next time the lights flash together is 8:01 or 1 minute after 8.

**5)** Observe that the numbers are listed in groups of 7 because there are 7 columns. Also observe that column B contains the multiples of 7. The first number in each of the other columns is the remainder which results when each of the numbers in the column is divided by 7. When 1000 is divided by 7, there is a remainder of 6. Then 1000 will be listed in column D.

| A | B | C | D | E | F | G |
|---|---|---|---|---|---|---|
| 1 |   | 2 |   | 3 |   | 4 |
|   | 7 |   | 6 |   | 5 |   |
| 8 |   | 9 |   | 10 |   | 11 |
|   | 14 |   | 13 |   | 12 |   |
| 15 |   | 16 |   | 17 |   | ... |

## Olympiad 79

**1)** Method 1

The train travels 1 mile in 1 minute 30 seconds. Then it will travel 2 miles in 3 minutes. Since 60 minutes contains 20 groups of 3 minutes, the train will travel $20 \times 2 = 40$ miles in 1 hour.

Method 2

The number of miles the train travels in 1 hour is equal to 60 minutes divided by 1.5 minutes. 60 divided by 1.5 = 40.

**2)**

|  |  | Number |
|---|---|---|
| 1-coin amounts: | 1,3,5,10 | 4 |
| 2-coin amounts: | 1+3, 1+5, 1+10, 3+5, 3+10, 5+10 | 6 |
| 3-coin amounts*: | 1+3+5, 1+3+10, 1+5+10, 3+5+10 | 4 |
| 4-coin amounts: | 1+3+5+10 | 1 |
|  |  | total: 15 |

*To determine the number of 3-coin amounts, realize that every time you use 3 coins, one coin is left over. There are only four ways that one coin can be left over. Therefore there are four ways to have 3-coin amounts.

**3)** Method 1

Let the number be represented by a rectangle divided into 6 congruent sections, each representing 1/6 of the number. Then 2 sections represent 2/6 or 1/3 of the number. Show on the diagram that 5 more than 1/3 of the number is 1/2 of the number. Clearly 5 is 1/6 of the number, which therefore is 30.

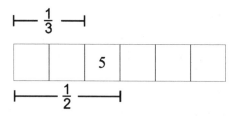

Method 2

The difference between 1/2 and 1/3 of the number is 5. Since $1/2 - 1/3 = 3/6 - 2/6 = 1/6$, 1/6 of the number is 5. The number is 30.

**4)** Since B is the midpoint of AC, AB = BC; mark each of these lengths as d. Since C is the midpoint of BD, BC = CD; mark CD as d. Since D is the midpoint of BE, BD = DE; mark DE as 2d. In terms of d, AE = 5d and also equals 20. Then d must be 4, and DE = 2d = $2 \times 4 = 8$.

## (Olympiad 79)

**5)**  Work from the bottom up. (See Appendix 2, section 3.)

$$\cfrac{1}{4+\cfrac{1}{2+\cfrac{1}{3}}}=\cfrac{1}{4+\cfrac{1}{\cfrac{7}{3}}}=\cfrac{1}{4+\cfrac{3}{7}}=\cfrac{1}{\cfrac{31}{7}}=\frac{7}{31}$$

## Olympiad 80

**1)**  The first four socks I pick could each have a different color. But the 5th sock I pick must have the same color as one of the first four socks I picked. Therefore five socks must be picked so that I can be absolutely certain that I have two socks of the same color among those picked.

**2)**

$$\frac{A}{3}+\frac{B}{4}=\frac{11}{12}$$
$$\frac{4\times A}{4\times 3}+\frac{3\times B}{3\times 4}=\frac{11}{12}$$
$$\frac{4A+3B}{12}=\frac{11}{12}$$
$$4A+3B=11$$

If A = 1, B is not a counting number. If A = 2 and B = 1, then the condition that 4A+3B = 11 is satisfied. Answer: A = 2 and B = 1.

**3)**  <u>Method 1</u>
Make a tree-diagram for all three-letter code words starting with A. Each path from the top to the bottom contains 3 letters, which is one of the code words beginning with A. There are 9 such code words. Clearly, there are 9 code words starting with B and 9 starting with C. In all, there are 27 code words.

<u>Method 2</u>
There are 3 choices for the first letter of the code word. Similarly there are 3 choices for each of the 2nd and 3rd letters. Therefore there are 3 × 3 × 3 = 27 three-letter code words.

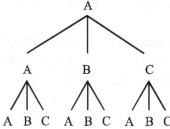

**(Olympiad 80)**

4)  The largest result occurs when ABC is as large as possible and DEF is as small as possible. The largest value of ABC is 987 and the smallest value of DEF is 102. The result of subtracting DEF from ABC in this instance is 885.

|      |       |
|------|-------|
| ABC: | 987   |
| DEF: | − 102 |
|      | 885   |

5)  Let I, II, and III denote the areas of the triangles as shown on the diagram. The area of DABC can be obtained by subtracting I+II+III from the area of the rectangle.

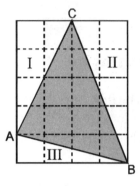

I = 4 × 2/2 = 4, II = 5 × 2/2 = 5, III = 1 × 4/2 = 2; I+II+III = 4+5+2 = 11.
Area △ABC = Area of rectangle − (I+II+III)
Area △ABC = 4 × 5 − 11 = 9.

The area of △ABC is 9 square units.

# APPENDIXES

Proofs and solutions appear in the last section of most appendixes.

## BASIC CONCEPTS FOR YOUNG MATHLETES

## BASIC CONCEPTS FOR YOUNG MATHLETES

### 1. Reading Numbers, Sequences, and Series

<u>Numbers:</u> Use "and" before a fraction or decimal.

Read $305\frac{1}{4}$ as "three hundred five and one-fourth".

Read 1001.2 as "one thousand one and two-tenths".

<u>Sequences and Series:</u> Use three dots ( ... ) to mean "and so forth."
Read the sequence 2, 4, 6, ... as "two, four, six, and so forth."
Read the series $1 + 2 + 3 + \cdots$ as "one plus two plus three, and so forth."
Read the series $1 + 2 + 3 + \cdots + 10$ as "one plus two plus three, and so forth, up to ten."

### 2. Digits

A *digit* is any one of the ten numerals 0, 1, 2, 3, 4, 5, 6, 7, 8, 9. The number 358 is a three-digit number; its *lead-digit* is 3. The lead digit of a counting number may not be 0;  0358 is considered to be a three-digit number.

### 3. Expanded Form of a Number

A counting number may be written in expanded form as follows:

|  <u>Standard Form</u>  |  <u>Expanded Form</u>  |
|---|---|

### 4. Sets of Numbers

$$358 = \begin{cases} 300 + 50 + 8, \text{ or} \\ 3 \times 100 + 5 \times 10 + 8 \times 1, \text{ or} \\ 3 \times 10^2 + 5 \times 10 + 8 \times 1 \end{cases}$$

*Whole Numbers* = {0,1,2,3, ... }

*Counting Numbers* = {1,2,3, ... }

*Rational Numbers* are numbers which can be written in the form A/B where A and B are whole numbers and B does not equal zero.
<u>Examples:</u>   7/15, 2¾(= 11/4),   .9 (= 9/10)
Note that all whole numbers are rational. For example, 3 is a rational number because 3 = 3/1 or 6/2 and so forth;  0 is rational because 0 = 0/1 or 0/2 and so forth.

## 5. Fractions

A *common* or *simple fraction* is a fraction in the form A/B where A and B are whole numbers and B is not equal to zero. Note that all common fractions are rational numbers.

A *unit fraction* is a common fraction with numerator 1.

A *proper fraction* is a common fraction in which A is less than B.
Examples: 2/5 and 1/3.

An *improper fraction* is a common fraction in which A is greater than or equal to B.
Examples: 5/2, 3/3, 7/1.

A *complex fraction* is a fraction whose numerator or denominator (or both) contains a fraction. See Appendix 2 for more on complex fractions.

Examples:
$$\frac{\frac{2}{3}}{5}, \quad \frac{5}{\frac{3}{4}}, \quad \frac{\frac{3}{8}}{\frac{4}{5}}, \quad \frac{3+\frac{1}{2}}{2-\frac{1}{3}}$$

The fraction A/B is *simplified* or *reduced to lowest terms* if A and B have no common factor other than 1.

## 6. Order of Operations

When computing the value of an expression involving two or more operations, the following priorities must be observed in the order listed:
1. do computations in parentheses, braces, and brackets, THEN
2. do multiplications and divisions in order from left to right, THEN
3. do additions and subtractions in order from left to right.

Examples:
1): $3 + 4 \times (8 - 6) \div 2 = 3 + 4 \times 2 \div 2 = 3 + 4 = 7$
2): $3 + 4 \times 8 - 6 \div 2 = 3 + 32 - 3 = 32$
3): $3 + (4 \times 8 - 6) \div 2 = 3 + (32 - 6) \div 2 = 3 + 26 \div 2 = 3 + 13 = 16$

## 7. Average

The *average* of N numbers is the sum of the N numbers divided by N.
Example: The average of 3, 4, 8, and 9 is $(3+4+8+9) \div 4 = 24 \div 4 = 6$.

## 8. Basic Definitions for Number Theory

Let A and B be counting numbers. We say that *A divides B exactly* if the remainder is zero when the division B÷A is performed.
See Appendix 3, section 6 for equivalent expressions.

A *prime* is a counting number greater than 1 that is divisible only by itself and by 1.
Examples: The first eight prime numbers are 2, 3, 4, 7, 11, 13, 17, and 19. Some larger primes are 43, 101, 20147, and 20149. Notice that 2 is the only even prime number, and that 2 and 3 are the only two consecutive numbers that are each prime.

A *composite* is a counting number that is the product of 2 or more primes.
Examples: $18 = 2 \times 3 \times 3$, $35 = 7 \times 5$, and $91 = 7 \times 13$. The first eight composite numbers are 4, 6, 8, 9, 10, 12, 14, and 15. All counting numbers which are not prime and not 1 are composites.

The number 1 is called a *unit*. It is neither prime nor composite, and is a factor of all counting numbers.

A counting number is said to be *factored completely* when it is expressed as a product of prime numbers.
Example: Since $72 = 2 \times 2 \times 2 \times 3 \times 3$, then $2 \times 2 \times 2 \times 3 \times 3$ represents the *complete factorization* or *prime factorization* of 72. This can also be written as $2^3 \times 3^2$.

The *Greatest Common Factor (GCF)* of two counting numbers A and B is the largest counting number that divides both A and B exactly.
Example: GCF(12,18) = 6. See Appendix 5 for methods of computing the GCF.

Two counting numbers are *relatively prime* or *co-prime* if their GCF equals 1.
Examples:  8 and 15 are relatively prime because GCF(8,15) = 1; 27 and 35 are relatively prime; 995 and 996 are relatively prime. Note that any two consecutive numbers are relatively prime.

The *Least Common Multiple (LCM)* of two counting numbers A and B is the smallest counting number that is divisible by both A and B.
Example: LCM(9,12) = 36. See Appendix 6 for methods of computing the LCM.

## 9. Terms and Formulas from Geometry

*Angles:* degree-measure, acute, right, obtuse, straight, reflex

*Triangles:* acute, right, obtuse, scalene, isosceles, equilateral

*Quadrilaterals:* parallelogram, rectangle, square (a special rectangle), rhombus, trapezoid

*Polygons:* triangle, quadrilateral, pentagon, hexagon, octagon, decagon, dodecagon, icosagon

*Area* is the number of square units contained in a closed region.

*Perimeter* is the length of the boundary of a closed plane figure.

*Circumference* is the perimeter of a circle.

*Congruent Figures* are plane figures that have exactly the same size and shape. If two polygons are congruent, their corresponding sides and angles will have the same measures.

### Geometry Formulas

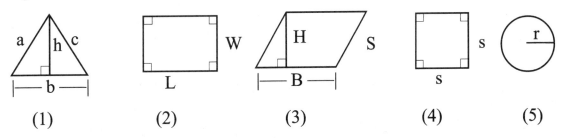

(1)    (2)    (3)    (4)    (5)

| Plane Figure | Perimeter (P) | Area (A) |
|---|---|---|
| (1) Triangle | $P = a + b + c$ | $A = \frac{1}{2} b \times h$ or $\frac{1}{2} bh$ |
| (2) Rectangle | $P = 2L + 2W$ | $A = L \times W$ or $LW$ |
| (3) Parallelogram | $P = 2B + 2S$ | $A = B \times H$ or $BH$ |
| (4) Square | $P = 4 \times s$ or $4s$ | $A = s \times s$ or $s^2$ |
| (5) Circle | $C = 2\pi r$ | $A = \pi \times r \times r$ or $\pi r^2$ |

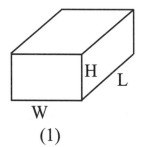 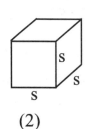 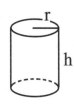 

(1)          (2)          (3)          (4)

| Solid | Volume(V) |
|-------|-----------|
| (1) Rectangular Solid | $V = L \times W \times H$ or $LWH$ |
| (2) Cube | $V = s \times s \times s$ or $s^3$ |
| (3) Cylinder | $V = \pi \times r^2 \times h$ or $\pi r^2 h$ |
| (4) Cone | $V = \frac{1}{3} \times \pi \times r^2 \times h$ or $\frac{1}{3}\pi r^2 h$ |

## 10. Notes Regarding Answers

After reading a problem, it is helpful to determine exactly what is called for, and to immediately note this at the bottom of the worksheet. For example, suppose a problem requires that the values of A and B be determined. Place "$A = \square$ and $B = \square$" in the space where the answer will be given.

Another worthwhile practice is to write the answer in a simple declarative sentence. <u>Example:</u> "The average speed is 54 miles per hour". This practice usually requires the problem solver to reread the question carefully.

Units of measure may not be required in an answer. Any unit of measure that is included in an answer must be correctly stated. Otherwise the answer is considered to be wrong.

## Appendix 2

# RECIPROCALS AND FRACTIONS

## Appendix 2

## RECIPROCALS AND FRACTIONS

### 1. Reciprocal of a Number

The reciprocal of the nonzero number $N$ is $\dfrac{1}{N}$. Observe that the product of a nonzero number and its reciprocal is always 1: $N \times \dfrac{1}{N} = \dfrac{N}{N} = 1$.

Examples: The reciprocal of 2 by definition is $\dfrac{1}{2}$. By definition, the reciprocal of $\dfrac{1}{2}$ is

$\dfrac{1}{\frac{1}{2}}$ which is equal to $\dfrac{1 \times 2}{\frac{1}{2} \times 2} = \dfrac{2}{1} = 2$. Similarly, the reciprocal of $\dfrac{2}{3}$ is $\dfrac{1}{\frac{2}{3}}$ which likewise is

equal to $\dfrac{1 \times \frac{3}{2}}{\frac{2}{3} \times \frac{3}{2}} = \dfrac{3}{2}$.

**Rule: The reciprocal of the nonzero fraction a/b is equivalent to b/a.**
Another name for reciprocal is *multiplicative inverse*.

Problems:

    1. What is the reciprocal of $3\dfrac{1}{2}$?

    2. What is the reciprocal of 2.7?

### 2. Complex Fractions

A complex fraction is a fraction whose numerator or denominator (or both) contains a fraction. See Appendix 1, section 5. A complex fraction can be simplified and expressed as an equivalent simple fraction.

Example: $\dfrac{5}{\frac{3}{4}} = 5 \times \dfrac{4}{3} = \dfrac{20}{3}$. Note that instead of dividing the numerator by 3/4, we

multiply the numerator by the reciprocal of 3/4. (This is commonly referred to as "invert and multiply".) The following shows why this is mathematically correct:

$$\frac{5}{\frac{3}{4}} = \frac{5 \times \frac{4}{3}}{\frac{3}{4} \times \frac{4}{3}} = \frac{5 \times \frac{4}{3}}{1} = 5 \times \frac{4}{3}$$

Problems:

1. Express $\dfrac{\frac{3}{8}}{\frac{4}{5}}$ as a simple fraction.

$\dfrac{3}{8} \div \dfrac{4}{5} \qquad \dfrac{3}{8} \times \dfrac{5}{4} = \dfrac{15}{32}$

2. Express $\dfrac{6}{3\frac{1}{2}}$ as a simple fraction.

$\dfrac{6}{1} \div \dfrac{7}{2} \qquad \dfrac{6}{1} \times \dfrac{2}{7} = \dfrac{12}{7} = 2\frac{2}{7}$

3. Express $\dfrac{3\frac{1}{4}}{5}$ as a simple fraction.

$\dfrac{13}{4} \times \dfrac{1}{5} = \dfrac{13}{20}$

## 3. Extended Fractions

In this book, an example of an "extended fraction"* is $\cfrac{1}{5+\cfrac{1}{5+\frac{1}{5}}}$. This fraction can

be written as a simple fraction by simplifying it "from the bottom up":

$$\cfrac{1}{5+\cfrac{1}{5+\cfrac{1}{5}}} = \cfrac{1}{5+\cfrac{1}{\frac{26}{5}}} = \cfrac{1}{5+\frac{5}{26}} = \cfrac{1}{\frac{135}{26}} = \frac{26}{135}$$

Problem: What simple fraction is equal to $\cfrac{1}{2+\cfrac{1}{3+\frac{1}{4}}}$ ?

$\cfrac{1}{2+\cfrac{1}{\frac{13}{4}}} = \cfrac{1}{2+\frac{4}{13}} = \cfrac{1}{\frac{30}{13}} = \dfrac{13}{30}$

_____

*In the literature, this topic falls under the category of "Continued Fractions".

## 4. Solutions

Section 1:

Problem 1.   $3\frac{1}{2} = \frac{7}{2}$. The reciprocal of $\frac{7}{2} = \frac{2}{7}$.

Problem 2.   $2.7 = 2\frac{7}{10} = \frac{27}{10}$. The reciprocal of $\frac{27}{10} = \frac{10}{27}$.

Section 2:

Problem 1.   $\dfrac{\frac{3}{8}}{\frac{4}{5}} = \frac{3}{8} \times \frac{5}{4} = \frac{15}{32}$.

Problem 2.   $\dfrac{6}{3\frac{1}{2}} = \dfrac{6}{\frac{7}{2}} = 6 \times \frac{2}{7} = \frac{12}{7}$.

Problem 3.   $\dfrac{3\frac{1}{4}}{5} = \frac{13}{4} \times \frac{1}{5} = \frac{13}{20}$.

Section 3:

Problem   $\dfrac{1}{2 + \dfrac{1}{3 + \frac{1}{4}}} = \dfrac{1}{2 + \dfrac{1}{\frac{13}{4}}} = \dfrac{1}{2 + \frac{4}{13}} = \dfrac{1}{\frac{30}{13}} = \frac{13}{30}$.

# FACTORS OF A NUMBER

## FACTORS OF A NUMBER

**In this appendix, the word *number* always refers to a counting number.**

### 1. Factors of a Number

A factor of a number N is a number which divides N exactly. <u>Example:</u> the factors of 12 are 1, 2, 3, 4, 6, and 12. Notice that every number N has itself and 1 among its factors. Recall that when a number is greater than 1 and has just itself and 1 as factors, the number is *prime*.

### 2. Pairing the Different Factors of a Number

When all the different factors of a given number N are listed, they usually can be paired so that the product of each pair is N. Consider the factors of 30.

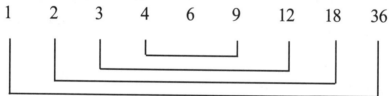

In the above diagram, notice that the eight different factors of 30 can be paired so that the product of each pair is 30: 1×30, 2×15, 3×10, 5×6.

Consider the different factors of 36.

The above pairing reveals that there is an odd number of factors. Since 36 is a square number, 6 must be paired with itself to yield the product 36.

**<u>Rule:</u> A square number always has an odd number of different factors.**

<u>Problem:</u> Which of the numbers from 1 to 200 have an odd number of different factors?

### 3. Factoring Completely

A number is factored completely when it is expressed as a product of primes. <u>Example:</u> $90 = 2×3×3×5$. The right side, $2×3×3×5$, is the *complete factorization* of 90. The factors of 90 can be written as 1, 2, 3, 5, 6, 9, 10, 15, 18, 30, 45, and 90, (or as 1, 2, 3, 5, 2×3, 3×3, 2×5, 3×5, 2×3×3, 2×3×5, 3×3×5, and 2×3×3×5).

## 4. Exponents

Suppose the complete factorization of a number is $7 \times 7 \times 7 \times 7 \times 7$. It is convenient to write this as $7^5$. Here the small 5 placed to the upper right of 7 tells us that $7^5$ represents a product in which 7 appears as a factor 5 times. The small number 5 in this case is called the *exponent* and the number 7 which appears as a factor is called the *base*. Clearly, the factors of $7^5$ are 1, 7, $7 \times 7$, $7 \times 7 \times 7$, $7 \times 7 \times 7 \times 7$, and $7 \times 7 \times 7 \times 7 \times 7$. The factors of $7^5$ can also be represented using exponents: 1, $7^1$, $7^2$, $7^3$, $7^4$, and $7^5$. From these *exponential forms*, one can see that $7^5$ has 6 different factors.
(See Appendix 7 for more on exponents.)
**Rule: If P is a prime number, then $P^N$ has N+1 different factors.**

## 5. How Many Factors Does a Number Have?

Example: How many different factors does 400 have?

Factor 400 completely in exponential form:
$400 = 2 \times 2 \times 2 \times 2 \times 5 \times 5 = 2^4 \times 5^2$
$2^4$ has 5 different factors and $5^2$ has 3 different factors.
The number 400 will have $5 \times 3 = 15$ different factors.

A listing of the different factors is instructive. The factors of $2^4$ are 1, 2, 4, 8, 16; the factors of $5^2$ are 1, 5, 25. The different factors of 400 are presented in the following tables:

| In factored form | | | Same results simplified | | |
|---|---|---|---|---|---|
| 1×1 | 1×5 | 1×25 | 1 | 5 | 25 |
| 2×1 | 2×5 | 2×25 | 2 | 10 | 50 |
| 4×1 | 4×5 | 4×25 | 4 | 20 | 100 |
| 8×1 | 8×5 | 8×25 | 8 | 40 | 200 |
| 16×1 | 16×5 | 16×25 | 16 | 80 | 400 |

The table at the left shows each of the 15 factors as a product of two factors. Observe the pattern of the entries in this table both vertically and horizontally. The table at the right shows each of the 15 factors in standard form. These entries can be used to make the following ordered list of the 15 factors:  1, 2, 4, 5, 8, 10, 16, 20, 25, 40, 50, 80, 100, 200, 400.

**Rule:  If $N = P^a \times Q^b \times R^c \times \cdots$ where P, Q, R, ... are different primes and a, b, c, ... are exponents, then N has $(a + 1) \times (b + 1) \times (c + 1) \times \cdots$ factors.**

Problem: Find the number of different factors in each of the following.
  a) 648     b) 1000     c) 1024

## 6. Factors, Multiples, and Divisibility

If F is a factor of N, then *F divides N exactly*, *N is divisible by F*, and *N is a multiple of F.*

Example. The following statements are equivalent.

> 1) 6 is a factor of 30
> 2) 6 divides 30 exactly
> 3) 30 is divisible by 6
> 4) 30 is a multiple of 6

## 7. A Card Problem

Select the following 10 cards from a deck of cards: Ace, 2, 3, 4, ... , 9, 10. Let the Ace be equal to 1. Place the ten cards in a row from left to right in order from 1 to 10. Turn each card of the row face down. To change the status of a card that is face-down (D) to face-up (U), turn the card face-up. Similarly, the status of a card that is face-up (U) can be changed to face-down (D). So to begin with, all cards are face down and each has status D. We are going to make changes in the status of various cards and use the following table to keep record of the changes described below. Check the entries in the table with the directions given below. (R stands for row number, and C for card number.)

### STATUS OF CARDS

| R\C | 1 | 2 | 3 | 4 | 5 | 6 | 7 | 8 | 9 | 10 |
|---|---|---|---|---|---|---|---|---|---|---|
| **1** | U | U | U | U | U | U | U | U | U | U |
| **2** |   | D |   | D |   | D |   | D |   | D |
| **3** |   |   | D |   |   | U |   |   | D |   |

Row 1: Change the status of each card. (Since we began with every card face-down, change the status from D to U as shown in row 1 of the table.)

Row 2: Change the status of every second card. (Change the preceding status of the 2nd, 4th, 6th, 8th, and 10th cards.)

Row 3: Change the status of every third card. (Change the preceding status of the 3rd, 6th, and 9th cards.)

Copy the table given above and its entries. Complete the entries for rows 4 through 10 as directed below.

Row 4: Change the status of every fourth card. (Change the preceding status of the 4th and 8th cards.)

Row 5: Change the status of every fifth card. (Change the preceding status of the 5th and 10th cards.)

Complete the entries for rows 6 through 10. Then compare your completed table with the one given in section 8.

Notice that the final status of every card is given on the diagonal of the table and that some cards are face-up and some are face-down. Answer the following questions with reference to the complete table:

1a. Which cards are face-up?

  b. How many times was the status of each of the face-up cards changed?

  c. To what special class of numbers do the face-up numbers belong?

2a. Which of the face-down cards had their status changed just two times?

  b. To what special class of numbers do the numbers with only two changes in status belong?

3. In which rows was the status of the card numbered 6 changed? What connection is there between the row numbers and the card number?

4a. Make a table for cards numbered 1 through 16. Without using cards, see if you can complete rows 1 through 16 using the same kind of instructions given for the original table. (Row 1 will have all U's.)

  b. At the end, which cards are face-up?

  c. How many times was the status of cards 11 and 13 changed?

  d. How many times was the status of cards 12 and 16 changed? In which rows did a change of status occur for each of these card numbers?

**8. Answers**

Section 2: 1, 4, 9, 16, 25, 36, 49, 64, 81, 100, 121, 144, 169, 196
Section 5: a) 20   b) 16   c) 11

Section 7:

| R | 1 | 2 | 3 | 4 | 5 | 6 | 7 | 8 | 9 | 10 |
|---|---|---|---|---|---|---|---|---|---|----|
| 1 | U | U | U | U | U | U | U | U | U | U |
| 2 |   | D |   | D |   | D |   | D |   | D |
| 3 |   |   | D |   |   | U |   |   | D |   |
| 4 |   |   |   | U |   |   |   | U |   |   |
| 5 |   |   |   |   | D |   |   |   |   | U |
| 6 |   |   |   |   |   | D |   |   |   |   |
| 7 |   |   |   |   |   |   | D |   |   |   |
| 8 |   |   |   |   |   |   |   | D |   |   |
| 9 |   |   |   |   |   |   |   |   | U |   |
| 10 |   |   |   |   |   |   |   |   |   | D |

CARD STATUS

Answers to questions:

1a. 1, 4, 9

  b. 1 was changed one time, 4 and 9 were each changed three times.

  c. 1, 4, and 9 are square numbers. Every square number has an odd number of factors, and each of their cards had their status changed an odd number of times.

2a. 2, 3, 5, 7

  b. 2, 3, 5, and 7 are prime numbers. Every prime number has just itself and 1 as factors. Thus each of 2, 3, 5, and 7 had their status changed just twice.

3. The status of the card with number 6 was changed in rows 1, 2, 3, and 6. The row numbers in which the status of a card number was changed are the factors of the card number. Check this out for other face-down cards

4b. 1, 4, 9, 16

  c. 2 times

  d. 6 times and 5 times for card numbers 12 and 16, respectively;
    rows 1,2,3,4,6,12 for card number 12; and rows 1,2,4,8,16 for card number 16.

# Appendix 4

## DIVISIBILITY  THEOREMS

## DIVISIBILITY THEOREMS

**In this appendix, the word *number* always refers to a counting number.**

A *theorem* is a mathematical statement or rule that can be proved.

1. **Simple Divisibility Theorems**

   If a number ends in 0, 2, 4, 6, or 8, it is divisible by 2
   
   If a number ends in 0 or 5, it is divisible by 5.
   
   If a number ends in 25, 50, or 75, it is divisible by 25.
   
   If a number ends in 00, it is divisible by 4 and 25, or by $2^2$ and $5^2$.
   
   If a number ends in 000, it is divisible by 8 and by 125, or by $2^3$ and $5^3$.
   
   If a number ends in 0000, it is divisible by 16 and by 625, or by $2^4$ and $5^4$.
   
   **<u>Rule:</u> If a number ends in N zeros, it is divisible by $2^N$ and $5^N$.**

2. **Distributive Principles**

   **1)** $A \times (B+C) = A \times B + A \times C$      *(Distributive Principle for Multiplication Over Addition)*

   **2)** $A \times (B-C) = A \times B - A \times C$      *(Distributive Principle for Multiplication Over Subtraction)*

   **3)** $\dfrac{B+C}{A} = \dfrac{B}{A} + \dfrac{C}{A}$      *(Distributive Principle for Division Over Addition)*

   **4)** $\dfrac{B-C}{A} = \dfrac{B}{A} - \dfrac{C}{A}$      *(Distributive Principle for Division Over Subtraction)*

<u>Examples:</u>

$7 \times 32 = 7 \times (30 + 2) = 7 \times 30 + 7 \times 2 = 210 + 14 = 224$

$7 \times 28 = 7 \times (30 - 2) = 7 \times 30 - 7 \times 2 = 210 - 14 = 196$

$6 \times \$2.98 = 6 \times (\$3 - \$.02) = 6 \times \$3 - 6 \times \$.02 = \$18 - \$.12 = \$17.88$

The Distributive Principles can also be used in reverse.

$$\frac{15\frac{1}{2}}{3} = \frac{15}{3} + \frac{\frac{1}{2}}{3} = 5 + \frac{1}{6} = 5\frac{1}{6}$$

<u>Examples:</u>

$19 \times 83 + 19 \times 17 = 19 \times (83 + 17) = 19 \times 100 = 1900$

$83 \times 19 - 60 \times 19 = 19 \times (83 - 63) = 19 \times 20 = 380$

$$\frac{3\frac{1}{4}}{3} + \frac{5\frac{3}{4}}{3} = \frac{3\frac{1}{4} + 5\frac{3}{4}}{3} = \frac{9}{3}$$

3. **Divisibility by $2^N$**

   Problem 1: Is 5,472,381,539,672 divisible by 8?

   Recall that a number which ends in 000 is divisible by 8 or $2^3$. Rewrite the given number as the sum 5,472,381,539,000 + 672. The first addend ends in 000 and is therefore divisible by $2^3$. Since the second addend 672 = 8×84, 672 is also divisible by 8 or $2^3$. Then the sum of the addends (which is equivalent to the given number) is also divisible by $2^3$ according to the reverse of Distributive Principle 1. Notice that it is sufficient to divide just the last three digits of the given number to determine whether the given number itself is divisible by $2^3$.

   **Rule: If the number formed by the last N digits of a given number is divisible by $2^N$, then the given number is also divisible by $2^N$.**

   Problem 2: Is 5,472,381,539,672 divisible by 16?

4. **Divisibility by 9**

   Below are some multiples of 9 and the related digit-sum of each product.

   | Multiples of 9 | Digit-sums |
   |---|---|
   | 26×9 = 234 | 2+3+4 = 9 |
   | 217×9 = 1953 | 1+9+5+3 = 18 |
   | 1523×9 = 13707 | 1+3+7+0+7 = 18 |
   | 49420×9 = 444780 | 4+4+4+7+8+0 = 27 |

   From the evidence above, it seems reasonable to assume that if a number is a multiple of 9, then its digit-sum will also be a multiple of 9. The following rule is also reasonable to assume.

   **Rule: If the digit-sum of a number is a multiple of 9, then the number itself is also a multiple of 9.** (See section 6 for a proof for a special case.)

   The above rule is also true when 9 is replaced by 3.

   Problem 1: The number 526*147 has a missing digit. What digit should be inserted in the blank space (*) so that the resulting number will be divisible by: a) 9? b) 3?

   Problem 2: The five-digit number A845E is divisible by 72, and A and E are digits. What values do A and E have? (Hint: The number is also divisible by 9 and by 8. Apply the appropriate theorems beginning with divisibility by $2^N$.)

**5. Divisibility by 11.**

The following are some numbers that are each divisible by 11.

$$99 \quad 693 \quad 5324 \quad 39270 \quad 81609$$

The above numbers have something in common which is difficult to discover. Let us begin with two-digit numbers which are divisible by 11: 11, 22, 33, 44, and so forth. Each of the digit-sums is different from the others. But observe that each digit-difference is zero. How can we relate this to the following three-digit numbers which are each divisible by 11?

$$132 \quad 418 \quad 693 \quad 704 \quad 957$$

Before reading ahead, try addition and subtraction in each three-digit number. Observe that when you add the first and third digits and then subtract the second digit, the result is either 0 or 11.

How would you apply the pattern of sums and differences to the following four-digit numbers which are each divisible by 11?

$$1452 \quad 3982 \quad 4719 \quad 8030 \quad 9295$$

Observe that when you take the difference between the sum of the first and third digits and the sum of the second and fourth digits, you get either 0 or 11.

The following vocabulary will help you describe the pattern of sums and differences. Call the ones place an *odd-place* and the tens place an *even-place*. The consecutive places to the left of the tens place are called odd-place, even-place, odd-place, and so forth as shown at the right.

odd places

| | | |

8 5 3 6 9 1

even places

We now use the above vocabulary to state the divisibility theorem for 11:

**Rule: A number is divisible by 11 if the difference between the sum of the odd-place digits and the sum of the even-place digits is 0 or a multiple of 11.** (See section 6 for a proof for a special case.)

 Problem 1: 674N5 is a five-digit number which is divisible by 11. What digit does N represent?

Problem 2: A725B is a five-digit number which is divisible by 88. What values do A and B each have? (Hint: the number is also divisible by 8 and 11; first find the value of B.)

## 6. Solutions and Proofs

Section 3.

Problem 2: Rewrite 5,472,381,539,372 as 5,472,381,530,000 + 9372. Since the left addend ends in 0000, it is divisible by 16. The right addend 9372 must also be divisible by 16 if the given number is to be divisible by 16. However, 9372 is not divisible by 16. Therefore the given number is not divisible by 16.

Section 4.

Proof of the Divisibility Principle for 9 for three-digit numbers.

Proof: Let N be the three-digit number ABC, where A+B+C is a multiple of 9. We need to show that ABC is also a multiple of 9.

Write N in expanded form:

1) $N = 100A + 10B + C = 99A + A + 9B + B + C$

By regrouping and factoring:

2) $N = 99A + 9B + A + B + C = 9 \times (11A + B) + (A + B + C)$

It is given that A+B+C is a multiple of 9. Let $A+B+C = 9M$ where M is some counting number. Then:

3) $N = 9(11A + B) + 9M$

By the reverse of Distributive Principle 1:

4) $N = 9(11A + B + M)$

Clearly N is divisible by 9. This is what we had to prove.

Problem 1:   a) 2    b) 2, 5, or 8

Problem 2: The number A845E is divisible by 8 and by 9. Then 45E, the number formed by the last 3 digits of the given number, is divisible by 8. So E must be 6. To be divisible by 9, the digit-sum A+8+4+5+6 = A+23 must be 27. Then A must be 4.

Section 5.

Proof of the Divisibility Principle for 11 for four-digit numbers.

Definition: The difference of R and S = R – S if R > S and S – R if S > R.

Let N = ABCD = 1000A + 100B + 10C + D. Then associate each of the addends of the right side with the closest multiple of 11 as follows:

1) N = (1001A – A) + (99B + B) + (11C – C) + D

By regrouping:

2) N = 1001A + 99B +11C – A + B – C + D

By factoring and regrouping:

3) N = 11×(91A + 9B + C) – (A + C) + (B + D)

It is given that the difference between the sum of the odd-place digits and the sum of the even-place digits is 0 or a multiple of 11. If the difference is 0, then N is clearly a multiple of 11. Suppose that (B+D) is greater than (A+C). Then – (A+C) + (B+D) = 11M where M is a whole number.

4) N = 11(91A + 9B + C) + 11M.

By the reverse of Distributive Principle 1 (in section 2):

5) N = 11(91A + 9B + C + M).

If (A+C) is greater than (B+D), then:

6) N = 11(91A + 9B + C) – 11M.

By the reverse of Distributive Principle 2:

7) N = 11(91A + 9B + C – M).

In each case, N is a multiple of 11. This what we had to prove.

Problem 1: The sum of the odd place digits is 15; the sum of the even place digits is N+7. If N+7 = 15, then N = 8 and the difference of sums is 0. By the divisibility Principle for 11, the given number is divisible by 11.

Problem 2: A725B is divisible by 8 or $2^3$ if 25B is divisible by 8. Then B must be 6. The sum of the digits in the odd places of A7256 is A + 2 + 6 or A + 8. The sum of the digits in the even places is 7 + 5 or 12. If A + 8 = 12, then A = 4. Thus the difference between the sums is 0, and the given number is divisible by 11. Therefore A = 4 and B = 6.

# THE GREATEST COMMON FACTOR (GCF) OF TWO NUMBERS

## THE GREATEST COMMON FACTOR (GCF) OF TWO NUMBERS

**In this appendix, the word number always refers to a counting number.**

The Greatest Common Factor (GCF) of two numbers A and B is the largest number that divides both A and B exactly. There are many ways to find the GCF of two numbers. The following show some of these ways.

### 1. Listing

This is a simple but sometimes time-consuming method in which one lists all factors of each number, compares these factors , and then finds the greatest of these common factors.

Example 1:  Find the GCF of 24 and 30 [abbreviated GCF(24,30)].
Factors of 24: 1, 2, 3, 4, 6, 8, 12, 24
Factors of 30: 1, 2, 3, 5, 6, 10, 15, 30
The common factors are: 1, 2, 3, and 6.
Answer: GCF(24,30) = 6.

Example 2:  Find GCF(8,15).
Factors of 8: 1, 2, 4, 8
Factors of 15: 1, 3, 5, 15
Answer: GCF(8,15) = 1.

Definition: If GCF(A,B) = 1, then A and B are said to be *relatively prime* or *co-prime.*

### 2. Testing

Take the factors of the smaller number in order from largest to smallest, and divide each factor into the larger original number. The first factor which divides the larger number exactly is the GCF of the original two numbers.

Example:  Find GCF(16,56).
The smaller of the two numbers is 16.
Factors of 16 from largest to smallest are 16, 8, 4, 2, 1.
The first factor of 16 to divide 56 exactly is 8.
Answer: GCF(16,56) = 8.

## 3. Factoring

Factor each of the two given numbers completely into primes. The product of the primes common to both factorizations is the GCF of the given numbers.

Example: Find GCF(36,90).

Factor each number completely:

$$36 = 2 \times 2 \times 3 \times 3$$
$$90 = 2 \times 3 \times 3 \times 5$$

The common prime factors are one 2 and two 3s.

Answer: GCF(36,90) = $2 \times 3 \times 3$ = 18.

## 4. The Difference of Two Numbers

If two distinct numbers are each divisible by the difference of the numbers, the difference is the GCF of the two numbers.

Example: Find GCF(48,60).

Each of 48 and 60 is divisible by their difference 12.

Answer: GCF(48,60) = 12.

The above example is related to a special case of an important theorem in Number Theory. The general case of the theorem states that the largest number which divides any two given numbers with the same remainder is the difference of the two numbers. A proof for this theorem and the special case in which the remainder is 0 is given in section 7 of this Appendix.

## 5. The GCF of Three Numbers

Example: Find GCF(16,24,36).

Method 1: Factor each of the three numbers completely.

$$16 = 2 \times 2 \times 2 \times 2$$
$$24 = 2 \times 2 \times 2 \times 3$$
$$36 = 2 \times 2 \times 3 \times 3$$

The three numbers have just two 2s in common.

Answer: GCF(16,24,36) = $2 \times 2$ = 4.

Another general strategy for finding GCF(A,B,C) is to first find GCF(A,B). Suppose it is D. Now find GCF(C,D). The result will be GCF(A,B,C). This strategy is used in Method 2.

Method 2:  Find GCF(16,24,36).
GCF(16,24) = 8
GCF (8,36) = 4
Answer: GCF(16,24,36) = 4.

## 6. The Euclidean Algorithm (an *algorithm* is a systematic procedure)

Euclid of Alexandria lived about 300 B.C. and is famous as a Geometer. His book *Elements* is considered to be the most influential mathematics textbook ever written, and is one of the most historically significant works in mathematics. The Euclidean Algorithm appears in *Elements* as a process for finding the GCF of two numbers. In that book, it is presented in geometric form, but here we will show it in arithmetic form

Process for Finding GCF(A,B)  (See the examples below)
   **1.** Divide the smaller of the two numbers into the larger (be sure that the remainder is smaller than the divisor).
   **2.** Repeat the process using the preceding remainder as the new divisor, and the preceding divisor as the new dividend.
   **3.** Continue this process until the remainder is 0. The divisor that produced the 0 remainder is the required GCF.

Example 1:  Find GCF(15,42).

$$1)\ 15\overline{)42} \qquad 2)\ 12\overline{)15} \qquad 3)\ 3\overline{)12}$$

$$\begin{array}{c} \phantom{0}2 \\ 15\overline{)42} \\ \underline{30} \\ 12 \end{array} \qquad \begin{array}{c} \phantom{0}1 \\ 12\overline{)15} \\ \underline{12} \\ 3 \end{array} \qquad \begin{array}{c} \phantom{0}4 \\ 3\overline{)12} \\ \underline{12} \\ 0 \end{array}$$

Answer: GCF(15,42) = 3

Example 2:  Find GCF(391,713).

$$\begin{array}{c} \phantom{0}1 \\ 1)\ 391\overline{)713} \\ \underline{391} \\ 322 \end{array} \quad \begin{array}{c} \phantom{0}1 \\ 2)\ 322\overline{)391} \\ \underline{322} \\ 69 \end{array} \quad \begin{array}{c} \phantom{0}4 \\ 3)\ 69\overline{)322} \\ \underline{276} \\ 46 \end{array} \quad \begin{array}{c} \phantom{0}1 \\ 4)\ 46\overline{)69} \\ \underline{46} \\ 23 \end{array} \quad \begin{array}{c} \phantom{0}2 \\ 5)\ 23\overline{)46} \\ \underline{46} \\ 0 \end{array}$$

Answer: GCF(391,713) = 23

Problem: Reduce the fraction $\dfrac{679}{1261}$ to lowest terms.

## 7. Proofs and Solutions

Section 4.

Theorem: The largest number which divides any two given numbers leaving the same remainder is the difference of the two numbers.

Proof: Let A and B represent two numbers, A > B, and D a divisor of the numbers which leaves the same remainder R. Then D divides both (A–R) and (B–R) exactly. By the reverse of Distributive Principle 2, D divides [(A–R) – (B–R)] exactly. But (A–R) – (B–R) = A–B. Therefore, the greatest value that D can have is A–B. This is what we had to prove.

In the case where R, the remainder, is 0, D divides each of A and B exactly. Since the greatest value that D can have is A–B, then D = GCF(A,B) = A–B. This is also what we had to prove.

Section 6.

Problem: Reduce $\dfrac{679}{1261}$ to lowest terms.

We need to divide 679 and 1261 by their GCF. Use the Euclidean Algorithm to find the GCF.

$$
\begin{array}{lll}
\text{1)}\ 679\overline{)1261}^{\,1} & \text{2)}\ 582\overline{)679}^{\,1} & \text{3)}\ \ 97\overline{)582}^{\,6} \\
\quad\ \ \underline{679} & \quad\ \underline{582} & \quad\ \ \underline{582} \\
\quad\ \ 582 & \quad\ \ \ 97 & \quad\ \ \ \ 0
\end{array}
$$

97 = GCF(679,1261). Since 679 = 7×97 and 1261 = 13×97, $\dfrac{679}{1261} = \dfrac{7}{13}$.

# THE LEAST COMMON MULTIPLE (LCM) OF TWO NUMBERS

## THE LEAST COMMON MULTIPLE (LCM) OF TWO NUMBERS

**In this appendix, the word *number* always refers to counting number.**

The Least Common Multiple (LCM) of two numbers A and B is the smallest number that is divisible by both A and B. There are many ways to find the LCM of two numbers. The following show some of these ways.

### 1. Listing
This is a simple but sometimes time-consuming method in which one lists multiples of each number, compares these multiples, and then finds the least common multiple (LCM).

Example:  Find the LCM of 6 and 9.

Multiples of 6:   6,12,18,24,30,36,42,48,54,60, ...

Multiples of 9:   9,18,27,36,45,54,63,72,81,90, ...

Common multiples are: 18, 36, 54,  ...

Answer:  LCM(6,9) = 18.

### 2. Testing
Consider multiples of the larger number in order, starting with the number itself. Divide each multiple by the smaller of the original two numbers. The first multiple that the smaller number divides exactly is the LCM of the original two numbers.

Example:  Find LCM(6,14).

The larger of the two numbers is 14

Multiples of 14 starting with 14 itself:  14,28,42,56,70, ...

The first multiple that 6 divides exactly is 42.

Answer:  LCM(6,14) = 42.

### 3. Factoring
Factor each of the two given numbers completely into primes. The LCM of the given numbers is the product of the different prime factors that appear, each taken the greater number of times it appears in either factorization.

Example:  Find LCM(36,40)

Factor each number completely:

$$36 = 2 \times 2 \times 3 \times 3$$
$$40 = 2 \times 2 \times 2 \times 5$$

Answer:  LCM(36,40) = $2 \times 2 \times 2 \times 3 \times 3 \times 5$ = 360.

## 4. Relating GCF and LCM

It can be shown that for any two numbers A and B that:

**GCF(A,B) × LCM(A,B) = A×B**

<u>Example:</u> GCF(36,40) = 4; LCM(36,40) = 360.

The product of these numbers is 1440, which is the same as the product of the given numbers 36 and 40.

This shows us another way to find the LCM of two numbers:

$$LCM(A,B) = \frac{A \times B}{GCF(A,B)}$$

<u>Example:</u> Find LCM(24,30).

$$LCM(24,30) = \frac{24 \times 30}{GCF(24,30)} = \frac{24 \times 30}{6} = 120$$

## 5. Venn Diagram

A Venn Diagram usually consists of two overlapping ovals which are frequently used to show set relationships. In this application, the ovals of the Venn diagram are used to represent two numbers and their factors.

<u>Example</u> Use a Venn diagram to find LCM(30,42)

Factor the numbers completely:

        30 = 2×3×5

        42 = 2×3×7

The left oval is for the factors of 30; the right oval is for the factors of 42. Since GCF(30,42) = 2×3, and C is the region common to both ovals, place 2×3 in C. Place 5, the remaining factor of 30 in the A-region, and 7, the remaining factor of 42, in the B-region. The LCM is the product of the factors in regions A, B, and C.

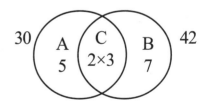

## 6. The LCM of Three Numbers

The LCM of three or more numbers is the product of the different primes that appear in the factorizations of the numbers, each prime being taken the greatest number of times it appears in any factorization.

Example: Find LCM(14,18,24)

Method 1: Factor each of the given numbers completely.

$$14 = 2 \times 7$$
$$18 = 2 \times 3 \times 3$$
$$24 = 2 \times 2 \times 2 \times 3$$

Answer: LCM(14,18,24) = $2 \times 2 \times 2 \times 3 \times 3 \times 7 = 504$.

Another strategy for finding the LCM(A,B,C) is to first find LCM(A,B). Suppose it is D. Now find LCM(C,D). The result will be LCM(A,B,C). This strategy is used in Method 2.

Method 2: Find LCM(18,24,14)

$$\text{LCM}(18,24) = \frac{18 \times 24}{\text{GCF}(18,24)} = \frac{18 \times 24}{6} = 72$$

$$\text{LCM}(14,72) = \frac{14 \times 72}{\text{GCF}(14,72)} = \frac{14 \times 72}{2} = 504$$

## 7. The LCM Algorithm

We will use two examples to show how the following algorithm is used to find the LCM of two numbers and then the LCM of three numbers.

Process For Finding LCM(A,B)  (See the examples that follow)

1. Find any prime, p, that is a factor of either of the original numbers. List that prime on line (1) under Prime.

2. Look at the numbers that are on the previous line in the last two columns. If p <u>does not</u> divide the number exactly, repeat that number onto line (1) in the same column. If p <u>does</u> divide the number, do the division and put the quotient onto line (1) in the same column.

3. Repeat this process as follows: Find any prime, q, that is a factor of either of the two numbers in the last two columns of line (1). List that prime on line (2) under Prime. Note: q may be the same prime as p.

4. Look at each of the numbers that are on the previous line in the last two columns. If q <u>does not</u> divide the number exactly, repeat that number onto line (2) in the same column. If q <u>does</u> divide the number exactly, do the division and put the quotient onto line (2) in the same column.

5. Continue to repeat this process until each of the numbers in the last two columns is a 1. Then the LCM of the two original numbers will be the product of the primes listed in the table under Primes.

Example 1: Find LCM(15,18).

| Line | Prime | 15 | 18 |
|------|-------|----|----|
| (1)  | 2     | 15 | 9  |
| (2)  | 3     | 5  | 3  |
| (3)  | 3     | 5  | 1  |
| (4)  | 5     | 1  | 1  |

Answer: LCM(15,18) = 2×3×3×5 = 90.

Example 2:  Find LCM(45,75,175).

| Line | Prime | 45 | 75 | 175 |
|------|-------|----|----|-----|
| (1) | 5 | 9 | 15 | 35 |
| (2) | 3 | 3 | 5 | 35 |
| (3) | 3 | 1 | 5 | 35 |
| (4) | 5 | 1 | 1 | 7 |
| (5) | 7 | 1 | 1 | 1 |

Answer: LCM(45,75,175) = 5×3×3×5×7 = 1575.

# WORKING WITH EXPONENTS

## WORKING WITH EXPONENTS

### 1. Reading Exponents and Powers

Sometimes a number is used as a factor several times, as in $6 \times 6 \times 6 \times 6 \times 6 \times 6 \times 6$. A short way to write this last expression is to use the symbol $6^7$. This is read as "six to the seventh power." In this example, the 6 (the factor that repeats) is called the *base* and the small 7 (which tells us how many times the factor repeats) is called the *exponent*. In general we read $B^N$ as "B to the Nth power." The form $B^N$ is called the *exponential form*.

When the exponent is 2 or 3, we may read the power in several ways. For example, $9^2$ may be read as "nine to the second power" or "nine square" or "nine squared." Similarly, $7^3$ is read as "seven to the third power" or "seven cube" or "seven cubed." When a number is written with no exponent, then the exponent is understood to be 1. Thus $5 = 5^1$, $6 = 6^1$, and so forth.

### 2. Multiplying Powers of the Same Base

The expression $3^4 \times 3^2$ means $(3 \times 3 \times 3 \times 3) \times (3 \times 3)$ which equals $3 \times 3 \times 3 \times 3 \times 3 \times 3$. The last expression may be written in exponential form as $3^6$. Compare this exponent with the original exponents. Notice that the exponent 6 is equal to the sum of the original exponents 4 and 2. We express this in the following form: $3^4 \times 3^2 = 3^{4+2} = 3^6$.
**First Rule of Exponents:** $B^R \times B^S = B^{R+S}$.

Caution: Remember that to use this rule, the bases must be the same!
Example: $2^3 \times 2^1 \times 2^2 = 2^6$. Notice that this actually says that $8 \times 2 \times 4 = 64$.

Problem: Show why $(5B^4) \times (6B^3) = 30B^7$.

### 3. Dividing Powers of the Same Base

The division $5^7 \div 5^3$ may also be written in the form $5^7/5^3$ which is equal to $\frac{5 \times 5 \times 5 \times 5 \times 5 \times 5 \times 5}{5 \times 5 \times 5} = 5 \times 5 \times 5 \times 5$. The last expression may be written in exponential form as $5^4$. Compare this exponent with the original exponents. Notice that the exponent 4 is equal to the difference of the original exponents 7 and 3. We express this in the following form: $5^7 \div 5^3 = 5^{7-3} = 5^4$.

**Second Rule of Exponents:** $B^R \div B^S$ or $B^R/B^S = B^{R-S}$, provided that $R > S$.

Caution: Remember that to use this rule, the bases must be the same!

<u>Example:</u>  $3^5 \div 3^2 = 3^{5-2} = 3^3$.

<u>Problems:</u>
1. Express $4^3 \div 4$ as a power of 4.
2. Express $(7^8 \times 7) \div (7^2 \times 7^4)$ as a power of 7.

## 4. The Zero Power of B

Let us extend our rule for division of powers of the same base to the case where the exponents are equal. For example $5^3 \div 5^3$ would equal $5^{3-3}$, which is $5^0$. What can such an exponent mean? Clearly $5^3 \div 5^3$ must equal 1 because any natural number divided by itself must equal 1. So it must be true that $5^0 = 1$. In general, $B^R \div B^R = B^{R-R} = B^0$, which logically must be 1.

**<u>Definition:</u>  $B^0 = 1$ for any $B > 0$.**

<u>Example:</u>  $(8^7 \times 8^2) \div (8^4 \times 8^5) = 8^9 \div 8^9 = 8^0 = 1$.

<u>Problems:</u>
1. Simplify $(5^5 \times 5) \div (5^0 \times 5^6)$.
2. Simplify $12^3 \times 12 \times 12^0 \times 12^2$.

## 5. Powers of Powers

Suppose we wish to find a power of a power as in the case $(B^2)^3$.
Read this as "the third power of B square" or as "the cube of B square".
Then $(B^2)^3$ equals $(B^2) \times (B^2) \times (B^2)$. This can be written more simply as $B^2 \times B^2 \times B^2$ which is equal to $B^{2+2+2} = B^6$. Notice that exponent 6 is equal to the product of the original exponents 2 and 3. This same result would follow if we write $(B^2)^3$ as
$(B \times B)^3 = (B \times B) \times (B \times B) \times (B \times B) = B \times B \times B \times B \times B \times B = B^6$.

**<u>Third Rule of Exponents:</u>  $(B^R)^S = B^{R \times S} = B^{RS}$ for any $B > 0$.**

<u>Example:</u>  $(10^2)^4 = 10^8$. Notice that this says that $100 \times 100 \times 100 \times 100 = 100,000,000$.

<u>Problems:</u>
1. Simplify $(9^5)^7 \div (9^7)^5$.
2. Simplify $(5 \times A^3)^2$.
3. Compare $5 \times (A^3)^2$ with the result in problem 2.
4. Show why $(A^2 \times B^5)^3 = A^6 \times B^{15}$.

## 6. Fermat's "Little" Theorem

Pierre de Fermat (1601-1665) was a French lawyer and mathematician. He communicated with many mathematicians relative to his discoveries in algebra, geometry, probability, calculus, and number theory. French academicians consider him to be one of the discoverers of Calculus. However his chief interest was number theory. The following example is related to one of his many discoveries.

Example: What is the remainder when $3^{20}$ is divided by 7?

We will look for a pattern by examining the sequence of remainders associated with $3^1$, $3^2$, $3^3$, $3^4$, and so forth.

### REMAINDERS WHEN $3^N$ IS DIVIDED BY 7

| Power | $3^1$ | $3^2$ | $3^3$ | $3^4$ | $3^5$ | $3^6$ | $3^7$ | $3^8$ | $3^9$ | $3^{10}$ | $3^{11}$ | $3^{12}$ |
|---|---|---|---|---|---|---|---|---|---|---|---|---|
| Remainder | 3 | 2 | 6 | 4 | 5 | 1 | 3 | 2 | 6 | 4 | 5 | 1 |

Shortcut: A remainder can be obtained by multiplying the preceding remainder by 3 and then dividing the result by 7. For example, to obtain the remainder for $3^5$, take the preceding remainder for $3^4$ and multiply it by 3. Divide the product by 7. The remainder is 5. Enter it in the table under $3^5$.

Notice that when 1 occurs as a remainder, the set of remainders begins to repeat in the same order until 1 occurs again, and will continue to repeat in this manner as the sequence of powers is extended. So we expect the remainders for $3^6$, $3^{12}$, and $3^{18}$ to be 1. Since $3^{20} = 3^{18} \times 3^2$, $3^{20}$ has the same remainder as $3^2$. Therefore $3^{20}$ has a remainder of 2 when divided by 7.

In the following table, we explore the effect 7 has when it divides powers of other number bases. We do not include 7 or a multiple of 7 as a base because the remainder is 0 when such bases are divided by 7.

## REMAINDERS WHEN $a^N$ IS DIVIDED BY 7

| a | $a^1$ | $a^2$ | $a^3$ | $a^4$ | $a^5$ | $a^6$ | $a^7$ | $a^8$ | $a^9$ | $a^{10}$ | $a^{11}$ | $a^{12}$ |
|---|---|---|---|---|---|---|---|---|---|---|---|---|
| 1 | 1 | 1 | 1 | 1 | 1 | 1 | 1 | 1 | 1 | 1 | 1 | 1 |
| 2 | 2 | 4 | 1 | 2 | 4 | 1 | 2 | 4 | 1 | 2 | 4 | 1 |
| 3 | 3 | 2 | 6 | 4 | 5 | 1 | 3 | 2 | 6 | 4 | 5 | 1 |
| 4 | 4 | 2 | 1 | 4 | 2 | 1 | 4 | 2 | 1 | 4 | 2 | 1 |
| 5 | 5 | 4 | 6 | 2 | 3 | 1 | 5 | 4 | 6 | 2 | 3 | 1 |
| 6 | 6 | 1 | 6 | 1 | 6 | 1 | 6 | 1 | 6 | 1 | 6 | 1 |
| 8 | 1 | 1 | 1 | 1 | 1 | 1 | 1 | 1 | 1 | 1 | 1 | 1 |
| 9 | 2 | 4 | 1 | 2 | 4 | 1 | 2 | 4 | 1 | 2 | 4 | 1 |
| 10 | 3 | 2 | 6 | 4 | 5 | 1 | 3 | 2 | 6 | 4 | 5 | 1 |
| 11 | 4 | 2 | 1 | 4 | 2 | 1 | 4 | 2 | 1 | 4 | 2 | 1 |
| 12 | 5 | 4 | 6 | 2 | 3 | 1 | 5 | 4 | 6 | 2 | 3 | 1 |
| 13 | 6 | 1 | 6 | 1 | 6 | 1 | 6 | 1 | 6 | 1 | 6 | 1 |

Observations:

1. Notice that $a^7$ has a remainder of **a** when **a** < 7, and a remainder of **a** – 7 when 7 < **a** < 14.

2. Observe that each entry in the $a^6$ and $a^{12}$ columns is 1 for all values of **a** relatively prime to 7.

3. When 1 occurs as a remainder in a row, 1 marks the end of a group of remainders that will repeat in the same order for higher powers of the base in the same row.

One form of Fermat's "Little" Theorem is related to the 2nd observation:
**If p is a prime, and a is relatively prime to p, then $a^{p-1}$ leaves a remainder of 1 when divided by p.**

Problem: What is the remainder when $6^{32}$ is divided by 11?

## 7. Solutions

Section 2

Problem: $(5B^4) \times (6B^3) = 5B^4 \times 6B^3$

$$= 5 \times 6 \times B^3 \times B^4 \text{ (regrouping)}$$

$$= 30B^{3+4} = 30B^7 \text{ (First Rule; simplifying)}$$

Section 3

Problems: (Second Rule, First Rule)

1. $4^3 \div 4 = 4^3 \div 4^1$

$$= 4^{3-1} = 4^2.$$

2. $(7^8 \times 7) \div (7^2 \times 7^4) = (7^8 \times 7^1) \div 7^6 = 7^9 \div 7^6$

$$= 7^{9-6} = 7^3$$

Section 4

Problems: (Definition $B^0$, First Rule, Second Rule)

1. $(5^5 \times 5) \div (5^0 \times 5^6) = 5^6 \div 5^6$

$$= 5^{6-6} = 5^0 = 1.$$

2. $12^3 \times 12 \times 12^0 \times 12^2 = 12^{3+1+0+2} = 12^6$

Section 5:

Problems: (Third Rule)

1. $(9^5)^7 \div (9^7)^5 = 9^{35} \div 9^{35} = 9^{35-35} = 9^0 = 1.$

2. $(5 \times A^3)^2 = (5 \times A^3) \times (5 \times A^3) = 5 \times 5 \times A^3 \times A^3 = 25A^6.$

3. $5 \times (A^3)^2 = 5A^6.$ In this case the exponent 2 acts only on $A^3$.
   In problem 2, the exponent 2 acts on both 5 and $A^3$.

4. $(A^2 \times B^5)^3 = (A^2 \times B^5) \times (A^2 \times B^5) \times (A^2 \times B^5)$

$$= A^2 \times A^2 \times A^2 \times B^5 \times B^5 \times B^5$$

$$= (A^2)^3 \times (B^5)^3 = A^6 \times B^{15}$$

Section 6

Problem: According to Fermat's Little Theorem, $6^{10}$ has a remainder of 1 when divided by 11. Since the remainders repeat after $6^{10}$ in the same order in groups of 10, $6^{32}$ has the same remainder as $6^2$. When $6^2$ is divided by 11, the remainder is 3. Therefore $6^{32}$ has a remainder of 3 when divided by 11.

# Problem Types

Types of problems are generally classified according to topic or strategy in the listing that follows. References are made to Olympiad contest number and problem number. For example, 26-3 represents Olympiad contest 26, problem 3. Page references for all Olympiad contest problems can be found on page 17; page references for all solutions on page 123. Note that not all problems are listed here. Some Olympiad problems have an algebraic technique as an alternate method for solution. These problems are listed under Algebra.

**Addition Patterns**  2-2, 3-5, 4-3, 14-2, 41-3, 41-5, 45-3, 46-2, 52-3, 72-4

**Algebra**  1-4, 2-2, 2-4, 8-2, 10-5, 11-5, 12-4, 13-4, 14-2, 15-3, 15-4, 16-2, 17-2, 18-1, 19-1, 20-5, 25-4, 32-3, 33-5, 36-4, 39-4, 39-5, 41-5, 43-5, 46-2, 48-2, 52-1, 53-2, 54-1, 66-2, 67-2, 68-1, 75-5, 77-4

**Area**  2-3, 5-2, 9-3, 14-1, 22-3, 29-2, 39-3, 40-4, 43-3, 49-2, 50-3, 54-5, 57-3, 58-4, 60-4, 65-2, 66-5, 68-4, 70-4, 72-2, 77-5, 78-2, 80-5

**Arithmetic Sequence**  3-5, 9-2, 14-3, 41-3, 41-5, 45-3, 46-2, 48-4, 52-3, 64-2, 72-4, 74-2

**Arithmetic Series**  1-3, 6-2, 15-1, 16-5, 34-1, 46-2, 48-3, 59-2, 65-5, 75-2

**Average**  2-4, 3-2, 6-3, 18-5, 19-1, 21-5, 23-1, 25-4, 32-2, 41-2, 42-3, 46-4, 47-3, 59-2, 60-1, 68-1, 68-5, 71-2, 72-3 74-3, 75-2, 77-1

**Book Pages**  2-5, 18-2, 29-5, 66-1

**Blindfold**  8-1, 53-1, 80-1

**Circumference**  30-3, 31-4

**Clock**  28-2, 33-4, 40-1, 41-1, 60-5, 69-3

**Coin**  2-2, 6-4, 7-2, 12-4, 13-5, 17-1, 21-1, 30-2, 32-5, 34-2, 43-5, 46-1, 52-3, 70-2, 72-4, 77-2, 79-2

**Combinations**  1-2, 7-2, 8-1, 11-4, 25-2, 32-5, 38-3, 53-1, 55-2, 55-3, 79-2, 80-1

**Consecutive Numbers**  14-3, 25-3, 48-3

**Consecutive Even Numbers**  5-1

**Consecutive Odd Numbers**  31-2, 60-1, 61-5

**Cubes, Towers of**
see Towers of Cubes

**Cryptarithms**  10-1, 13-2, 17-5, 21-2, 24-3, 27-3, 30-4, 31-5, 36-1, 43-4, 44-2, 46-5, 47-5, 52-4, 55-1, 56-5, 63-5, 65-3, 69-5, 75-3, 76-2

**Divisibility**  3-3, 49-1, 59-4, 64-4, 73-1

**Divisibility Combinations**  19-5, 25-5, 44-5, 53-3, 70-5

**Extended Fractions**  5-3, 54-2, 65-4, 79-5

**Factors**  10-2, 10-4, 29-3, 43-2, 48-5, 56-1, 62-1, 65-1

**Flashing Lights**  35-5, 60-3, 70-3, 78-4

**Geometric Sequences**
see Multiplication Patterns

**Magic Squares**  9-1, 14-5, 40-2, 45-2, 62-4

**Motion**  9-4, 20-1, 24-5, 37-5, 55-5, 66-3, 68-2, 73-5, 79-1

**Multiples**  3-1, 28-3, 29-1, 44-1, 51-2, 59-2, 67-1, 70-1, 73-1

**Multiplication Patterns**  15-5, 35-4, 38-2, 64-3

# Glossary

**A**

**acute angle** An angle with a measure between 0° and 90°.

**acute triangle** A triangle with three acute interior angles.

**algorithm** A systematic procedure. Example: Long Division.

**angle** The figure formed by two rays having the same endpoint (also known as the vertex of the angle).

**area of a region** The number of square units contained in the region.

**arithmetic sequence** A sequence of numbers in which each term after the first is obtained by adding a fixed number to the preceding term. Example: 1, 8, 15, 22. Note that the terms of a sequence are separated by commas.

**arithmetic series** The sum of the terms of an arithmetic sequence. Example: 1+8+15+22 = 56.

**B**

**base of a triangle** A side of a triangle, extended if necessary, to which an altitude is drawn from the opposite vertex.

**C**

**center of a circle** See circle.

**chord** A line segment joining any two points on a circle.

**circle** The set of all points in a plane equidistant from a given point in the plane. The given point is the center of the circle.

**circumference** A measure of the perimeter of a circle. (Sometimes used to denote the circle itself.)

**commutative property of addition** For any two numbers a and b, a + b = b + a.

**commutative property of multiplication** For any two numbers a and b, a × b = b × a.

**composite number** A number that is the product of two or more primes.

**congruent figures** Figures that have exactly the same size and shape.

**counting number** Any member of the set {1,2,3,4, ... }. (Sometimes also known as a natural number.)

**cryptarithm** An arithmetic problem in which different letters represent different digits.

**cube** A solid having six faces that are congruent squares.

**D**

**denominator** The expression written below the bar of a fraction.

**diagonal** A line segment that joins two non-consecutive vertices of a polygon or solid.

**diameter** A chord of a circle that contains the center of the circle. (Also a longest chord of the circle.)

**digit** Any one of the ten symbols 0, 1, 2, 3, 4, 5, 6, 7, 8, 9.

**divide exactly** If a number divides another number with remainder zero, the first divides the second exactly.

**dividend** A number which is divided by another number.

**divisible** A number is divisible by a second number if the second divides the first exactly.

**divisor** The number by which a dividend is divided.

## E

**edge** The line segment in which two faces of a solid intersect.

**endpoint** A point at the end of a line segment.

**equation** A mathematical sentence that has an equal sign in it.

**equilateral triangle** A triangle that has three congruent sides.

**equivalent equations** Equations that have precisely the same solution(s).

**equivalent expressions** Numbers or expressions that have the same value.

**even number** A whole number that is divisible by 2.

**exponent** A number that is placed at the right of and above another number called the base.

## F

**face** A flat surface of a solid.

**factor of a number** A counting number that divides the given number exactly.

**factored completely** A number is factored completely when it is expressed as a product of primes. (Also known as prime factorization.)

**fraction** A number that is in the form a/b.

## G

**geometric sequence** A sequence of numbers in which each term after the first is obtained by multiplying the preceding term by a fixed number. Example: 5, 10, 20, 40.

**geometric series** The sum of the terms of a geometric sequence.
Example: 5+10+20+40=75.

**greatest common factor of two numbers** The largest number that divides both of the given numbers exactly.

## I

**intersecting lines** Lines that meet in exactly one common point.

**isosceles triangle** A triangle that has two congruent sides.

## L

**least common multiple of two numbers** The smallest number that is divisible by each of the given numbers.

**line segment** Part of a straight line between two points of the line called the endpoints of the segment.

**M**

**midpoint of a line segment** The point of a line segment that divides the segment into two congruent line segments.

**mixed number** A number that has a counting number part and a fraction part written in a certain form. Example: 3½.

**multiple of a number** A number which is the product of the given number and another factor. Examples: 12 is a multiple of each of the numbers 1, 2, 3, 4, and 6.

**N**

**numerator** The expression written above the bar of a fraction.

**O**

**obtuse angle** An angle with a measure greater than 90° but less than 180°.

**obtuse triangle** A triangle having an obtuse angle.

**odd number** A natural number that is not divisible by 2.

**P**

**parallel lines** Lines in the same plane which do not intersect however far they are extended.

**perimeter** The length of a simple closed plane figure such as a circle, or the sum of the lengths of the sides of a polygon.

**pi(π)** Pi(π) is the ratio of the circumference of any circle to the length of its diameter. (It is approximately 3.14 or 22/7.)

**polygon** A closed figure formed by line segments joined at their endpoints with no other common points. (The segments are the sides of the polygon.)

**prime factorization of a number** The expression of a number as a product of prime factors. (Also know as complete factorization.)

**prime number** A counting number that is greater than 1 and divisible only by itself and 1.

**Q**

**quadrilateral** A polygon of four sides.

**R**

**radius of a circle** A line segment having one endpoint at the center of a circle, and the other endpoint on the circle.

**rational number** A number that may be written in the form a/b where a and b are whole numbers and b is not 0.

**ray** Part of a straight line extending from a point called the endpoint (or origin) of the ray.

**reciprocal** The reciprocal of a nonzero number N is 1/N. (Also known as multiplicative inverse.)

**rectangle** A quadrilateral having four right angles.

**regular polygon** A polygon having all sides congruent and all interior angles congruent.

**rhombus** A quadrilateral having four congruent sides.

**right angle** An angle whose measure is 90°.

**right triangle** A triangle having a right angle.

**S**

**scalene triangle** A triangle whose three sides have unequal lengths.

**similar figures** Figures that have the same shape but not necessarily the same size.

**sphere** A solid having the shape of a ball.

**square** A rectangle having four congruent sides.

**square number** The product of a counting number and itself.

**straight angle** An angle whose measure is 180°.

**T**

**theorem** A mathematical statement, rule, or principle that can be proved.

**trapezoid** A quadrilateral having only one pair of parallel sides.

**triangle** A three-sided polygon.

**V**

**Venn diagram** A drawing consisting of overlapping circles that is used to show relationships among sets of objects.

**vertex** A point at which two or more lines, rays, or segments meet. See angle. (Also known as a "corner" of a polygon or solid.) Plural: vertices.

**volume** The number of cubic units in the interior of a solid.

**Z**

**zero property of addition** The sum of 0 and any number N is always N: $N + 0 = N$.

**zero property of multiplication** The product of any number N and 0 is always 0: $N \times 0 = 0$.

# Index

When a page reference is given and followed by a number in parentheses, the latter denotes a section number on the page. For example, 248(2) represents page 248, section 2 (or problem 2). For definitions of terms see the Glossary. When a topic is listed below and shown in italics, it appears in Problem Types where references are made to Olympiad contest numbers and problem numbers. See pages 271 and 272.

# Index

# Index

## CREATIVE PROBLEM SOLVING
### IN SCHOOL MATHEMATICS, 2ND EDITION
*by Dr. George Lenchner.*

**SPECIFICATIONS:** *Paperback. 8.5 in by 11 in. 284 pages. 2005 edition. ISBN 1-882144-10-4. Library of Congress Control Number 2005927296. Call 866-781-2411 for prices. Shipping and handling charges apply.*

Based upon Dr. Lenchner's popular inservice course, this textbook is organized into four parts: techniques for teaching problem solving; strategies used to solve problems; problem solving within many topics in the standard curriculum; and, in the six appendices, extensions of some topics and explorations of others. The book extends elementary and middle school mathematics through approximately 400 non-routine problems into such topics as sequences, series, principles of divisibility, geometric configurations, and logic.

***Creative Problem Solving in School Mathematics, 2nd Edition*** is a valuable resource for teachers in our program and useful to parents who want to help their children grow mathematically. Each point made in the book is supported by a wealth of challenging problems, with detailed solutions. Further, the material in the second and third parts is organized into 50 sections, each of which can be presented as a full lesson.

## MATH OLYMPIAD CONTEST PROBLEMS
### VOLUME 2
*Edited by Richard Kalman*

**SPECIFICATIONS:** *Paperback. 8.5 in by 11 in. 309 pages. 2007 edition. ISBN 1-882144-11-2. Library of Congress Catalog Number: 2007908880. Call 866-781-2411 for prices. Shipping and handling charges apply.*

Volume 2 is the companion book to *Math Olympiad Contest Problems for Elementary and Middle Schools* by Dr. George Lenchner and contains the 425 problems that appeared on the 85 Olympiads from 1995 to 2005. Features include detailed solutions, hints, percents correct, a problem index, and a rich study guide for mathletes, coaches and parents. The strategy for every question is stated and extensions are provided for about half the problems.

**DESCRIPTIONS AND ORDER FORMS ARE ALSO AT OUR WEB SITE,** *www.moems.org.*

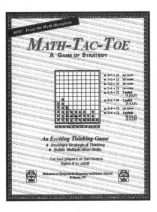

# *Order Form*

**Prices and charges:** Call 866-781-2411, visit *www.moems.org*, or email *info@moems.org* for current prices and charges. Domestic shipping charges apply to USA ZIP codes only. Foreign prices apply to all others. Most shipping is done through UPS Ground (USA) or Global Priority Mail (all other countries). UPS deliveries are tracked and guaranteed.

**Payments:** Orders sent to USA ZIP codes must prepay using a major credit card, check, or school purchase order. All orders sent to other than USA postal codes must prepay with a major credit card. Checks drawn on banks with a foreign address will be returned.

Name _____ School _____

School Address _____

City, State, Zip _____ Phone (Day) _____

Email _____

***PAYMENT:***   Check # _____   P.O.# _____   *(payable to **MOEMS**)*

Credit card: ❏ **MasterCard**   ❏ **Visa**   ❏ **Discover**   ❏**AMEX**

# _____ _____ _____ _____   Expires _____

Mail checks, P.O., or credit card information to: MOEMS, 2154 Bellmore Avenue, Bellmore, NY 11710-5645. *Or* fax P.O. or credit card information to: 516-785-6640. *Or* call with credit card information to: 866-781-2411.

| Books | (Shipping and Handling not included) | Quantity | Unit Price | Amount |
|---|---|---|---|---|
| Creative Problem Solving in School Mathematics | | | | |
| Contest Problems for Elementary & Middle Schools | | | | |
| Contest Problems, Volume 2 | | | | |
| *Special price if all three books are ordered together* | | | | |
| | | Add Shipping and Handling | | |
| | | | *Subtotal* | |

| Math-Tac-Toe | (USA: Shipping & Handling included) | Quantity | Unit Price | Amount |
|---|---|---|---|---|
| 1 set (5 pads) | | | | |
| 2-4 sets | | | | |
| 5 or more sets | | | | |
| *Foreign Orders: add $10 for Shipping and Handling* | | | *Subtotal* | |

| | | | |
|---|---|---|---|
| | | ***TOTAL*** | |